Essays in Social Psychology

Essays in Social Psychology

George Herbert Mead

Edited with an introduction by
Mary Jo Deegan

Transaction Publishers
New Brunswick (U.S.A.) and London (U.K.)

147768

Library of Congress Catalog Number:
ISBN: 0-7658-0082-9
Printed in the United States of America

Library of Congress Cataloging-in-Publication Data

Mead, George Herbert, 1863-1931.
    Essays in social psychology / George Herbert Mead ; edited and with an
introduction by Mary Jo Deegan.
        p. cm.
    Includes bibliographical references and index.
    ISBN 0-7658-0082-9 (alk. paper)
        1. Social psychology. I. Deegan, Mary Jo, 1946-. II. Title.

HM1033 .M43 2001
302—dc21   2001027891

To

Dennis R. Bozarth, M.D.
and his remarkable staff especially:

Thomas "Pat" Schmidt, PA-C
Charles E. Scholtes, PA-C
Chad Springer, PA

for their dedication, professionalism,
and humor

Contents

Preface

Many people generously aided me in completing this project that was started so many years ago by George Herbert Mead. Daniel Meyer, curator and archivist at the Department of Special Collections, Regenstein Library, the University of Chicago, supported this and many other projects over the past two decades. He and the staff at the library are excellent caretakers for the Mead collection. Elaine Trehaub, archivist for Mount Holyoke College, most generously copied many items for me on Elizabeth Storrs Mead and her tenure as president of that university. I gratefully acknowledge her gracious assistance on this and other projects. Irving Louis Horowitz and Mary Curtis of Transaction Publishers also provided vital support on this project, again as they have many times before. Laurence Mintz, my editor at Transaction Publishers provided a helpful eye and sound advice. The Mead family, first through the late Irene Tufts Mead, the daughter-in-law of Helen Castle and George Herbert Mead, and then Albert Castle, the great nephew of Helen Castle and George Herbert Mead, are generous and articulate allies for disseminating their relative's work. Their aid on this and other projects are also gratefully acknowledged. I have been fortunate in having talented and congenial help in the physical preparation of this manuscript, too. Joleen Deats has been skillful and cheerful over the many years of our association. Lori Ratzlaff and Nancy Knapp significantly helped to prepare the original Mead writings. Connie D. Frey and Carolette Norwood helped polish the introduction. Michael R. Hill provided critique, an intelligent ear, and driving skills needed for the many trips back and forth to the archives from our summer cottage in Michigan. I am fortunate to be surrounded by such good and talented friends.

Introduction:
George Herbert Mead's First Book

As I read this manuscript, I imagine George Herbert Mead is sitting at his desk on a cold but invigorating day in Chicago. It is early November, 1910. He has just received the galleys for his first book.[1] He is excited and pleased by the prospect. His years of careful thought and research are spread before him. He knows that a major project is almost complete. He wonders if it will be well received. He plans future projects based on this accomplishment. He is at a turning point in his career, but not the one he anticipates.

Now, I sit at my desk and it is almost a century later. Mead's galleys are spread before me. I am excited and pleased at the prospect of editing them for their first publication. I am also intrigued by the mystery that Mead's first book was never published. Or, if it was published, a copy cannot be found; it is not logged on computers, typed in card catalogs, or listed in the *National Union Catalog*.[2] The galleys have been saved in the "Mead Addenda" to his papers that were donated by the late Dr. Irene Tufts Mead, George Herbert Mead's daughter-in-law, to the Department of Special Collections at the Regenstein Library of the University of Chicago. Unfortunately it is now too late to ask her the provenance of the galleys, although she clearly intended to preserve them and give access to them.

The archivists' guide to the unfinished project stored in the Mead Addenda, Series III states that the box

> contains the manuscript and galley proofs of an important collection of Mead's writings that was to have been titled *Essays on Psychology*. The collection would have incorporated a number of Mead's shorter works on child psychology and education. Most of the material was still in original manuscripts and had not been previously published. (Note in the "Finding Guide to the Mead Addenda")

The reasons why the project was never completed remain unknown. Even the potential date of publication is unclear, but 1910 is the last date for a published manuscript in the collection and one set of galleys is stamped with that year.

I can only speculate on how different Mead's career would have been if his first book had been published. I believe he would have played an even more significant rôle in psychology, philosophy, pedagogy, and sociology than he did, especially during his lifetime. When he wrote these articles he called his work "psychology" and the field of "social psychology," in which he later played a central rôle, was in its infancy. He was clearly making a transition from "psychology" to "social psychology," and his book is closer to the subject area now called "social psychology." Mead titled this work *Essays on Psychology*, but I indicate my interpretation of the discipline's realignment of topic areas in my altered title to the essays. Mead's title, moreover, would be misleading to contemporary psychologists who emphasize the individual considerably more than Mead does, even at this early stage in his career. Each human being is social to Mead: there are no human beings without the web of others—institutions, language, community, and interaction, not just the family as so many psychologists stress.

I expand on the significance of this book for Mead's contemporary rôle as a theorist in my first section. I then present Mead's biography and follow this with a discussion of the myths surrounding his work and his so-called lack of publications during his lifetime. Finally, I introduce and contextualize the chapters included here. I hope the reader will enjoy discovering a new facet of the writings of George Herbert Mead as much as I did.

The Scholarly Significance of Mead's Missing Book

When I first discovered Mead's galleys, I recognized that his ideas on play, childhood, and education changed my previous understanding of his work. This aspect of his thought consumed me for several years and resulted in my introduction to and editing of his writings on *Play, School, and Society* (Mead 1999). I do not doubt that similar shifts in his ideas on other topics will occur as a function of publishing this lost book. I enumerate a few major alterations in Meadian scholarship here.

First, Mead is often interpreted as overly rational and lacking a theory of emotions. Contemporary scholarship on the "sociology of emotions," therefore, often traces its roots to the more recent work of Arlie Hochschild (1975, 1983). She considers this area of study as a function of the "feminine eye," a perspective congruent with women's interest and socialization (Hochschild 1975, 280). She states that in qualitative and experimental social psychology there is a dearth of theory on this topic (Hochschild 1975, 280). Her ideas on "emotional labor" were articulated also in *The Managed Heart* (1983), a book that drew on the work of Charles Darwin in a manner analogous to Mead's use of Darwin's ideas many decades earlier (see chapters 2 and 3 here). Combining Hochschild's work with Mead's newly discovered manuscript shows remarkable continuity in their sociology of human emotions, as well as differences, suggesting a new area of research and theory building.

Second, Mead's ideas are seen as located in a disembodied human being who is conceptualized too abstractly. Biology and "instincts" (as he called them here in chapter 1) or innate "impulses" (as he later called them) have a relatively minor status in his most popular book in sociology, *Mind, Self and Society* (although his work on "the biologic individual" is found in a supplementary essay there; 1934, 347-53). This disembodiment is corrected in this rediscovered manuscript.[3]

Third, sociologists use Mead as a central, abstract theorist of "micro-sociology" in an area that is now called "symbolic interaction," primarily because of the work of Mead's student and champion, Herbert Blumer (1969). Mead's intellectual apparatus emerged from an active, deliberately applied political sociology, however, and to portray him as an abstract, ivory tower theoretician of small groups characterized by face-to-face interaction is a profound error. I interviewed Blumer in August, 1979 and tried to discuss his interpretation of Mead as an apolitical theorist. But Blumer would not discuss these specific political actions and ideas. He even accused me of wanting to cause trouble and—literally—told me not to worry "my pretty little head" about these issues. He could not see my inquiries as a scholarly attempt to understand his interpretation of a series of political events shaping Mead's thought. Chapter 5 here is an excellent example of Mead's blend of historically based politics and theory.

Fourth, Mead's central rôle in the formation of the Laboratory Schools at the University of Chicago is systematically overlooked in the extensive literature on that successful enterprise (e.g., Cremlin 1964/c. 1961; De Pencier 1967). Mead was a major figure in the development of Dewey's brand of "progressive education" and chapters 11 to 18 here help establish that fundamental contribution opening another area for intellectual exploration. Mead's pedagogical, and intellectual commitment to education is documented here (see also Clayton 1943; Mead 1999; Petras 1968).

Fifth, Mead frequently wrote about childhood in his early career, at a time when his own child was growing into adulthood. Although I document it extensively elsewhere (Deegan 1999), this manuscript supports the Meadian study of childhood, early childhood education, play, and parenting. Because of the scholarly emphasis on Mead's posthumous books emerging from his later career, he has been incorrectly perceived as focusing primarily on adults. This interpretation can now be balanced by materials found here (see chapters 1 to 4, 6 to 12; see also Mead 1999).

Sixth, symbolic interactionists often portray Mead as anti-quantitative. This is due to the beliefs of two later sociologists, Robert E. Park and Herbert Blumer, who claim to be fundamental to the Chicago school of sociology (see Faris 1967; Matthews 1977; Shils 1994). Since Mead is supposedly a founder of this theoretical position (see Blumer 1969; Charon 1995; Manis and Meltzer 1980; Stone and Farberman 1970), many scholars attribute the anti-quantitative positions of Park and Blumer to Mead, but this is an error as the present volume documents. Mead was grounded in the experimental, scientific method and opposed the dichotomization of data collection techniques (see Deegan 1999).

Blumer, who studied with Mead in the late 1920s until the latter's death in 1931, frequently led an acrimonious battle between quantitative and qualitative researchers where Blumer defended "humanistic" methods against the tide of vulgar statisticians. Mead was fascinated with the laboratory model, however, and his concentration on the natural and physical sciences is often overlooked because of the Blumerian influence. The writings included here reflect that early, quantitative concentration in Mead's work.

Seventh, many scholars connect Mead's work to sociologists (e.g., Blumer 1969; Manis and Meltzer 1980; Stone and Farberman 1970), and philosophers (e.g., Campbell 1992; Rucker 1969), especially at the University of Chicago (see also Lewis and Smith 1980). This book, however, strongly documents Mead's work in more psychological domains, and most importantly with his German mentor,

Wilhelm Wundt (see Blumenthal 1973; Joas 1985). He clearly wrestled with the theoretical ideas of the following psychologists before 1910: William James, whom he knew at Harvard; James Mark Baldwin and G. Stanley Hall, both students of James with Hall a student of Wundt as well; James McDougall, and Edward Lee Thorndike.[4]

Finally, Mead is often temporally categorized as a sociologist who worked after the early era of sociology that emerged between 1890 and 1920, because his posthumous publications all appeared after 1932. His early work was perceived as "lost" to any sociologist who did not have him as a teacher. His early work, therefore, survived only as an oral tradition. (This required a dismissal of the 125-plus articles that Mead did write, however.) Thus the concepts of the "early Mead" were available only to those who studied with him, and his early students gained stature as the only authorities on this aspect of Mead's corpus. This "disciple pattern" had a major influence in the history of ideas because of the ideological and institutional dominance of the University of Chicago in the development of sociology (e.g., Faris 1967; Fine 1995; Kurtz 1984; D. Smith 1988).

Mead's "first" book, however, clearly locates him as a major figure in the classical, founding years of the profession; the bulk of this manuscript was written between 1892 and 1910. Mead's major concepts can now be seen as emerging over several decades instead of appearing for the first time during the 1930s. One major drawback of depending on his posthumous books is that they are the product of a mature scholar: authoritative, rarely footnoted, and usually a result of an oral lecture. This manuscript, however, reveals a scholar trying to sort through the literature of his era, sometimes thirty or forty years before the posthumous books appeared.

The evolution of Mead's thought, his early study of emotions and instincts, his place in the development of distinct disciplines, his relation to Dewey's ideas, and much more, are found in this early work. This manuscript is fundamental to a major reconsideration of Mead and the development of social psychology and sociology. This early work is rooted in his often neglected biography, my next topic.

George Herbert Mead (1863-1931)

George Herbert Mead formed deep and life-long friendships with many people, and most notably here, with John Dewey and many of his students. In fact, Mead inspired his students so greatly that they collected several sets of verbatim class notes to generate four, posthumous books (Mead 1932, 1934, 1936, and 1938).[5] Mead was also a well-loved family man, husband to Helen Castle from 1891 until her death in 1929 (Deegan 1999), and the father of Henry Castle Albert, born in 1893. Henry was a young child and adolescent during the years when most of the articles reprinted here were written (see H.C.A. Mead 1938). The Meads had a large extended family who made frequent visits for extended periods, and they also influenced his thoughts on community and the self (Deegan 1999).

Mead was active in numerous civic activities where he applied his ideas on the unity between society and the self. I have summarized many of these endeavors elsewhere, including his work on immigration, war, the conscientious objector, labor unions, education, and women's rights (Deegan 1988, 1999). In this biographical section, I focus on his interest in physiology, emotions, children, and education as social psychological questions. I address the reform context for these issues later in this introduction.

Childhood and Youth (1863-1879)

Both of Mead's parents were educators who espoused religious and liberal values. They came from established New England families with the social responsibilities and benefits associated with that status in the nineteenth century. Mead's father, Hiram Mead, graduated from Middlebury College in Vermont and from Andover Seminary in Massachusetts (Cook 1993, 1). After an appointment in New Hampshire, the Reverend Hiram Mead became the pastor of the Congregational Church in South Hadley, Massachusetts where he met Elizabeth Storrs. She had been educated at Mount Holyoke Seminary, one of the few institutions available for women's advanced education during this era. She then taught school for several years in Northampton, Massachusetts and cofounded a school for young "ladies" in Andover, Massachusetts. Hiram and Elizabeth married on 5 August 1858. A year later Hiram was appointed a trustee of Mount Holyoke Seminary (Cole 1940, 205). He held this position until 1873, and his connection with this women's school was continued by his wife many years later. In 1859, a daughter Alice was born. Four years later, in 1863, a young son, George Herbert, was born—perhaps named after the poet (Benson 1971).

Hiram Mead was "called" to Oberlin College in 1869. Here, he held the Chair of Sacred Rhetoric and Pastoral Theology until his death in 1881. This college was noted both for its religious dedication and for its then radical stance of educating women and African Americans (Joas 1985). From 1881 until 1883, the well-known educator and then widow, Elizabeth Storrs Mead, taught English composition at Oberlin (Mead, Elizabeth Storrs [Billings] 1893). (It is not surprising that George stressed the importance of the "vocal gesture" and language given his parents' academic specialties.) In fact, Mead's mother gained greater fame than his father (e.g., she was listed in *Who Was Who in America*, 1943, like her son, but Hiram was not). Despite her eminence, most male scholars barely mention Mead's mother while they stress the occupation and influence of his father (e.g. Joas 1985, 15; Miller 1973, xi; Cook 1993 devotes only one paragraph to both parents, p. 1, and two sentences to Mead's mother on pp. 6 and 11).

Undergraduate and Graduate Training (1879-1891)

George entered Oberlin's Preparatory Department in 1876 and matriculated as a freshman at Oberlin College in 1879. In 1877 he met Henry Northrup Castle, from Honolulu, Hawaii, who was also enrolled in the preparatory program. They were apparently casual acquaintances at that time. Henry was a descendant of religious New Englanders, transplanted to Hawaii for missionary work with the indigenous people. Henry's father was also one of the founders of the powerful Castle and Cooke Company of Hawaii, and he inherited considerable wealth as a result (Cook 1993, 2).

By 1882, in their junior year, George and Henry were best friends and roommates. They were active on campus, writing letters to the student newspaper and short articles. Both young men struggled with their religious backgrounds, social questions, identity, and the increasing secularization characterizing American life. They shared philosophical interests and intensely questioned their instructors and delighted in flummoxing them. Henry also loved literature and poetry and taught George how to passionately appreciate it. In the fall of 1892, Helen Kingsbury Castle, Henry's sister, also attended Oberlin and roomed with her brother at their aunt's home (Mead and Mead, 1902). In 1883, both George and Henry graduated from Oberlin and started down different career paths.

Mead worked in a series of makeshift jobs after graduation: He taught high school briefly, worked in railroad construction, was a surveyor, and a private tutor. None of these jobs satisfied him and a depression ensued: "The feeling that life is absurd brought about a long-lasting existential crisis and left Mead with no guidance in his selection of professional and personal goals" (Joas 1985, 16).[6] Meanwhile, Castle was growing restless in Hawaii, and temporarily resolved his conflicts by entering Harvard Law School. Mead looked upon this decision "with something akin to horror" (Cook 1993, 11), but in January 1887 Henry began his Harvard studies anyway.

From 1881 until 1883, Mead's widowed mother taught at Oberlin College until her son graduated. She then taught successfully at Abbott Academy in Andover, Massachusetts (Mead Elizabeth Storrs [Billings] 1893). Because it was highly unusual for a woman to have a good job at this time, she might have worried occasionally about her finances. Clearly Mead experienced anxiety about his mother's financial security in the summer of 1883, but this was an unnecessary concern. Mead did need to finance his own advanced education, however, and this was a significant burden for an intellectual and ambitious young man. With Henry's advice and a loan from a family friend (Cook 1993, 198, fn. 61), George entered Harvard University for further academic study. After a year's study at Harvard with Josiah Royce (see Mead 1917), the Christian neo-Hegelian, Mead switched from a philosophy major to physiological psychology. Cook argues that Mead left Harvard before completing his studies there because of a summer infatuation with William James' sister-in-law. For some reason, this relationship was seen as unsuitable by James and he strongly suggested that Mead begin his studies in Germany for a doctorate (Cook 1993, 15-19). Because James had studied with Wilhelm Wundt and modeled his physiological laboratory after Wundt's, he might have recommended that Mead study with Wundt. Whatever his advice to Mead on his program of advanced study, James became central to Mead's understanding of instinct, emotions, and the formation of the child (see chapters 1 to 12 here). Mead also often noted the work of the students of James and Wundt, as noted earlier, reflecting a strong Wundtian influence that has rarely been noted (for exceptions to this statement see Blumenthal 1973; Joas 1985; Feffer 1993).

Mead then studied under Wilhelm Wundt in Leipzig, Germany in the winter of 1888-1889. Wundt's work on folk psychology and the interaction between the person and the community became significant questions for Mead as a result (see Mead 1904, 1906c, and chapters 1 to 12 here). "Drawing on advances in physical anthropology, evolutionary theory, brain physiology, and anatomy" (Feffer 1993, 54), Wundt established a laboratory to test his ideas. Mead established similar laboratories at the universities of Michigan[7] and Chicago (Deegan 1988, 111-12).

Mead transferred after one semester to the University of Berlin where he studied under the psychologists Wilhelm Dilthey, Hermann Ebbinghaus (a follower of Wundt, Whimster 1987, 273), and Frederich Paulsen, and the socialist Gustav Schmoller. With Dilthey as his doctoral advisor, Mead asserted that the psychology of the child's early moral development was the most vital field of research, and he planned to translate a volume of articles on this subject (Joas 1985, 19). Although Mead did not complete this project, his commitment to the study of play and early childhood is evident in the readings included here. The Germanic influence on Mead is particularly strong in the first set of papers on the biologic individual (see chapters 1 to 5 here).

Henry Castle joined Mead in Germany, deepening their intense tie. Henry's sister and George's future bride, Helen Castle, was also studying in Germany, and the three friends boarded with a woman named Frau Stechner. Henry fell in love with Frida Stechner, their landlady's daughter, whom he married in 1889. In January 1891, George and Helen became engaged, further cementing the bonds between George and the Castle family.

Henry's young wife Frida, and the mother of their infant daughter Dorothy, died tragically in 1891 when she was thrown from her carriage by a runaway horse. Henry and Helen experienced profound grief following Frida's death, and Helen later claimed that George "saved her life or reason" in the aftermath of the tragedy (H.C.A. Mead 1938, lxxiv). On 1 October 1891, George and Helen married in Berlin.

Teaching at the University of Michigan: (1891-1894)

Mead was offered a position in late 1891 to teach philosophy and psychology at the University of Michigan in Ann Arbor. He quickly accepted this post and left Berlin without completing his doctorate. Helen also interrupted her advanced studies on languages and never completed her degree.[8]

Mead's long depression was resolved through his new relationship with Helen and life in Ann Arbor. He was swept into the intellectual spirit of this department, especially with the professional and personal relationships he established with John Dewey and Alfred Lloyd. Mead taught courses and seminars in general psychology, physiological psychology, and advanced psychology, and offered training in special laboratory research topics. He also taught a course on matter and motion and on Herbert Spencer (see list in Cook 1993, 200 n. 33).

These were happy years for both the Meads and the Deweys. The Mead's son Henry Castle Albert was born in 1893, while the Deweys also had three young children. Both Mead and Dewey analyzed early childhood when they were young parents (see Deegan 1999 for more analysis on Mead and children, and see chapters 1 to 10 here). These early studies dramatically shift the dominant interpretation today that Mead was interested primarily in adult behavior. This focus on children, moreover, connected Mead's and Dewey's interest in early education.

Teaching at the University of Chicago and Life in Chicago: (1894-1931)

In 1894, Dewey was offered the chair of the Department of Philosophy with extensive psychology work in the classroom and laboratory at the University of Chicago. When Dewey accepted the Chicago position, he argued forcefully for Mead being hired as well. This auspicious partnership ultimately established a distinct type of philosophy, social psychology, sociology, education, and worldview (James 1904, Rucker 1969). It was forged by the deep intellectual and personal ties between Dewey and Mead. This friendship and mutual influence have been greatly underestimated despite massive literatures on each of them, and an exciting world of theory and application has been hidden in the process (see Deegan 1987, 1988, 1999). A further sign of this interlocking, interdisciplinary world is the fact that Mead and Dewey worked in departments aligned simultaneously with psychology, philosophy, and education.

The *Annual Register* (p. 41) for July, 1893-July, 1894, already listed Dewey as head professor of philosophy, and Mead as an assistant professor of philosophy. "experimental psychology" courses were offered by James Angell, assistant professor of experimental psychology, while Mead taught a course on "comparative psychology" and another on "methodology of psychology" (pp. 44-45). The psychology laboratory was situated next to the physiological laboratory and down the hall from a physics laboratory for vision experiments (p. 45). A model of the brain, charts illustrating the brain and sense organs, and various apparatuses to test the senses were found there. "For the study of vision, Kühen's artificial eye, Helmhotz's phakoscope, Ewald's pseudoscope, Rother's triple color-wheel, a complete set of Hering's apparatus for the study of color, Wheatstone's photometer, Helmhotz's stereoscope, Ludwig's tropostereoscope, a perimeter, zoetropes, test types, skeins for color blindness, etc." (p. 45) were also on hand. These experimental aids were clearly designed by German scholars and probably also available in Wundt's laboratory. Mead specifically praises the advances of Kühen and Helmholtz in chapter 17 here, demonstrating his familiarity with these devices. Thus Mead and Dewey continued their overlapping vision of philosophy and psychology when they transferred from Michigan to Chicago.

Unfortunately, shortly after the Meads moved to Chicago, their life was devastated by another death in the family. Their beloved brother and friend Henry Castle had recovered from his first wife's death and remarried. He and his second wife, Mabel Wing, had a daughter, Elinor. While Henry and Dorothy were returning to Hawaii after an extended visit to Germany, they were drowned when their ship sank in the North Sea on 30 January 1895. Henry's mother, Mary Tenney Castle, established a memorial in the form of a kindergarten following their deaths.[9] George's interest in early childhood education became central to his work as well, and the papers collected here reflect that deep commitment more than any of his other books (see also Deegan 1999; see chapters 1 to 12 here).

On a happier note, the 1890s were busy years for Mead's mother, Elizabeth Storrs Mead. During this decade she served first as the president of Mount Holyoke Seminary. She then guided its transition and growth to its new status as a college, thereby becoming the first president of Mount Holyoke College. She enacted far-reaching changes during her tenure there, including the establishment of a popular department of pedagogy (*President's Annual Report, 1899-1900*, 5-6, Mount Holyoke College Library, Archives). In 1900 she resigned her post and retired to Florida.[10]

The 1890's were also lively and controversial years at Chicago's famous social settlement, Hull-House. Anarchists, Marxists, socialists, unionists, and leading social theorists congregated there to discuss ideas, promote social justice, and form a socially and culturally diverse community. Dewey and George Herbert Mead, among others, were frequent visitors, lecturers and close friends of its charismatic head, Jane Addams (Deegan 1988, 1999). Mead even gave a talk on "brains" here, continuing his physiological and reform interests (Deegan 1988, 120). Hull-House gained a national and international reputation as a radical, innovative, and successful institution. Oriented towards social change, Addams articulated an American dream, particularly adapted to bright, educated, Anglo women who wanted a new rôle in life and society. Addams did not limit her influence to women, however, as noted. Mead's analysis of temperance (see chapter 5 here) reveals how he combined controversial social issues with philosophical and psychological interpretations of social behavior.

Mead's many intellectual ties with Addams are difficult to trace, but they are expressed in a letter he wrote her in 1910. In this note, he complimented her on the excellence of a recently published book, probably *Twenty Years at Hull-House* (1910). He continued: "May I add my affectionate appreciation——the appreciation which I feel whenever I think of what you are to Chicago and to those who are fortunate enough to feel that they belong to the circle of your friends" (Mead to Addams, 1 December, 1910, 1-2, cited in Deegan 1999, lxxxiii).

Mead's professional admiration for Addams is eloquently expressed in the following passage written to Addams in 1908 (after the bulk of his first book was completed) in response to a speech she delivered:

> I presume that you could not know how deep an impression you made last night by your very remarkable paper. My consciousness was, I presume, in the same condition as that of the rest of your audience—completely filled with the multitude of impressions which you succeeded in making, and the human responses which you called out from so many unexpected points of view. (Mead to Addams, 12 April, 1908, 1, cited in Deegan 1999, lxxxiv)

This passage is more than a friend's compliment. It is an intellectual, self-reflective analysis of his changed "consciousness," and her ability to "call out" new "responses" from her innovative point of view (i.e., "perspective"). These concepts are all defined and developed in Mead's corpus (e.g., 1934, 1938; Deegan and Hill 1987).

These vital professional ties were cemented further through their intimate friendship. Combining all these factors, Mead and Addams had a life-long relationship encompassing both personal and professional ties. They shared common interests in kindergartens (Deegan 1999), women's rights, juvenile delinquency, public education, war and peace, democracy, and immigration. They each contributed to the other's thought. They helped to found major organizations and shaped the social thought known as American pragmatism. These influences went beyond the application of their ideas and extended to an intellectual relationship as well (Deegan 1988, 1999).

Although I concentrate here on Addams, a number of women at Hull-House influenced Mead. These women formed a core group who lived at the settlement, wrote together, gathered statistics, investigated factories and industries, conducted health examinations, examined sanitary conditions, lobbied for legislative and political reform, and organized for social betterment in their congested, immigrant, working-class district. Out of this welter of activity, Addams was the charismatic leader who translated the "facts" into everyday language, articulating the problems and needs of the community, and forming American ideals and social thought. Mary McDowell was one of these early residents, for example, and Mead worked closely with her through the University of Chicago Social Settlement (Mead 1929; Deegan 1999).

From Functional Psychology to Chicago Pragmatism

During the 1890s, the men in the philosophy/psychology/education cluster at the University of Chicago were seen as engaged in "functional psychology." The origin of this approach is traced to Dewey's publication of an influential article in 1896 called "The Reflex Arc Concept in Psychology." Here he critiqued the concept of an "arc" connecting physiology and thought as a static and narrow idea. Dewey stressed, instead, a holistic view of behavior and its processual nature. Dewey's "instrumental" view of behavior, called "functional psychology" especially before 1905, gradually evolved into a more coherent format embracing all the philosophy and psychology faculty at Chicago. Mead was struggling with the connection between physiology and consciousness through most of the first ten chapters here. These early writings, then, are part of Mead's "functional psychology" when he was making the transition to "Chicago pragmatism."

Functional psychology stressed "the coordination of the living organism in some activity—the act....Function, then, rather than organism or environment, is the thing to be considered in psychology" (Karpf citing Charles Ellwood, 1932, 329). Functions involve coordination or adaptation. Established coordination becomes a "habit," and interrupted and changed habits are "reconstructed." "The resulting interpretation of the facts of the psychical life yields a psychology whose chief categories are coordination, adaptation, habit, instinct selection, evaluation, and the like; in an *evolutionary* psychology (Karpf citing Charles Ellwood, 1932, 330).

Mead's functional psychology was directly tied to the work of Wundt, Baldwin, E.L. Thorndike, James, Johann Friedrich Herbart, John Fiske, and, of course, Dewey and Angell. Darwin and Spencer are also fairly prominent. In Mead's later work, John Watson and Charles Horton Cooley gain more prominence while only Dewey and Wundt remain central figures in comparison to these other, early colleagues and questions.

During Dewey's ten years at Chicago from 1894 to 1904, he visited Mead almost daily. This interpersonal relationship was buttressed through their work at the Laboratory School. Here the Deweys, John and his wife Alice Chipman,[11] and Mead implemented their ideas on following the nature of the child and studying the success of various pedagogical techniques (see chapters 11 to 18 here).

In addition to the highly successful Laboratory School, Dewey and his colleagues developed the "Chicago school of pragmatism." The first public, and powerful, recognition of their unique work was a complimentary article written by William James, who announced in 1904 that a "Chicago School of Thought" had emerged. This new, identifiable philosophy was summarized in a series of studies published in 1903 by the Chicago faculty (see Dewey 1903). Although James criticized the Chicago group as lacking a fully developed understanding of biological processes, the area Mead examined in the essays published here, James praised their epistemology on "consciousness" and their unitary approach to function and behavior.

Pragmatism is often slippery to define due to its intentional open–endedness and all–encompassing vision (Deegan 1988; Rucker 1969). Campbell (1992, 2), nonetheless, offers an excellent summary of these characteristics:

> Pragmatism offered a metaphysics emphasizing process and relations, a naturalistic and evolutionary understanding of intellectual activity as problem–oriented and as benefiting from historically developed methods, and an emphasis upon the democratic reconstruction of society through educational and other institutions.

Thus Mead's concern with evolutionary issues, scientific methods, experimentation, and education permeates his essays included here. Many of them were written, moreover, in the decade before James announced the emergence of the new school of pragmatism. The route to establishing this school is documented, therefore, in these early writings by Mead.

Chicago pragmatists who were or had been faculty at the university before 1910 included: James Rowland Angell, John Dewey, Addison Moore, and Ella Flagg Young. The latter two scholars studied with Mead and Dewey, and Angell and Dewey are frequently mentioned in Mead's work here.

Social reform, or the application of Mead's ideas in everyday life as "working hypotheses" (Mead 1899; Campbell 1992), was crucial to Mead's lifework. His analyses of alcohol (see chapter 5 here) and industrial education (see chapter 18 here) reflect this interest. Mead's editorial work for *The Elementary School Teacher* also illustrates how the worlds of the academy and the community sometimes overlapped in his everyday life (Deegan 1999). Combining all of Mead's circle of friends, family, colleagues, and activists, it is easy to see how his scholarly interest in the biologic individual, the beginning of social acts, and education emerged. The University of Chicago anchored this rich "world of Chicago pragmatism" (Deegan 1999, xxiii-xxxi).

Mead as Teacher and His Coursework at the University of Chicago, 1894-1910

Mead ultimately and justifiably became famous for his course on "social psychology" which he taught at the University of Chicago from 1900 to 1931, when he died (Lewis and Smith 1980, 263-85). This course shaped his ideas and that of his many students. In the essays he collected for his first book, however, he emphasized topics in several other courses, as well. Between 1894 and 1910, Mead taught courses in psychology, philosophy, philosophy of science, movements of thought, methodology of psychology, philosophy of ethics, and comparative psychology (see appendix 1, Lewis and Smith 1980, 262-71) among others. Mead regularly taught his course on comparative psychology from 1894 to 1911 (Cook 1993, 44), but it disappeared after the latter date and his social psychology courses, both general and advanced, increased in importance. (More details on his laboratory work in comparative psychology are discussed later.) Mead dramatically changed his teaching topics in 1911, after his book was completed in galley format in November 1910. Perhaps these facts are related, but no firm evidence establishes how or even if they are linked.

George Herbert Mead is best known through his four brilliant, posthumous books and his courses in social psychology. His first, uncompleted book documents his twenty years of teaching and research that were completed before his more famous work that was based primarily on the last twenty years of his life. The first half of his career, however, was significantly influenced by Wundt, and their fundamental ties are the next topic of interest.

Wundt and Mead: A Significant German Tradition

During the early years of Mead's career, from his German graduate studies in 1888 until 1910, Wundt was a central figure in Mead's courses, laboratory work, writings, and publications. Only Dewey had a more important influence on Mead than Wundt during this period. Mead's broad group of psychological colleagues were profoundly influenced by Wundt as well.

Wundt is internationally hailed as a founder of experimental psychology, one of Mead's areas of specialization between 1888 and 1910. Wundt was also a major sociologist, a facet of his work that is not well recognized today (see Barnes 1948, 216-26 for an analysis of this work and its neglect). As noted earlier, many scholars relate Mead to both sociologists and philosophers, but he is rarely analyzed in relation to Wundt. Wundt is acknowledged as the inspiration for Mead's concept of "the gesture" in *Mind, Self and Society*

(Mead 1934, 42-51), but Wundt's influence is far wider and deeper than that. I briefly trace below the recurrent, significant influence of Wundt on Mead's early writings.

The Germanic influence on Mead is particularly strong in the first ten chapters here. One important Wundtian influence is the American cohort trained by Wundt whom Mead frequently cited. In addition to James and his students, Mead grappled with other American students of Wundt—Edward Lee Thorndike, J.M. Cattell, G. Stanley Hall, and Edward B. Titchener (the latter was a major American popularizer of Wundt).[12] This list of psychologists comprise the majority of references in Mead's first book, and even Dewey, who was mentored by Wundt's student Hall, was inspired by Wundt (see Karpf 1932).

This collective influence is further accentuated by the number of concepts used by Mead after they were developed by Wundt (see table 1). Although Mead increasingly criticized Wundt, primarily focusing on Wundt's overemphasis on the individual, Mead used and modified Wundt's ideas throughout his lifetime. Except for the concepts of "folk-psychology" and "psychological eras or ages," all the concepts in table 1 are found in Mead's major posthumous book, *Mind, Self and Society* (1934), which reflected his mature social psychology. A careful, detailed exegesis of each of these concepts needs to be done to understand Wundt's influence on Mead, and Mead's modification of Wundt's concepts. This would require another book to explore, but I provide a model of such an analysis here by focusing briefly on their concept of "play" (see my extensive analysis in Deegan 1999).

Wundt's concept of "play." Wundt's concept of "play" was extremely important to, albeit sometimes different from, Mead's concept of "play," especially in Mead's articles written in the 1890s. Thus Wundt clearly defined play as integral to labor. He wrote, for example, that "Play is the child of work" (Wundt 1897a, 208). He assumed that play reflected some form of serious employment, "for work is one of the necessities of life" (ibid.). Play, in contrast, is pure enjoyment, an imaginative transformation. Play has a "ritualistic element" (Wundt 1897a, 209) reflecting a non-serious enactment of work. Games also arise from rituals, including "games of chance," "ceremonial games," "work games," and "gymnastic or athletic sports" (Wundt 1897a, 209-210). Children's play and games, how-

Table 1
Wundt's Concepts Used by Mead in *Mind, Self and Society* unless Otherwise Noted

---

apperception
community (Wundt 1901)
comparative psychology
consciousness
    individual****
    collective
    social*****
ethics (Wundt 1897a,b, 1901)
    Aristotelian (Wundt 1897b)
experimental psychology
folk-psychology (Mead 1906c)
genetic psychology ***
gesture
    communicative*
    natural*
    social*
human horde or community**
language
    community of**
    human (ideational content)*
mind
    collective
    social**
play (Wundt 1897a)
psychogenesis*****
psychological eras or ages (Mead 1936)
    primitive man
    totemic age
    ages of heroes and gods
    the age that is coming to be ***
stages of mental development

---

*Karpf 1932, 61
**Karpf 1932, 62
***Karpf 1932, 59

****Karpf 1932, 58
*****Karpf 1932, 64

ever, "are the most important means of education" (Wundt 1897a, 211). Aesthetics and art also emerged from ritual contexts and evolved into separate activities, becoming forms of work for artists who specialize in this aspect of life (Wundt 1897a, 213-14). Thus Wundt moved from a macro-analysis of the social origins of games and art, while Mead examined their emergence within the individual self, a distinction explored more below.

Mead's concept of "play." Mead (1896, 369; see chapter 12 here) also believed there were "three general types of human activity, work, art, and play." The "pure play" of the little child is characterized by an attitude and an activity. "When a child (at play) does assume a rôle he has in himself the stimuli which call out that particular response or group of responses" (Mead 1934, 150). The play attitude and activity emerge from the child and are not organized to respond to others' activities or social meanings, because this early form of play precedes the development of the child's mind and self. "Pure play" emerges from the unsocialized "I" and is associated with creativity, innovation, and a flowing unity of time, emotion, and experience (Mead 1896). Although play is essential to the child's activities Mead argued, like Wundt, that adults can and should play, too.

Mead's concept of play as a phase in the genesis of the self is the best known, and often the only known, aspect of his concept. In this model, play precedes the development of activities defined as games in which the player is able to take the rôle of the other in a situation of rules and coordinated action. This ability of a child to "take the rôle of others" is crucial in understanding others, rules, and cooperation (see Mead 1999, 15-17). When the child learns how to participate in a complex conversation of gestures with others, the ability to take the rôles of others can be organized in the game. Learning rules, meaning, and physical skills are crucial acts for becoming a socialized member within a larger group. But the child wants to learn more than rules. Each person wants spontaneity, creativity, and rule–breaking, too. The artistic impulse expresses this other side of rules, even in the small child. Mead discussed this playing with rules in his fragment on "The Art Impulses and the Child" (see Mead 1999, 6).

Mead, again echoing Wundt, saw "The essence of the child–act is play" (see chapter 12 here, p. 95-96). Play has a defining rôle in the behavior of the child, but it is more than a step in the development of the self. It is an organizing, identifiable, human activity that begins in childhood and is needed throughout life. Its pivotal rôle in the child is due to its initiating the connections between emotions and rational attitudes toward society and aesthetics. Play enables symbols to be transformed into meaning and behavior. It helps train the senses and the rational ability to discriminate between actions and ideas.

Play is essential, therefore, to the process of educating children. Here, too, Mead echoes Wundt. This process of play is built into the biological nature of the child and is part of education. Mead argued that the Germanic institution of kindergartens[13] were (and continue to be) the only major institution throughout the educational system that allow play to organize the child's learning. Kindergartens draw on the child's playfulness, and they are integral to early learning and the development of the child (see chapter 11 here).

Play, according to Mead, helps generate intelligence and vocal gestures. Play also allows the child's emotions to develop. Through the increasingly complex organization of detached acts, emotions are ordered and grow more meaningful and multidimensional. By making the connection between an act and an emotion explicit throughout most of his early essays (see chapters 1 to 11 here), Mead integrated his ideas on emotions and acts into this larger body of thought.

Mead, again in a manner analogous to Wundt, believed that play, along with work and art, comprise the context for meaning and being. Each has a different relationship to means and ends: Play is spontaneous and does not emerge from either a means or an end while work is goal directed and art is oriented to the harmony of means and true representation (see chapter 11 here). Of the three types of behavior, play appears first in the individual. Both play and playfulness are needed to generate the ability and motivation to work or create art. Play is the most fundamental step for subsequently developing the skills needed to engage in these socially indispensable behaviors (Mead 1896, 1934). Once these later forms emerge, play remains a vital form of behavior, nonetheless. Mead discusses the appearance of the artistic impulse in the child before the development of the self and as a component of play (see Mead 1999, 6). He never suggests, however, that artistic impulses cease after the development of the self.

Dewey also shared this Wundtian/Meadian emphasis on play. Dewy wrote that "Children do not normally play for the sake of amusement, any more than for the sake of anything beyond the action itself. They live in their actions, and these actions are called play because of certain qualities they exhibit" (Dewey 1913, 726). Dewey also shared Mead's interest in kindergartens and progressive education (Deegan 1999) and even trained kindergarten teachers.

Combining Wundt and Mead's concept of "play." The dual analyses of Wundt and Mead on play are quite exciting. Their concepts generally overlap, while Mead's added innovative insights. Thus both theorists examine the concepts of play, games, athletics, education, work, and art and use these concepts quite similarly. Simultaneously, Mead adds to Wundt's theory the practices of the kindergarten, progressive education, and labor in the modern city. Mead also connects his work to that of Dewey and other students of Wundt in an American context.

Together, however, the combination of Wundt's macro-level analysis of the sociological and anthropological origins of play and Mead's micro-level analysis of the social psychological origins of play, games, and the self is even more powerful than either theorists' work considered separately. A few chapters (see chapters 2, 3, 13, and 14 here) explicitly begin this weaving of a micro-macro connection between Wundt's folk-psychology and Mead's genesis of the self. But a more extensive and complex interconnection is needed to fully understand their sometimes joint and sometimes distinct ideas. This play analysis is an example of the tremendous change in Meadian scholarship that could emerge from a concentrated study of Mead's first book.

To summarize only the Wundtian influence examined in this section, Mead was personally trained by Wundt and influenced by two of his students, Ebbinghaus and James. He cited a wide range of psychologists who studied with Wundt, and he worked with colleagues at Chicago also influenced by Wundt.[14] Mead worked in psychological laboratories modeled after Wundt's and for two decades he taught Wundt's most significant specialization, comparative psychology. Finally, Mead's early and mature social psychology amply employed Wundtian concepts. In summation: Mead's ideas were shaped profoundly and extensively by Wilhelm Wundt.

Introducing the Chapters

Mead divided this early book into three topics: the first concerns the biological and physiological foundation for human beings; the second spirals around the issue of the uniqueness of these acts and the most fundamental components of human actions; and the third examines the development of education through various institutions throughout the life course.[15]   Each section begins with the most basic issues and questions and then builds to an increasingly complex analysis within that section.

I. The Biologic Individual

Although instincts are by definition innate, Mead defines these drives as socially oriented and shaped by others, especially during the interactions between infants and parents. Mead's assumption that instincts are fundamentally social dramatically revises the endless arguments between "nature versus nurture." Instincts are *both* biologically given and shaped by their environment (see chapter 1). Thus instincts have a social character, and this assumption is developed more in Dewey and Angell and their functional psychology (see Cook 1993; Feffer 1990). Like Dewey, Mead rejected the "reflex arc" concept; i.e., that a physical stimulus is necessary to create a mental response. Mead assumed, instead, that a physiological and mental state comprise a unified act (see Dewey 1896; Cook 1993; Feffer 1993). Conscious communications depend on unconscious instincts and emotions, and the self emerges from emotional consciousness. These statements are not found in Mead's later work, raising important questions of whether he changed his mind about these issues or assumed they were decided and did not need to be discussed again. Mead does exhibit continuity in his belief that rationality could change consciousness and action, and that the ability to take the rôle of the other emerged after the development of earlier, less rational forms of consciousness. This chapter may be the earliest piece that Mead wrote in this collection and reflects popular ideas in the early to mid-1890s.

In 1908, E.A. Ross wrote an important textbook on *Social Psychology*. Mead was fascinated by Ross's conception of the field and even reviewed this book (Mead 1998). Mead found that, like his own former teacher Royce, Baldwin also underestimated the significance of sociality or the social impulse in human behavior (see chapter 2 here). James, Cooley (1902), and Angell, however, had a conception of the self and the other that were closer to Mead's. Mead, nonetheless, found Wundt's definition of the gesture as a segment of vocalization and language to be a critical insight. Mead believed that "the other" generates meaning and values for an act which then creates an attitude. Acts gain meaning when they call out a response in the other where "thought" is a form of subliminated conversation. The social group, in turn, structures consciousness. All these ideas received further development in Mead's mature social psychology. At this point in his career, nonetheless, Mead still viewed social psychology as a counterpart to physiological psychology, a close association he ultimately discontinued.

Mead viewed consciousness as an independent factor within the individual and not just a phase within a larger, general process (see chapter 3 here). Mead calls his perspective "functional psychology" and links it to his work in "The Definition of the Psychical," (1903).16 Functional psychology examined the purposive character of conscious processes that emerged form a new evolutionary development. Consciousness was a phase of reality and not an island connected to physiological responses and stimuli. The selves of others, moreover, exist for the individual because they are social objects with similar experiences. Since the self and the other emerge from similar social processes, this creates intersubjective understanding. Again, Mead emphasized Wundt's concept of the gesture as part of a shared social process. Mead explored the meaning of language, gestures, and stimuli, and he subsequently employed all these concepts in his model of the genesis of the self (Mead 1912, 1934).

The rôle of social objects, moreover, was vital to Mead's social psychology. In addition to Wundt, Mead aligned himself here with McDougall and Cooley. He had even more in common with Dewey, Royce, and Angell who shared his belief in meaning as a process emerging from the consciousness of an attitude. Consciousness of meaning, in turn, emerged from an image of gestures associated with an inhibited act. Here, Mead blended the ideas of these theorists with his own original concepts. Thus meaning refers to an object that exists only in the context of social experience. Psychologists had to account for the social nature of objects which, in turn, structured consciousness.

In the next essay (see chapter 4 here), Darwin's study of emotions and instincts becomes Mead's starting point for analyzing the most basic human needs to move, eat, and reproduce. Human intelligence, however, changes emotions and instincts and brings in issues of increasing complexity, control, and meaning. Primitive passions give way to more social interests in humans, making people's emotions and instincts distinct from those of animals.

Drinking patterns surrounding alcohol reflected this union of biological and social processes. At this time, prohibition of such intoxicants was a major social issue in Chicago's reform circles. In fact, the national headquarters of the Women's Christian Temperance Union in the 1890s, led by Frances Willard after the 1870s (Willard 1889; Dillon 1971), was located in a Chicago suburb, Evanston. In 1919, a few years after Mead edited his book, the disastrous Eighteenth Amendment was passed, prohibiting the sale and manufacture of liquor. Prohibition became the law of the land, and gangsterism across the nation followed with especially disastrous consequences in Chicago. Crime became highly organized here and infiltrated the police and judicial system (Addams 1930), and the names of Al Capone and his FBI nemesis Eliot Ness notoriously shaped the American experience.

Mead entered this political arena in his never-before-published essay on stimulants and intoxicants (see chapter 5 here). Instead of taking a position that either opposed or supported the drinking of alcohol, Mead asked what is the nature of the experience created by this drug? He criticized revivalist methods that defined excessive drinking as a matter of will and ignored the multiple factors generating the situation and its complex meanings. The desired state of consciousness emerging from imbibing is complex and "colors" the whole world. This exhilarating experience has the capacity to transform ordinary situations into extraordinary ones.

Cults and other ritualized situations used changed emotional states to heighten experience (Wundt 1912). These ceremonial occasions link intoxication and its emotional, artistic, and symbolic associations to the social order. Intoxication in modern societies, in contrast, lacks this definition, certitude, and symbolic connection. Thus ancient Epicureans enjoyed the sensations created by alcohol, but individuals in the modern world often drink liquor without a social use for intoxication. Stimulating emotions without changing actual conditions creates a false sense of solidarity that is bound to fail to sustain the emotion after the intoxicant fades. An unsatisfactory situation particularly calls out for a stimulant but fails to create the conditions for change.

Mead's enjoyable experiences with good food and drink,17 especially during his graduate training in Germany, gave him a standpoint to critique the temperance movement when it was a powerful social movement in many reform circles in which he moved in Chicago. Simultaneously, Mead did not endorse meaningless and destructive drinking and he analyzed the dire consequences of such behavior in modern society.

II. The Beginning of Social Acts

Mead always advanced the fundamental epistemological assumption that humans are unique in comparison to all other life forms. Our distinctive ideas, emotions, and consciousness underlie our conduct. Comparing humans to animals, insects, or any living species is by definition, therefore, incorrect. Although human conduct may resemble a segment of overt action exhibited by another life form, the meaning and conversation of gestures generating that human segment are always different from an animal's action.[18]

To Mead, the topic of comparative psychology (see chapter 6 here) involved two comparisons: between animals and humans and between physiology and mental states. This functional psychology was also explored by Mead's colleagues at Chicago. Human beings, unlike animals, have a will to eat, intelligence, and the ability to control emotions. Humans define social objects (as discussed in chapter 5 here) and the meaning of acts, topics he more fully developed in *The Philosophy of the Act* (Mead 1938). Symbols, images, and the physiological ability to manipulate objects were also distinctive in humans. Animals and humans, therefore, had fundamentally different physiologies and mental capacities. Wundt was recognized as the international leader in this area of study (Karpf 1932), revealing once more a close tie between him and Mead. The psychological laboratory at Chicago often measured these human and animal responses, as well.

Higher cognitive processes are also employed in the rationality of humans. These abilities emerge from the perceptions unique to humans in comparison to animals (see chapter 7 here). Animal's perceptions were studied by a series of psychologists, like G.F. Stout, E.L. Thorndike, and C.L. Morgan (see Mead's review of Morgan's *An Introduction to Comparative Psychology*, 1912), who could not demonstrate that animals had either the power to manipulate objects or the consciousness of meaning that made human acts distinct from animals. Human perception draws on a wide field of associations, meanings, and memories that make human reason a mediator of physical events.

This analysis of comparative experiments continued in the next chapter (see chapter 8 here). Mead began by examining the experiments of L.T. Hobhouse [1901], a Fabian sociologist (see Deegan 1988, 263-6, on Fabian and Chicago sociology) who also studied animals and their ability to learn through a changed perception.19 On the one hand, Mead believed Hobhouse (and Morgan) overemphasized animal intelligence. Thorndike's [1898] studies of animal behavior, on the other hand, did not ascribe consciousness or intelligence to animals and Mead supported these findings and interpretations. Animal behavior, argued Mead, depends more on an automatic stimulus-response pattern than human behavior does. People also rely on reflective judgment employed during an act. Human perceptions are more than imitation or unreflexive acts. More careful animal experiments would be needed to show similarities between human and animal perceptions.

John Fiske's (1893) emphasis on the length of human infancy and the complexity of human learning complemented Mead's interest in human evolution and biology (see chapter 9 here). The early years of childhood require food, nurturance, exercise, and limited excitement. A new phase appears when puberty triggers sexual interest. The natural instinct to reproduce is essential to human life and should be incorporated in all models of human behavior. Early sexual education therefore, is necessary and should be integrated with other learning. Children's mental development should view life as an integrated system where ethical and mental maturation emerged simultaneously.

Like Dewey (1900/c. 1899), Mead advocated following the spontaneous interests of the child (see chapter 11). This spontaneity is not isolated within the child but effects people around him or her (see chapter 10 here; see also Addams 1909). This key rôle for children in generating society is often overlooked because of their dependence on the care of adults around them, especially mothers. The environment of children shapes them while they, in turn, shape it (Mead 1999). Mead also wrote about modern pedagogy as a joint editor for the *Elementary School Teacher* from 1908 to 1909 and for the *School Review*.20

The next, and last, section of Mead's first book focused on progressive education for students, teachers, and pedagogists.

III. Education from the Kindergartens to the University

Mead organized his readings on education here according to the life course: beginning with kindergartens and progressing though the training of college teachers. The last chapter addresses the industrial education of workers and their need for holistic training and practices.

The first two chapters (see chapters 11 and 12 here) are central to Mead's concept of play and its significance during early childhood (Mead 1999). The pure play period of the little child is characterized by an attitude and an activity: "When a child (at play) does assume a rôle he has in himself the stimuli which call out that particular response or group of responses" (Mead 1934, 150). The play attitude and activity emerge from the child and are not organized to respond to others' activities or social meanings, because this early play stage precedes the development of the child's mind and self. "Pure play" emerges from the unsocialized "I" and is associated with creativity, innovation, and a flowing unity of time, emotion, and experience (Mead 1896, see chapter 12 here). Although play is essential to the child's activities, adults can and should play, too. To paraphrase a cliche, all work and no play makes dull and deadened adults (see also Addams 1909; J. Dewey and E. Dewey 1915).

Play exhibits this holistic response of the child: "Play is the normal activity of the child" (see chapter 9 here, p. 80). Play develops the mind and physiological abilities, and it involves the whole child, including emotions, impulses, habits, and the other. Separating the child from his dependence on others introduces differentiation too soon and requires the imposition of motivation from outside the child. Dewey's concept of a "psychological fallacy," when adults think they can make a child learn or focus on an activity when the child is really learning about punishment and rewards, applies to this situation. "Life," wrote Mead, "should always be made to appeal to the child as a rational whole that falls within the scope of his comprehension" (see chapter 8 here, p. 138). This is the idea beyond Chicago's Laboratory Schools, and Mead built this concept based on the model of growth begun in the womb.

After kindergarten, organized around Froebel's concept of "mother-play" (Deegan 1999), the child's attitude toward play no longer structured classroom learning. This turns teaching and learning in elementary schools sites for power struggles. Industrial education, in particular (see chapter 18 here), brought the adults' work attitudes into the school and estranged the child's mind and body. In this situation, the meaning of the act is disassociated from the behavior needed to produce a capitalist commodity. The worker–to–be incorporates this alienating and artificially segmented view of work into his rôle in the workplace, the community, and everyday life. Mead's play model, in contrast, followed the child from the earliest steps in learning to the end of the elementary school in the eighth grade (Dewey 1900/c.1899). Play was, moreover, fundamental to the development of all subsequent behavior and education.

This "social situation" in the school shaping the mind of the child (see chapter 13 here) shared several characteristics similar to nonmodern forms of thought and social organization. Thus nonmodern forms (what Mead, following Wundt, called "primitive" forms) generated types of consciousness that can be studied to learn about children's social situation in the modern society's educational system. Again drawing on Wundt's work, and that of Mead's former student and colleague W.I. Thomas (1903, 1909), Mead examines the process of a *rite de passage* in nonmodern society. The child identifies with the group in this emotionally charged setting and learns to organize emotions within a communal context. Schools that defined education as an abstract process of learning separated themselves from the home, family, and workshop, and from institutional patterns that shaped the self, emotions, and meaning.

Thus play, children, playgrounds, the male academy, the female–defined social settlement, family, and gender were intertwined in Mead's study of play and in his study of emotions. This gendered aspect of Mead's life and work has been seriously neglected in the scholarship on him with few exceptions (e.g., Deegan 1988, 1991, 1999; Deegan and Hill 1987; Diner 1978; Ferguson 1980). Mead's concept of play emerged from this dense community of men and women who worked in Chicago and struggled for kindergartens, playgrounds, the natural emotional development of the child, and the child's right to play. The multiple focus on play, as well as juvenile delinquency and the elimination of child labor, provided a complex setting that generated a definition of play from a pragmatic perspective (see my discussion of "the world of Chicago pragmatism," Deegan 1999, xxiii-xxxi).

Within this *lebenswelt* (Schutz 1971), they developed a new, sophisticated pedagogy. The university faculty they trained, in turn, trained others to teach, but the larger university often separated pedagogy and the school of education from the enterprises of generating academic prestige and gaining access to resources (see chapters 14 and 15 here). Few universities, therefore, developed pedagogy as a specialty that was as important as other areas of knowledge and training. Mead and Dewey systematically concentrated on improving this neglected area of knowledge.[21] Although the university faculty often distanced itself from elementary school training, faculty, and work, Mead argued that these two forms of education were linked. Only a concentrated study of education as an academic subject could end this artificial division of knowledge.

Knowledge was changing as a function of science, the academy, and social interaction, and textbooks needed to incorporate this new knowledge and thereby transform the classroom. In both chapters 15 and 16, Mead discusses the new textbooks that were more accurate, holistic, and interesting to the student than the textbooks of an earlier age. Textbooks were dramatically changing as he spoke. University scholars, and not educational specialists, needed to articulate this new knowledge.[22]

The natural and physical sciences, in particular, must be on the forefront of new facts. This did not mean, however, that the holistic curiosity of an earlier date, exemplified in the discoveries of a scientist like Benjamin Franklin, should be discarded. Science fiction, too, captured the scientific imagination that was often stunted in the overly abstract study of science in the high school. Thus Mead recommended that books by Jules Verne[23] be combined with the latest scientific information and the use of mathematics.

Mead's discussion of teaching science in the high school (see chapter 16 here) as a holistic, naturally engaging study instead of as a highly differentiated, mathematically abstract analysis was given to three natural scientists at the University of Chicago when it was published in *Science* in 1906. In this public debate, Forest Ray Moulton (1906), of the Department of Astronomy; Robert Andrews Millikan (1906), of the Department of Physics and a Nobelist; and Charles R. Barnes (1906), of the Department of Botany, concurred with Mead's view of science, adolescence, and student interest. They were all familiar with badly trained and disaffected students. These eminent professors wanted to share their knowledge with students and teach a receptive audience that science was fascinating instead of teaching a disaffected group that misperceived science as boring and incomprehensible.

Mead's dedication to the natural sciences is often avoided or dismissed by sociologists who debate qualitative versus quantitative research methods, an argument fueled by Blumer's view of Mead's work. Mead, however, was interested in the physiological basis for behavior (see chapters 1 to 10 here), Einstein's theory of relativity and time (Mead 1938), and the history of science (see chapters 16 and 17 here). The teaching of mathematics was distorted in Mead's era, and this same distortion plagues educators today. Ironically, many sociologists who claim to enjoy and follow Mead often share this same misperception and apprehension.

The teaching of science in college (see chapter 17) is also critiqued in a lengthy paper that Mead delivered in 1906 to the Chicago chapter of Sigma Chi. Mead noted the unpopularity of sciences on the collegiate level, and this remains a contemporary problem. The divorce of the natural sciences from the students' interest occured on all levels of training. Showing the human side of the natural sciences was necessary to recruit scientists to a type of labor that could be learned, like all labor, as an apprentice (see Mead 1999).

Mead's last essay in this section, on "Industrial Education, the Working Man, and the School" (see chapter 18 here), appears to be an unexpected excursion from college students studying the hard sciences to laborers. But it was exactly this dichotomized perception of ideas and labor that Mead opposed. Workers also need holistic, interesting education. Vocational education was often disassociated from the whole human being, and this socially constructed pedagogy limited the life and vision of laborers. Vocational education to

Mead, and his colleagues Dewey and Addams, involved a dense appreciation of the unity of theory and application. The unity of things that are often separated was an epistemological assumption that permeated his work on education and social reform, as well. I briefly examine this connection here, while I recommend reading my fuller examinations of this reform context elsewhere (e.g., Deegan 1988, 1999).

Mead and his Working Hypotheses on Physiology and Social Reform

As noted, Mead was committed to laboratory and experimental work in progressive education located at the Laboratory Schools (see Cremlin 1961; De Pencier 1967; Deegan 1999; and Dewey 1900/ c. 1899). These multi-dimensional laboratory interests melded in a local school for disabled children, as well: the Chicago Physiological School. This institution was founded by Mary R. Campbell who approached officials at the University of Chicago in 1899. Members of the first board included William R. Harper, the president of the University of Chicago, Dewey, Angell, and Henry H. Donaldson, chief consulting neurologist at the university where he headed the physiological laboratory. Mead served as the president of the board during the school's five years of existence.

This experimental setting was also linked to the Psychological Laboratory, headed by Angell at the University of Chicago, and based on the natural science concept of a quantitative experiment. Again, as noted earlier, many contemporary scholars interpret Mead as opposed to such a setting, but it was vital to the early writings of the functional psychologists and was reflected in Mead's work here. Mead wanted to extend this setting, moreover, to a population of children with physical and mental challenges.

One study, by Robert Kelley and Angell (1903) compared the behavior and functioning of students from the two types of "laboratory schools." Angell and other colleagues intended further studies, but the school's finances were increasingly precarious due to the poverty of the children and the expensive care they required (see Deegan 1988, 112). The Chicago Physiological School was unstable financially, and the board saw Campbell as at least partially at fault in the fiasco. One crisis came to a head in 1903 when Harper, Donaldson, and Mead personally helped pay a pressing debt. This could not be a continual policy, however, and a new head and board members were needed. In 1904, the school came to a crashing halt, the same year that Dewey's Laboratory Schools were devastated by his fiery exit from the University of Chicago because of Harper's meddling and refusal to adequately fund that prestigious institution (see discussion in Deegan 1999, lxx-lxxi). Perhaps Mead felt the "other" Laboratory Schools were more important, and one school had to be sacrificed in this new crisis. Mead continued to argue for the need for a school for disabled children and an accompanying laboratory, nonetheless, until 1908.[24]

Mead's essays published here were largely written during the years of the unsuccessful physiological school, when he frequently offered coursework on comparative physiology. Thus Mead was interested in what is now considered "special education" although he does not explore this population in his more general essays on education (e.g., see chapters 11 to 18 here). We can only speculate on what might have happened to Mead's interests in disability and its impact on the self and education if this school had been adequately financed.

In addition to Mead's commitments to the Laboratory Schools, he chaired the Education Committee at the Chicago City Club, a male reform and social group that was extremely influential in Chicago politics and policymaking (Diner 1980). In this capacity, Mead addressed the practical issues of applying his more abstract ideas within a public, civic arena. In 1912, shortly after her wrote this book of essays, Mead joined other members of the Chicago City Club to document the need to keep children in school until sixteen years of age instead of fourteen (see Mead, Weidt, and Broggan 1912). This work complemented that of the Hull-House residents and University of Chicago sociologists Sophonisba Breckinridge and Edith Abbott (e.g., 1912; Mead, Weidt, and Broggan 1912).

Similarly, Mead participated in a garment workers' strike initiated by women in 1910, and this effort shows his commitment to women's leadership, unionization, and paid labor, as well as the rights of the working class (Buhle 1976; Deegan 1988, 115–116). He also joined in a similar garment workers' strike in 1915 (see Ickes, Mead, and Tucker 1915). Many female Hull–House residents were major figures during the course of both strikes, when Mead again joined the fight for social justice for laborers.

In addition, Mead served many years as a member of the board of the Immigrants' Protection League (IPL), which was organized at Hull-House. This group was organized to shield young women from men who took advantage of the women's confusion upon arriving in America (Deegan 1988, 211). Mead thereby joined women in yet another struggle for increasing women's right to a wider public voice.

Thus Mead consistently applied his ideas discussed in these essays, often during and after the time he wrote them. This work often complements his later writings, but sometimes it contradicts them indicating a shifting, complex intellectual and political apparatus over the course of Mead's life. Sorting out the relationship between the early and late writings, therefore, is a challenge to be addressed in future scholarship. Publication of Mead's first book opens up entirely new scholarly questions about his epistemology, intellectual networks, institutional ties, and politics.

Conclusion

George Herbert Mead was a dedicated scholar who intended his brilliant, early essays to be published as a book. This dream never materialized, and the course of his career and ideas were dramatically reshaped as a result. Indeed, many of his early essays were never published, and the essays that were published were placed in a different context than the one he intended. Mead's central interests in physiology, emotions, early psychologists (especially Wundt), mathematics, pedagogy, and early childhood were consequently less visible.

Mead must be reconceptualized as a sociologist, social psychologist, and theorist as a result of these essays. I edited an anthology of his work on play after reading only one new article (Mead 1999; see chapter 11 here). It caused me to reread, reorganize, and ultimately reconceptualize his notions of play and the self, children and adults, play, work, and art. Other previously unknown articles will have the same impact. It is tempting to explore these new avenues, but it is more important at this point to share these essays with the wider scholarly community.

This reconsideration of Mead opens up new connections to Germanic thought, especially to Wundt, to physiological and mathematical models of human behavior, and the relation of gender to the social creation and application of knowledge. Mead's rôle in progressive education must also be revised and more strongly linked to Dewey. Mead anticipated and amplified many of Dewey's ideas concerning progressive education and this rôle can now be understood in more detail. Mead's concept of labor and education can also be reconsidered and placed in the broader context of Chicago's labor unions, teachers' unions, and the meaning of a liberating education for detached and alienated workers. All these topics and more are opened to new analyses as a result of Mead's first book, a volume finally available almost a century after its galleys were completed.

Part I

The Biologic Individual

1

The Social Character of Instinct [1]

The primitive instincts of the human animal are practically all social. It is at best a difficult task to isolate and define human instincts, but whatever group one gathers together is bound to refer to conduct that is determined by the movements of other individuals whose conduct is like our own. In fact, the earlier history of the race and the history of childhood shows us that primitive consciousness even of the physical world is social, and only becomes a physical consciousness with the growing powers of reflection.

A recently published list of human instincts, that of William McDougall [1908] in his *Introduction to Social Psychology*, enumerates flight, repulsion, curiosity, pugnacity, subjection, self-assertion, the parental instinct, that of reproduction, the gregarious instinct, and the instincts of acquisition, and construction. If the objects of instinctive flight and curiosity were defined, their predominantly social character would be evident. Excepting the questionable instincts of acquisition and construction, we find the instinctive conduct here presented taking place within a social environment. This conduct might be more sharply defined as that which is mediated by the movements of other individuals, to which our own movements are instinctively adjusted, though this definition does not necessarily imply the presentation of such individuals as objects. This is, as has already been suggested, the type of conduct which earliest appears in the infancy of the form or the race. The earliest adjustments of the child are to the movements of the mother, and for primitive people the changes of the whole surrounding world are socially interpreted before they can be scientifically determined. And yet psychologists, such as [James Mark] Baldwin [1897],[2] have suggested that the child early distinguishes the social object from the physical by its unreliability.

3

Within this field of social consciousness arise gradually objects—social objects, the selves, the me, and the others. I wish to discuss for a few moments the process by which these objects arise. That these instinctive social processes are intimately connected with the emotions, that many of the so-called expressions of the emotions are vestiges or early stages of instinctive reactions, has been recognized in all psychological treatment of the emotions and the instincts, but, so far as I know, the function which these expressions of the emotions may have in the process of mediating social conduct and then in forming the objects within social consciousness has not been adequately studied.

I will assume the point of view given in Dewey's [1894, 1895a, b] articles on the emotions, in the first and second volumes of the *Psychological Review*—or rather the still more admirable and succinct statement of this position in [James Rowland] Angell's *Psychology* [e.g., 1907].[3] The so-called expressions of the emotions are physiologically traced either to the valuable instinctive activities themselves or to evidences of preparation on the part of the system, through blood-flow, the rhythm of breathing, and like organic changes, for such instinctive processes. This theory assumes that such a physiological explanation could be offered for all the expressions of the emotions, and that [Charles] Darwin's [1872] own position could be rendered more consistently Darwinian than the form in which he left it. It assumes further that emotional situations which are responsible for the so-called expressions of the emotions imply some break—some barrier to action—and that this break or inhibition of immediate overt action is due to the conflict of impulses mediated by the same situation. At this point the interpretation of the James-Lange [Lange and James, 1967/c. 1922][4] theory of the emotions demands that we account for the emotional consciousness by the stimulation of those expressions of the emotions, the preparation for the act and the earlier stages of the act itself. These physiological processes themselves produce the emotion—or rather the emotion is the feel of these physiological processes. Over against this bald statement Dewey and Angell insist that in the process of recognizing and building up of the object as fearful, for example, our consciousness of the physiological processes are essential. A cold-blooded attitude would never lead to the presentation of an object of emotion. Our own physiological condition is, then, evidence to us of how fearful the object is. Thus, at least to the individual who experiencing the emotion, this theory recognizes that the so-called expressions of the emotions are valuable functionally, even when they may be vestiges of acts no longer executed. But this revelation of the emotional nature of the situation to the subject himself is not the only mediating function which these expressions of the emotions may perform. As already indicated, they are all of them early stages in the act or evidences of organic preparations for instinctive acts. As evidences of an on-going act, they are of the highest value as the very cues to which other individuals in the group respond.

We have already defined social conduct as that in which the acts are adjusted to the movements of others. Perfection of adjustment implies response to the earliest indications of the overt act. Just as the fencer reads in the eye of his opponent the coming thrust and is ready with the parry before the thrust is made, so we are continually reading from the attitude, the facial expressions, the gestures, and the tones of the voice the coming actions of those with reference to whom we must act. Such beginnings of acts, and organic preparations for action, which have been called expressions of emotion, are just the cues which have been selected and preserved as the means of mediating social conduct. Before conscious communication by symbols arises in gestures, signs, and articulate sounds, there exists in these earliest stages of acts and their physiological fringes the means of co-ordinating social conduct, the means of unconscious communication. And conscious communication has made use of these very expressions of the emotion to build up its signs. They were already signs. They had been already naturally selected and preserved as signs in unreflective social conduct before they were specialized as symbols.

To recur to the situation out of which the emotion arises, we find it one in which inhibition through conflicting impulses makes readjustment necessary. The situation is a social situation. Its readjustment will be a social readjustment. The first objects that must be presented are social objects. What will be the material out of which these social objects will be constructed? As our physical objects later come to be built up out of sensuous stuff, and fundamentally out of the sensuous experiences of contact, so must we not assume that the stuff out of which selves are constructed is emotional consciousness?

In the first place, the emotional consciousness belongs at the beginning of the reflective process. It comes before the possibility of thought or of reflective action. It arises immediately upon the inhibition of the act. It is the earliest stuff out of which objects can be built in the history of presentative consciousness, and this earliest instinctive consciousness is primarily social. The first objects that must be presented are then social objects. The first adjustments and readjustments must be made to social stimulations, and these social stimulations must be first constructed into social objects. Secondly, introspection reveals that our thoughts and our volitions are referred to selves whose content is affective. Thought and volition develop and interpret the situation that is first of all emotional. It is the emotion that is most particular, most definitely referred to, or rather made a part of the individual self and the other selves. Thought and action demand universality for their own validity. To generalize and universalize the emotion deprives it of the very content which enables it to function.

It is, then, further through these cues of social conduct, these so-called expressions of the emotions, that the social objects are first differentiated. These were the instinctive means of organizing social conduct. The earliest readjustments had to be in terms of those stimulations. We find them in our experience in the value which human faces and attitudes and facial expressions have for us, when the individuals are complete strangers, when we would be unable to define intellectually one of the values to which we instinctively respond. We go to strange cities and move about among unknown men without perhaps presenting to ourselves the ideas of one of them, and yet successfully recognize and respond to each attitude and gesture which our passing intercourse involves. There is in all of us a fund of unexplored social organization which enables us to act more surely in a social environment than in the physical. This content of consciousness is one of feeling. It is not sensuous. What we see in the faces and attitudes of others is not the face or the body. It is the indication of certain sorts of conduct, and the evidence of the feeling that conduct involves. We see the coming acts and feel the values which express themselves in those actions.

We feel, first of all, to be sure, the tendency to respond to the social stimulus and the emotional content that accompanies it, when momentarily checked. The presentation of the social stimulus to this response follows, first of all, in terms of the response itself. It is the organization of the response or the various responses that determines the construction of the object—the social stimulus. The social object is then constructed out of this emotional material which accompanies the inhibited social impulses in their earlier phases. It follows from this that the self loses its peculiar content when intellectualized. The average man, the economic man, the man in the street are not selves in the meaning of our social consciousness. These selves have the same immediacy as the "me." They are made out of the same stuff.

The distinction between the me and the alteri is given in the nature of the instinct. In the instinct of pugnacity the object is a hateful one, i.e., the content of the emotion arising from the checking of the hostile impulse. The primitively hateful individual is the one who, at least for the moment, successfully checks the instinct to attack. Just what that content will be depends upon the ground of the inhibition. If indications of superior prowess check the attack, the content of the alter is the objectified emotional content of one's impulse to escape from certain indications of dangerous action surcharged with that emotional content which answers to the inhibited pugnacity, i.e., anger built around the indications of prowess and vulnerability, and the me is the consciousness of the inhibited efforts both to escape and attack in terms of the same emotional contents. The alter in this social consciousness is quite as immediate as the me. There is no projection nor ejection of subjectivity from the self into the other. It is only a secondary process which leads to the projection of oneself into the other, putting oneself in his place. The object self of the protective instinct is the objectified group of social indications of the action of the child or the helpless member of the family or larger group, placed for the moment at least beyond our fostering care and surcharged with the tender emotion. A detailed analysis is, of course, in place here that must be postponed.

To sum up. We find a great group of primitive instincts which are social in the sense that the responses arise in answer to indications of various movements in other individuals of the group. That these indications are all the early stages in activities which when checked give rise to emotional experiences, in the individual, and answering responses in other members of the group. Their importance as indications of socially important conduct is vital, and has led to their selection and preservation and final development into the language of signs and articulate speech. Furthermore, the earliest stage in the reflective process, the earliest objectification in the child and the race, has been among theses social instincts, and here the objectification has been mediated by those early stages in the act which inevitably give rise to emotion, so that the content of the object is and must be emotional, and that these indications of the on-going act have both the function of stimulating the social response and indicating the import of the act to the individual and the *socii* [other selves]. I would convert the proposition and insist that all objects whose content is emotional are selves—social objects—for which position the psychology of art, the theory of *Einfühlung* [feeling], would afford abundant illustration.

2

Social Psychology as Counterpart to Physiological Psychology[1]

There is the widest divergence among psychologists as to the nature of Social Psychology. The most recent text-book under this title—the *Social Psychology* [1908, 1][2] of Professor [E.A.] Ross—opens with this sentence: "Social Psychology, as the writer conceives it, studies the psychic planes and currents that come into existence among men in consequence of their association" That is, it must confine itself to the "uniformities in feeling, belief, or volition—and hence in action—which are due to the interaction of human beings" (ibid.). Here we find a certain field of human experience cut off from the rest, because men and women influence each other within that field. There result certain uniformities from this interaction and this makes the subject-matter of the science of social psychology. In the same manner one might investigate the psychology of mountain tribes because they are subject to the influence of high altitudes and rugged landscape. Sociality is for Professor Ross no fundamental feature of human consciousness, no determining form of its structure.

In the Introduction to *Social Psychology* of [William] McDougall [1908],[3] which appeared but a few months before the treatise we have just mentioned, human consciousness is conceived of as determined by social instincts, whose study reveals sociality not as the result of interaction but as the medium within which intelligence and human emotion must arise.

If we turn to standard treatises on psychology, we find the social aspect of human consciousness dealt with in very varying fashion. [Josiah] Royce, both in his psychology and in the volume, *Studies in Good and Evil* [1898], makes out of the consciousness of oneself over against other selves the source of all reflection. Thought, ac-

9

cording to Professor Royce, in its dependence upon symbolic means of expression, has arisen out of intercourse, and presupposes, not only in the forms of language, but in the meanings of language, social consciousness. Only through imitation and opposition to others could one's own conduct and expression gain any meaning for one's self, not to speak of the interpretation of the conduct of others through one's own imitative responses to their acts. Here we stand upon the familiar ground of Professor [James Mark] Baldwin's [1895, 1897] studies of social consciousness. The *ego* [the self] and the *socius* [the self of the other] are inseparable, and the medium of alternative differentiation and identification is imitation. But from the point of view of their psychological treatises we feel that these writers have said too much or too little of the form of sociality. If we turn to the structural psychologists, we find the social aspect of consciousness appearing only as one of the results of certain features of our affective nature and its bodily organism. The self arises in the individual consciousness through apperceptive[4] organization and enters into relation with other selves to whom it is adapted by organic structure. In Professor [William] James's [1890, vol. 1, chapter 10] treatise the self is brilliantly dealt with in a chapter by itself. Within that chapter we see that, as a self, it is completely knit into a social consciousness, that the diameter of the self waxes and wanes with the field of social activity, but what the value of this nature of the self is for the cognitive and emotional phases of consciousness we do not discover. In the genetic treatment given by Professor [James Rowland] Angell [1907], the last chapter deals with the self. Here, indeed, we feel the form of sociality is the culmination, and the treatment of attention, of the impulses, and the emotions, and finally of volition involves so definite in a social organization of consciousness, that in the light of the last chapter, the reader feels that a rereading would give a new meaning to what has gone before. If we except Professor [Charles H.] Cooley,[5] in his *Human Nature and the Social Order* [1902], and his *Social Organization* [1909] the sociologists have no adequate social psychology with which to interpret their own science. The modern sociologists neither abjure psychology with [Auguste] Comte [1853], nor determine what the value of the social character, of human consciousness is for the psychology which they attempt to use.

To repeat the points of view we have noted, some see in social consciousness nothing but uniformities in conduct and feeling that result from the interaction of men and women, others recognize a consciousness that is organized through social instincts, others still find in the medium of communication and the thought that depends upon it a social origin for reflective consciousness itself, still others find the social aspect of human nature to be only the product of an already organized intelligence responding to certain social impulses, while others find that an organized intelligence in the form of a self could arise only over against other selves that must exist in consciousness as immediately as the subject self, still others are content to recognize necessary social conditions in the genesis of volition and the self that expresses itself in volition.

Now it is evident that we cannot take both positions. We cannot assume that the self is both a product and a presupposition of human consciousness, that reflection has arisen through social consciousness, and that social intercourse has arisen because human individuals had ideas and meanings to express.

I desire to call attention to the implications for psychology of the positions defended by McDougall, by Royce and Baldwin respectively, if they are consistently maintained. The positions I have in mind are the following: that human nature is endowed with and organized by social instincts and impulses; that the consciousness of meaning has arisen through social intercommunication; and finally that the *ego*, the self, that is implied in every act, in every volition, with reference to which our primary judgments of valuation are made, must exist in a social consciousness within which the *socii*, the other selves, are as immediately given as is the subject self.

[William] McDougall [1908] lists eleven human instincts: flight, repulsion, curiosity, pugnacity, subjection, self-display, the parental instinct, the instinct of reproduction, the gregarious instinct, the instinct of acquisition, and the instinct of construction. Six of these are social, without question: pugnacity, subjection, self-display, the parental instinct, the instinct of reproduction, and the gregarious instinct. These would probably be the instincts most widely accepted by those who are willing to accept human instincts at all. Four of the others, repulsion, curiosity, acquisition, and construction, would be questionable, or conceivably to be resolved into other instincts. The fact is that McDougall has his doctrine of instincts so essentially bound up with a doctrine of emotions and sentiments that he is evidently forced to somewhat strain his table of instincts to get in the proper number of corresponding emotions. But the fact that is of moment is that the psychologist who recognizes instincts and impulses will find among them a preponderating number that are social. By a social instinct is meant a well-defined tendency to act under the stimulation of another individual of the same species. If self conscious conduct arises out of controlled and organized impulse, and impulses arise out of social instincts, and the responses to these social stimulations become stimuli to corresponding social acts on the part of others, it is evident that human conduct was from the beginning of its development in a social medium. The implication is highly important for its bearing upon the theory of imitation, which, as is indicated above, plays a great part in current social psychology.

There are two implications of the theory that important social instincts lie behind developed human consciousness—two to which I wish to call attention. The first is that any such group of instincts inevitably provides the content and the form of a group of social objects. An instinct implies first of all a certain type of stimulus to which the organism is attuned. This sensuous content will attract the attention of the individual to the exclusion of other stimuli. And the organism will respond to it by a certain attitude that represents the group of responses for which such an instinct is responsible. These two are the characteristics of an object in our consciousness—a content toward which the individual is susceptible as a stimulus, and an attitude of response toward this peculiar type of content. In our consciousness of this sensuous content and of our attitude toward it, we have both the content of the object as a thing and the meaning of it, both the perception and the concept of it, at least implicit in the experience. The implication of an organized group of social instincts is the implicit presence in undeveloped human consciousness of both the matter and the form of a social object.

The second implication has to do with the theory of imitation. Social instincts imply that certain attitudes and movements of one form are stimuli in other forms to certain types of response. In the instinct of fighting these responses will be of one sort, in that of parental care another. The responses will be adapted to the stimulus and may vary from it or may approach it in its own form or outward appearance. It may be that, as in the case of the gregarious instinct, the action of one form may be a stimulus to the other to do the same thing—to the member of the herd, for example, to run away in the direction in which another member of the herd is running. We have no evidence that such a reaction is any more an imitation than if the instinctive response were that of running away from an enemy which threatened the animal. Furthermore, a group of well-organized social instincts will frequently lead one form to place another under the influence of the same stimuli which are affecting it.[6]

Thus a parent form, taking a young form with it in its own hunting, subjects the instincts which the child form has inherited to the same stimuli as those which arouse the hunting reaction in the parent form. In various ways it is possible that the action of one form should serve directly or indirectly to mobilize a similar instinct in another form where there is no more question of imitation than there is in the case in which the action of one form calls out, for the protection of life, a diametrically opposite reaction. Another phase of the matter is also of importance for the interpretation of the so-called imitative processes, in lower animal forms and in the conduct of young children. I refer to what Professor Baldwin has been pleased to call the circular reaction, the instance in which, in his terminology, the individual imitates himself. One illustration of this, that of mastication, which sets free the stimuli which again arouse the masticating reflexes, is a purely mechanical circle, similar to that which is responsible for the rhythmical processes of walking, but which has no important likeness to such processes as that of learning to talk. In the latter experiences the child repeats continually a sound which he has mastered, perhaps without being perceptibly influenced by the sounds about him—the da-da-da, the ma-ma-ma, of the earliest articulation. Here we have the child producing the stimulus which in a socially organized human animal calls for a response of another articulation.

We see the same thing probably in a bird's insistent repetition of its own notes. The child is making the first uncertain efforts to speak—in this case to himself; that is, in response to an articulate sound which operates as a stimulus upon his auditory apparatus as inevitably as if the sound were made by another. The bird is responding to the note he sings himself as definitely as if he responded to a note uttered by another bird. In neither case is there any evidence that the sound which is the stimulus operates by its quality to induce the child or the bird to produce a sound which shall be like that which is heard. Under the influence of social instincts, animals and young children or primitive peoples may be stimulated to many reactions which are like those which, directly or indirectly, are responsible for them without there being any justification for the assumption that the process is one of imitation—in any sense which is connoted by that term in our own consciousness. When another self is present in consciousness doing something, then such a self may be imitated by the self that is conscious of him in his conduct, but by what possible mechanism, short of a miracle, the conduct of one form should act as a stimulus to another to do, not what the situation calls for, but something like that which the first form is doing, is beyond ordinary comprehension. Imitation becomes comprehensible when there is a consciousness of other selves, and not before. However, an organization of social instincts gives rise to many situations which have the outward appearance of imitation, but these situations—those in which, under the influence of social stimulation, one form does what others are doing—are no more responsible for the appearance in consciousness of other selves that answer to our own than are the situations which call out different and even opposed reactions.

Social consciousness is the presupposition of imitation, and when Professor Royce, both in the eighth chapter of *Studies of Good and Evil* [1898], and in the twelfth chapter of his *Outlines of Psychology* [1903], makes imitation the means of getting the meaning of what others and we ourselves are doing, he seems to be either putting the cart before the horse, or else to be saying that the ideas which we have of the actions of others are ideo-motor in their character, but this does not make out of imitation the means of their becoming ideo-motor. The sight of a man pushing a stone registers itself as a meaning through a tendency in ourselves to push the stone, but it is a far call from this to the statement that it is first through imitation of him or some one else pushing stones that we have gained the motor-idea of stone-pushing.

The important character of social organization of conduct or behavior through instincts is not that one form in a social group does what the others do, but that the conduct of one form is a stimulus to another to a certain act, and that this act again becomes a stimulus to first to a certain reaction, and so on in ceaseless interaction. The likeness of the actions is of minimal importance compared with the fact that the actions of one form have the implicit meaning of a certain response to another form. The probable beginning of human communication was in co-operation, not in imitation, where conduct differed and yet where the act of the one answered to and called out the act of the other. The conception of imitation as it has functioned in social psychology needs to be developed into a theory of social stimulation and response and of the social situations which these stimulations and responses create. Here we have the matter and the form of the social object, and here we have also the medium of communication and reflection.

The second position to which I wish to call attention, and whose implications I wish to discuss, is that the consciousness of meaning is social in its origin. The dominant theory at present, that which is most elaborately stated by Wundt in the first volume of his *Volkerpsychologie* [1900],[7] regards language as the outgrowth of gesture, the vocal gesture. As a gesture, it is primarily an expression of emotion. But the gesture itself is a syncopated act, one that has been cut short, a torso which conveys the emotional import of the act. Out of the emotional signification has grown the intellectual signification. It is evident that but for the original situation of social interaction the bodily and vocal gestures could never have attained their signification. It is their reference to other individuals that has turned expression, as a mere outflow of nervous excitement, into meaning, and this meaning was the value of the act for the other individual, and his response to the expression of the emotion, in terms of another syncopated act, with its social signification, gave the first basis for communication, for common understanding, for the recognition of the attitudes which men mutually held toward each other within a field of social interaction. Attitudes had meanings when they reflected possible acts. And the acts could have meanings when they called out definite reactions which call out still other appropriate responses: that is, when the common content of the act is reflected by the different parts played by individuals, through gestures—truncated acts, Here is the birth of the symbol, and the possibility of thought. Still, thought remains in its abstractest form sublimated conversation. Thus reflective consciousness implies a social situation which has been its precondition. Antecedent to the reflective consciousness within which we exist, in the beginnings of the society of men and in the life of every child that arises to reflective consciousness, there must have been this condition of interrelation by acts springing from social instincts.

Finally, Professor Baldwin [1895, 1897] has abundantly exemplified the interdependence of the *ego* and the *socius*, of the self and the other. It is still truer to say the self and the others, the *ego* and the *socii*. If the self-form is an essential form of all our consciousness, it necessarily carries with it the other-form. Whatever may be the meta-physical impossibilities or possibilities of solipsism, psychologically it is nonexistent. There must be other selves if one's own is to exist. Psychological analysis, retrospection, and the study of children and primitive people give no inkling of situations in which a self could have existed in consciousness except as the counterpart of other selves. We even can recognize that in the definition of these selves in consciousness, the child and primitive man have defined the outlines and the character of the others earlier than they have defined their own selves. We may fairly say a social group is an implication of the structure of the only consciousness that we know.

If these positions are correct, it is evident that we must be as much beholden to social science to present and analyze the social group with its objects, its interrelations, its selves, as a precondition of our reflective and self-consciousness, as we are beholden to physiological science to present and analyze the physical complex which is the pre-condition of our physical consciousness. In other words, a social psychology should be the counterpart of physiological psychology. In each case the conditions under which certain phases of consciousness arise must be studied by other sciences, because the consciousness which the psychologist analyzes presupposes objects and processes which are preconditions of itself and its processes. It is true that our reflection can sweep the very physical and social objects which the physical and social sciences have presented within itself, and regard them as psychical presentations. But in doing this it is presupposing another brain that conditions its action, and whose defection would bring collapse to the very thought that reduced the brain to states of consciousness. In the same manner we may wipe the *alteri* out of existence and reduce our social world to our individual selves, regarding the others as constructions of our own, but we can only do it to some other audience with whom our thought holds converse, even if this self is only the I and the Me of actual thought, but behind these protagonists stand the chorus of others to whom we rehearse our reasonings by word of mouth or through the printed page.

The evolutionary social science which shall describe and explain the origins of human society, and the social sciences which shall finally determine what are the laws of social growth and organization, will be as essential for determining the objective conditions of social consciousness, as the biological sciences are to determine the conditions of consciousness in the biological world. By no possibility can psychology deal with the material with which physiology and the social sciences deal, because the consciousness of psychological science arises within a physical and a social world that are presuppositions of itself. From a logical point of view a social psychology is strictly parallel to a physiological psychology.

3

What Social Objects Must Psychology Presuppose?[1]

There is a persistent tendency among present-day psychologists to use consciousness as the older rationalistic psychology used the soul. It is spoken of as something that appears at a certain point; it is a something into which the object of knowledge in some sense enters from without. It is conceived to have certain functions—in the place of faculties. It is as completely separated from the physical body by the doctrine of parallelism as the metaphysical body was separated from the metaphysical soul by their opposite qualities.

Functional psychology has set itself the program of assimilating the purposive character of conscious processes—or of consciousness as it is termed—to the evolutionary conception of adaptation, but instead of making consciousness in human individuals a particular expression of a great process, as is demanded of a philosophy of nature, it comes in generally as a new and peculiar factor which even demands a new formula of evolution for its explanation, it involves a new evolution superinduced upon the old.

In spite of much philosophizing, the field which is open to introspection is identified in current psychological practice with consciousness and the object of knowledge is placed within this field, and related to the physical world—spoken of as an external field of reality—by a parallelistic series. This psychological practice tends to accept the conceptual objects of science, the atoms, molecules, other vortex rings, ions, and electrons, as the substantial realities of the physical world, and by implication at least, to relegate the sensuous content of objects of direct physical experience to this separate field of consciousness. The old-fashioned idealist has, then, only to point out the thought structure of these hypothetical objects of science to

19

sweep triumphantly with one stroke of his wand the whole world of nature within this limited field of the consciousness open to introspection. Whereupon the solipsistic spook arises again to reduce one's world to a nutshell.

The way out of these crude psychological conceptions, in my mind, lies in the recognition that psychical consciousness is a particular phase in development of reality, not an islanded phase of reality connected with the rest of it by a one to one relationship of parallel series. This point of view I have elsewhere developed somewhat obscurely and ineffectually, I am afraid.[2]

What I wish to call to your attention in the few moments at my disposal is another phase of this situation which is itself psychological in its character—the presupposition of selves as already in existence before the peculiar phase of consciousness can arise, which psychology studies. Most of us admit the reality of the objects of direct physical experience until we are become [sic] too deeply entangled in our psychological analyses of cognition.

Unless we subject ourselves to the third degree of criticism, the parallelism of which we speak lies between the processes of brain tissues which can be seen and smelt and handled and the states of consciousness which are conditioned by them. While this admission guarantees the physical bodies of our fellows as equally real, the self is relegated to the restricted field of introspected consciousness and enjoys not the reality of a so-called, external object, but only that of a combination of states of consciousness. Into the existence of those states of consciousness in another, we are solemnly told we can only inferentially enter by a process of analogy from the relations of our own introspected states and the movements of our bodies to the movements of other bodies and the hypothetical conscious states that should accompany them. If we approach the self from within, our analysis recognizes, to be sure, its close relationship to, if not its reality with, the organization of consciousness, especially as seen in conation, in apperception,[3] in voluntary attention, in conduct, but what can be isolated as self-consciousness as such reduces to a peculiar feeling of intimacy in certain conscious states, and the self gathers, for some unexplained reason, about a core of certain value and seemingly unimportant organic sensations—a feeling of contraction in the brow, or in the throat, or goes out to the muscular innervations all over the body which are not involved directly in what we are doing or perceiving. And yet when we proceed introspectively the whole field of consciousness is ascribed to this self, for it is only in so far as we are self-conscious that we can introspect at all.

But what I wish to emphasize is that the other selves disappear as given realities even when we are willing to admit the real objects of physical experience. The self arises within the introspected field. It has no existence outside that introspected field, and other selves[4] are only projects and ejects of that field. Each self is an Island, and each self is sure only of its own Island, for who knows what mirages may arise above this analogical sea.

It is fair to assume that, if we had exact social sciences which could define persons precisely and determine the laws of social change with mathematical exactness, we would accept selves as there in the same sense in which we accept physical objects. They would be guaranteed by their sciences—for in the practice of thought, we are as convinced as the Greeks that exact knowledge assures the existence of the object of knowledge.

It is evident that the assumption of the self as given by social science in advance of introspection would materially and fundamentally affect our psychological practice. Consciousness as present in selves would be given as there, outside the field of introspection. Psychological science would have to presuppose selves as the precondition of consciousness in individuals just as it presupposes nervous systems and vascular changes. In actual psychological analysis we should condition the existence and process of states and streams of consciousness upon the normal presence and functioning of these selves, as we condition the appearance and functioning of consciousness upon the normal structure and operation of the physical mechanism that our psychology presupposes.

In a manner we do this in treatises on mob-psychology, in such a treatise on social psychology as that of [Charles H.] Cooley's *Human Nature and the Social Order* [1902]. [William] McDougall's book *Social Psychology* [1908] prepares the way for it, in carrying back the processes of consciousness to social impulses and instincts—to those terms in which somewhat vaguely selves are stated in an evolutionary theory of society.

The economic man of the Dismal Science was an attempt to state the self in terms of an objective and exact social science. But fortunately the economic man has proved spurious. He does not exist. The economic man is as little guaranteed by the orthodox political economy as *Realia* [real things, realities] were by the metaphysics of scholasticism.

Social science in anthropology, in sociology pure and impure, dynamic and static, has not as yet found its scientific method. It is not able to satisfactorily define its objects, nor to formulate their laws of change and development. Until the social sciences are able to state the social individual in terms of social processes, as the physical sciences define their objects in terms of physical change, they will not have risen to the point at which they can force their object upon an introspective psychology. We can to-day foresee the possibility of this. Eugenics, education, even political and economic sciences, pass beyond the phase of description and look toward the formation of the social object. We recognize that we control the conditions which determine the individual. His errors and shortcomings can be conceivably corrected. His misery may be eliminated. His mental and moral defects corrected. His heredity, social and physical, may be perfected. His very moral self-consciousness through normal and healthful social conduct, through adequate consciousness of his relations to others, may be constituted and established. But without awaiting the development of the social sciences it is possible to indicate in the nature of the consciousness which psychology itself analyzes the presupposition of social objects, whose objective reality is a condition of the consciousness of self.

The contribution that I wish to suggest toward the recognition of the given character of other selves is from psychology itself, and arises out of the psychological theory of the origin of language and its relation to Meaning.

This theory, as you know, has been considerably advanced by Wundt's formulation of the relation of language to gesture.[5] From this point of view language in its earliest form comes under that group of movements which, since [Charles] Darwin [1872], have been called expressions of the emotions. They fall into classes which have been regarded as without essential connection. Either they are elements—mainly preparatory—beginnings of acts—social acts,— actions and reactions—which arise under the stimulation of other individuals, such as clenching the fists, grinding the teeth, assuming an attitude of defense—or else they are regarded as outflows of nervous energy which sluice off the nervous excitement or reinforce and prepare indirectly for action.

Such gestures, if we may use the term in this generalized sense, act as stimuli to other forms which are already under social stimulation. The phase of the subject which has not been sufficiently emphasized is the value which these truncated acts, these beginnings of inhibited movements, these gestures, have as appropriate stimulations for the conduct of other individuals.

Inevitably forms, that act and react to and upon each other, come to prepare for each other's reaction by the early movements in the act.[6] The preliminaries of a doe or cock fight amply illustrate the sensitiveness of such individuals to the earliest perceptible indications of coming acts. To a large degree forms, which live in groups or in the relation of the animals of prey and those they prey upon, act upon these first signs of oncoming acts. In all gestures, to whatever class they belong, whether they are the beginnings of the outgoing act itself, or are only indications of the attitude and nervous tension which these acts involve, have this value of stimulating forms, socially organized, to reactions appropriate to the attack, or flight, of wooing, or suckling, of another form.

Illustrations are to be found in human conduct, in such situations as fencing, where one combatant without reflection makes his parry from the direction of the eye and the infinitesimal change of attitude which are the prelude to the thrust.

Gestures, then, are already significant in the sense that they are stimuli to performed reactions before they come to have significance of conscious meaning. Allow me to emphasize further the value of attitudes and the indications of organic preparation for conduct, especially in the change of the muscles of the countenance, the altered breathing, the quivering of tense muscles, the evidence of circulatory changes in such minutely adapted social groups, because among these socially significant innervations will be found all those queer organic sensations about which the consciousness of the self is supposed to gather as a core.

Human conduct is distinguished primarily from animal conduct by that increase in inhibition which is an essential phase of voluntary attention, and increased inhibition means an increase in gesture in the signs of activities which are not carried out; in the assumptions of attitudes whose values in conduct fail to get complete expression. If we recognize language as a differentiation of gesture, the conduct of no other form can compare with that of man in the abundance of gesture.

But the fundamental importance of gesture lies in the development of the consciousness of meaning—in reflective consciousness. As long as one individual responds simply to the gesture of another by the appropriate response, there is no necessary consciousness of meaning. The situation is still on the level of that of two growling dogs walking around each other, with tense limbs, bristly hair, and uncovered teeth. It is not until an image[7] arises of the response which the gesture of one form will bring out in another that a consciousness of meaning can attach to his own gesture. The meaning can appear only in imaging the consequence of the gesture.

To cry out in fear is an immediate instinctive act, but to scream with an image of another individual turning an attentive ear, taking on a sympathetic expression, and an attitude of coming to help, is at least a favorable condition for the development of a consciousness of meaning.

Of course, the mere influence of the image, stimulating to reaction, has no more meaning value than the effect of an external stimulus, but in this converse of gestures there is also a consciousness of one's own attitude, of readiness to act in the manner which the gesture implies. In the instance given the cry is part of the attitude of flight. The cry calls out the image of a friendly individual. This image is not merely a stimulus to run toward the friend, but is merged in the consciousness of inhibited flight. If meaning is consciousness of attitude, as [John] Dewey, [Josiah] Royce,[8] and [James Rowland] Angell among others maintain, then consciousness of meaning arose only when some gesture that was part of an inhibited act itself called up the image of the gesture of another individual. Then the image of the gesture means the inhibited act to which the first gesture belonged. In a word, the response to the cry has the meaning of inhibited flight.

One's own gestures could not take on meaning directly. The gestures aroused by them in others would be that upon which attention is centered. And these gestures become identified with the content of one's own emotion and attitude. It is only through the response that consciousness of meaning appears, a response which involves the consciousness of another self as the presupposition of the meaning in one's own attitude. Other selves in a social environment logically antedate, then, the consciousness of self which introspection analyzes. They must be admitted as there, as given, in the same sense in which psychology accepts the given character of physical organisms as a condition of individual consciousness.

The importance for psychology of this recognition of others, if thus bound up with the psychology of meaning, may need another word of emphasis. Consciousness could no longer be regarded as an Island to be studied through parallel relations with neuroses. It would be approached as experience which is socially as well as physically determined. Introspective self-consciousness would be recognized as a subjective phase, and this subjective phase could no longer be regarded as the source out of which the experience arose.

Objective consciousness of selves must precede subjective consciousness, and must continually condition it, if consciousness of meaning itself presupposes the selves as there. Subjective self-consciousness must appear within experience, must have a function in the development of that experience, and must be studied from the point of view of that function, not as that in which self-consciousness arises and by which, through analogical bridges and self-projections, we slowly construct a hypothetically objective social world in which to live.

Finally, meaning in the light of this recognition has its reference not to agglomerations of states of subjective consciousness, but to objects in a socially conditioned experience. When, in the process revealed by introspection, we reach the concept, we have attained an attitude which we assume not toward our inner feelings, but toward other individuals whose reality was implied even in the inhibitions and reorganizations which characterize this inner consciousness.[9]

4

Emotion and Instinct[1]

In the analysis of the act to find the place of emotion within it, we have the work of [Charles] Darwin [1872] to start with. He has shown that the so-called emotions belong to a number of primitive acts. Of these we have love lying back of the sexual act of reproduction, fear behind that of flight, and anger behind that of fighting; besides these we should have the love of offspring in the mother behind the suckling of the child-form, and other acts of protection and feeding which may be necessary at any point in animal development. Beyond these primitive emotions it is difficult to go without entering into the wearisome classifications which since the time of [Baruch] Spinoza,[2] have added practically nothing to our comprehension of the passions and their derivatives.

There is, however, another side to this investigation that promises more valuable and interesting results, and that is the relation between the emotions and interest. We recognize the essentially emotional character of interest, but the affinity and the developmental relationship between them is not so plain. One distinction between them is evident almost at the first view. This is their positions within the act. Interest underlies the going after and struggle for the end, while the emotion characterizes the immediate grasping and enjoyment of the object sought. Both anger and fear seem to be exceptions to this classification. In the case of anger, however, the emotion arises when conscious direction of the activity of getting food and protection of the self or what belongs to it has ceased. The same thing is true of fear. Fear, as distinguished from a paralyzing terror, is found when an activity undirected by consciousness has effected the removal from the dangerous object. In each of these cases, and this applies to all actions in so far as they are predominantly passionate, the consciousness is occupied with the emotion and the activity approaches reflex action, and in all of these cases the emotion answers to the immediate presence of and appropriation of the object sought—an appropriation that takes place by means of instinctive processes that are not present in consciousness as means to an end, but as parts of the end and resultant itself. On the other hand, in so far as the activity represents the means of intentionally reaching and getting the end, the emotional side of the act is found in interest. Emotion in so far as it is passionate belongs to the instinctive appropriation of the object. Interest belongs to the deliberate overcoming of the spatial, temporal, and other obstacles that lie between the individual and the object sought.

If now we trace all activities back to their biological source, we find this in the expenditure of energy for the food and reproductive processes, including the going after objects and their immediate appropriation. Of these acts it is the opinion of biologists that the reproductive is (to use a mathematical phrase) a function of the food process. The withdrawal from danger is a special adaptation of the process of movement involved in getting food—it is the negative side of the act. The activity of fighting is an adaptation of the act of appropriation. The processes of protection from the inclemency of the weather and enemies combines, as does that of home-building for the young, the two activities of movement for the young, and two activities of movement after the object and appropriation of it. So, out of comparatively simple processes in the primitive unicellular form, we have growing a gradual complication of acts. The expression of intelligence in these acts we find in movements toward the objects sought rather than in their ultimate appropriation. The greater the distance, and the more complicated the path between the form and its food, the more intelligent we consider it. Of course, this applies also to the negative side of protection as well.

If now we look at the process of development of these activities, we find that those of ultimate appropriation do not become in any degree so complicated as the others of attaining the objects desired. And furthermore, the organization and development of the latter arise through the evolution of means of getting which have been abstracted from means of appropriation. The use of the jaws and bills for holding and manipulating, and the final development of the hand passed the food to the mouth to that which performed infinitely complicated processes in the mediation of the food, protective and reproductive acts indicate this. For, while the actual eating remains much the same in the highest and lowest forms, what goes before this is hardly open to comparison, so great is the difference between them. Much the same may be said of locomotion. We give to this under ordinary circumstances as little consciousness as, *mutatis mutandis* [the necessary changes being made], the lower forms may expend upon it, but upon what the hand does—this derivative of the primeval appropriating process—we cannot expend conscious directed energy enough. Take again the senses in this same connection. The distance senses as revealing the object that is to be immediately appropriated do begin to represent such analysis, such study, such intelligence in so far as they mediate those hand processes, as that which in a higher form of society lies between us and the object sought. We may express this in a somewhat different form in saying that, so long as the actual contact values for consciousness are exhausted in locomotion and immediate appropriation, there is comparatively little intelligence expressed in them, but, when they themselves become means for the attaining of more distant and difficult ends, they become that in which intelligence is chiefly expressed. And finally, as it is in control that not only appropriates but determines the existence of the objects that are sought that the highest intelligence appears, the contact with the object must be developed into a contact with the environment out of which the object springs that determines it.

We have, then, a constant succession of evolution of contact processes that have been appropriations into those that become determinative of the appearance of the desired object, and there must follow in this case an evolution of what had been on the emotional side chiefly passionate into that which is characterized by interest. The development of intelligence necessarily involves this evolution. The passions of one period are the reservoirs of the interests of those that follow it. It also follows that the interest is much more definitely social in its organization than is the emotion. For the appropriation has a most direct individual evaluation, but the intelligent act, must, in so far as it is objective, partake of the social organism of which the form is a metaphor.

5

A Psychological Study of the Use of Stimulants[1]

The Sociologist and the Criminologist have done a great deal toward the awakening of popular consciousness to the conditions out of which crime springs. We see in the slums of our great cities, the breeding-places of social and unsocial human beings. We find in the isolation and dry-rot of much of country life causes which produce similar results. We begin to understand that education must supply interest in the details of work, if we are to produce the morality which depends upon industry. We recognize what enormous sums are annually expended upon the inadequate suppression of crime and, comparing it with the relatively very small number of criminals, are encouraged to expend money toward the removal of the conditions out of which crime springs. But there has been surprisingly little done toward adequate comprehension of the conditions out of which intemperance arises. In so far as it is associated with crime, misery, and poverty, there has been light shed upon it by social statistics. We have comparisons of the amounts spent for alcoholic liquors with those given out for bread and education, and we know to what extent alcohol is mixed up with crime and the degree to which it follows upon the heels of general misery and degradation. But just what there is in these conditions that breeds intemperance has not been further analyzed aside from calling attention to the good-fellowship in drinking, the proverbial drowning of sorrows, and the momentary release from the drudgery of mechanical routine labor. It is possible that these grounds in some sense represent all the causes of drunkenness, but, as they stand, they are without any adequate social valuation. One of the reasons for this lies in the very personal and emotional methods of our temperance organizations.

The revivalistic methods imply the ability of the drunkard by an act of an indeterminist will to stop drinking, and thus practically denies the very social character of the demand for stimulants. This is quite apart from any theory of moral action. I refer simply to the ignoring of the situation out of which the drunkenness arises, which is involved in the effort to get signatures to a pledge. To some extent, there is an effort to assist persons in individual cases out of the conditions which led to drinking, but these are in the nature of the case sporadic. In general, the assumption is that the whole use or disuse of stimulants depends upon a "will" or "won't" on the part of the individual. As long as we occupy this standpoint it is impossible to appreciate the social character of the evil, except in its consequences. It is essential to the propaganda that all that is of positive meaning in the use of stimulants—supposing that there are such elements—should be ignored, and that the whole effort should be to make the use as hideous as possible. The great value of this method of attack upon the evil has been the formation of a strong public sentiment opposed to drunkenness. It would not be easy to overestimate the value of this, but, apart from this, temperance work has contributed hardly anything toward the comprehension of the social conditions out of which the use of alcoholic stimulants has arisen, and therefore of the reconstruction that must take place that we may be rid of the evils it involves; while positively it has darkened the minds of the public to what is certain to be the great positive meaning of a habit that has been and still is so integral a part of the life of humanity.

The same holds, of course, to the prohibition movement. It denies the value of the demand for stimulants even in so far as they show a deeper-seated evil. For we can hardly be in a condition to study and appreciate the meaning of stimulants, if our whole attention is concentrated upon destroying, root and branch, the very existence of the stimulant. Under these circumstances such a study could have only a scholastic and abstract value. It is poor policy to give the devil his dues if we are occupied in exorcising him.

I suppose that there can be no doubt that much of the decrease in drunkenness has been due to the substitution of malt liquors and light wines for distilled liquors during the past generation. However, the temperance worker who would simply stop the use of stimulants in *toto* is unable to give attention to this most interesting fact; on the contrary, he must almost regard it as a misfortune since it seems to weaken his own statement of the case. The same criticism must be made of the efforts to educate the rising generation through physiological statements of the effects of alcohol. It is necessary that the teaching should be clear and give no uncertain sound. On the other hand, we are, as yet, too ignorant of the very chemical processes within which these effects must take place to be able to give any satisfactory battle note from the trumpet of science. The result has been crude physiologies in the schools, which ultimately may do as much harm as good.

Both the status of the prohibition movement and that of education confess the necessity of giving a social statement of the situation, and they show as well the impossibility of doing this in an adequate way, while our attitude is that of seeing nothing of positive meaning or value in the whole phenomenon.

It seems to me that the beginning of such a study of this phenomenon would be the determination of the psychical states induced by the use of alcoholic stimulants, and then the functions of those states under normal conditions. It might then be possible to ascertain what is the nature of the social situation that leads so irresistibly to the artificial production of these, and how this situation can be changed. It might be also possible to learn whether the use of stimulants has had any valuable social function in the past or is serving any purpose at the present time.

In the first place, the state of consciousness, which is sought by the use of stimulants, is an emotional one of great complexity. It is important to recognize this, for our common conception is that of satisfying a so-called appetite. We think of the drinker as on a level with the child who gorges himself with sweets. It is true that the pleasure that comes from the palate is of the nature of emotion, or at least it is impossible to separate completely the two classes from each other. There is no necessity of mixing ourselves up here in the theory of the emotions, for all that is necessary for our purposes is admitted by all psychologists. In popular terminology we distinguish between the pleasurable state consequent, for example, upon the satisfaction of the palate, and the emotional states consequent on the complex activities, such as those of love and war. When the expression "emotional state" was used above we referred to the latter, and, whether the distinction be a qualitative or quantitative one or whatever its nature, we all recognize its fundamental character. The palate indeed plays some part, especially in the enjoyment of the finer kinds of wines and liquors, but it is the general exhilaration that is sought and not the flavor. It is just here that our analysis fails us. For we class this exhilaration with the satisfaction of the palate in the point of its functional value in the organism. The test lies in the objects that are affected by the stimulus. In the pleasures of the table we ascribe the flavor and the emotional value—the pleasure—to the viands themselves. It is only in the slightest degree, that our attitude toward the important things in our world are, even for the time being, affected by the results of eating. Overlooking the unusual persons whose view of life is utterly changed by a good dinner or the dyspeptic whose mental eyes are colored by indigestion, the emotional value of eating is very slight.

The result of the alcoholic stimulant, on the contrary, is not confined to the objects drunk. The effect is to color the whole world, especially its social aspects. The values of the social relations, whether pleasant or unpleasant, are emphasized and exaggerated. Our projects become more worthy and desirable, and the hopes and anticipations become much more promising. It is only necessary to refer to the customary metaphorical expressions of intoxicated with love, with success, or ambition, to show how the exhilaration of the alcoholic stimulant goes over into our entire life and gives an added emotional value to what ordinarily may be but dull and gray.

It is, of course, not remarkable that so powerful and comprehensive an agent as this should produce contrary and perverse effects. Now these exhilarating emotional effects under normal conditions are, as we have learned from the works of Darwin and others, the accompaniments of the most important and intense activities. We can study them best in primitive actions and, even to some degree, in animals. For here we have the activity reduced to its simplest terms while it is yet most complete in its absorption of interest and consciousness. The battle fury that Homer[2] portrays, the madness of the lover, the passion of the one who is carried away by great achievement in any direction,—such as that which shook Sir Isaac Newton's hand when he was making the final computations on the path of the moon, that should demonstrate the law of gravitation— are all examples of such emotional states under normal conditions, and we can see that they represent the climaxes of life—that in them we find the emotional valuation of our actions and the world that surrounds us. But even when they do not appear at such important points of life, there is an accompaniment of loss violent emotion that arises from the interest with which we work at what we are doing and from the success with which our efforts are crowned. In the presence or absence of this emotional accompaniment of our activities lies, more than anything else, our conscious valuation of what we are doing and of life itself and all its elements. Enough has been said here to show of how fundamental importance this emotional side of life is and how complex a phenomenon it is—representing the fruit and meaning of experience.

It is not strange that there should be among human institutions and instruments means of inducing these emotional states, apart from the activities with which they naturally appear. The first of these institutions is the Cult, which lies at the basis of all mythology and religious ceremony. One of the best illustrations of these is the war dance. Here we have a selection of various of the typical acts of war with reference to their capacity for arousing the emotions that accompany the full war activity. This selection depends upon the emphasizing of the rhythmical features and the grouping of the stimuli for the different senses. There are also the harvest and vintage cults representing the agricultural activities, at the times of their culmination, by symbolic acts, which are arranged to call out the emotions answering to these fundamental food processes. These cults developed in two directions in the ancient world. As they became gradually separated from their original social activities the artistic value, as in the drama, arose from their symbolic representation of human life, and from their power over the emotions arose the orgies and mysteries in which the complete abandonment to the emotion was interpreted as possession by divinity. Wine was an important element in the orgiastic celebrations, and was considered in its action in early society as divine. A third means of gaining control over the emotions, apart from the immediate activities out of which they spring, is found in the other arts, especially poetry. Here we have the selection of various mental images whose motor tendencies arouse appropriate emotions reinforced by rhythmic measure.

In general, we may say that religious and other social ceremonial and service, the fine arts, and finally alcoholic and other allied stimulants, all depend upon their capacity for arousing emotions origi-

nally belonging to more or less specified acts and making them perform other functions. It is evident at once, however, that we have
varying degrees of normality in these different agents not only among
the agents, but also in the types of religious and artistic expression.
We generally feel that those are healthful that react back at once into
life either through the reinforcement of moral action or through the
perfection and consequent reality of representation. That emotional
expression which cannot be brought in these ways into immediate
relation to life, we are apt to consider sentimental and disintegrating.

This brings us then to the function of emotion when indepen-
dently aroused apart from immediate activity. Let me repeat the former
position. The emotion originally is but an accompaniment of an act—
as anger with fighting, or fear with flight—it does not exist apart
from the act. However, the emotions are the means through which
we estimate the meaning and value of our acts to ourselves. Whatever the reason may say as to the value of an act to the community
or to oneself, viewed from an objective standpoint, its immediate
subjective value is always expressed in terms of emotion. Whatever
the function of pleasure and pain may be, it lies ultimately along this
line, of estimating to ourselves the value of actions and all objects
that are bound up with actions. Finally, there are certain human institutions and artistic processes, together with certain stimulants,
which enable us to summon up these emotional states with a minimum of the original activity—and this generally of but a symbolic
character. We regard some of this control over the emotions as normal and valuable and some of it as baneful. The question is what is
the basis of the attitude and this distinction.

As already indicated, we assume that healthful religious emotion
reacts immediately back into ethical action, and healthful artistic
emotion into our processes of perceiving and grouping our perceptions of nature and human conduct. From this standpoint we might
criticize the use of stimulants. For the emotion that arises under their
influence is evanescent and frequently out of all harmony with our
standards of conduct, while the sensuous interpretations of the world,
which they call forth, are as frequently lacking in fundamental truth
and unable to make us see, hear, and feel more of the beauty and
meaning of the world. Indeed, this distinction is that which is drawn
between the legitimate use of our direct control over our emotional
states and self–indulgence. We insist that emotional expression, apart

from its original action, must still have organic value for us, else it is disintegrating and sets up habits of continuously summoning these emotional states which, being out of relation with human action, tend to swallow up all conscious effort in themselves. The assumptions of an ascetic life are that only religious emotion can have this value, while the Puritan would even control severely this religious emotion. The frequent assumption of the apostle of beauty and culture is that the religious emotions distort our view of the world, while only the aesthetic emotion can react back into it as whole. It is characteristic of the Epicurean that he denies the value of any of these emotional contents apart from their immediate experience. His motto is:

"Drink, for we know not whence we come! Drink for we know when we go!"

But we have still to understand the psychology of the use of abstracted emotional contents. How can an emotional expression that belonged originally to an overt act have value for later action, which would in turn have its own emotional content? An illustration may shed some light on this. Out of the spontaneous social acts of consideration and kindly appreciation for others, in a child's family life, there develops or should develop a social attitude involving a like consideration for others in all relations. This might be called a generalizing of particular family activities into a universal attitude toward all mankind. Now such a generalization meets with great difficulties. The actually existing rivalries and enmities among nations, communities, families, and individuals make an intellectual statement of such an attitude well-nigh impossible. The fight for existence is as necessary for life as the recognition of others. How can we state a technique of life which will recognize such vital rivalries—seemingly the springs to our most important actions—and yet enunciate the universal principle of human brotherhood? It is beyond doubt that it is easier to generalize the emotional side of the act than the intellectual—or to express it in concrete terms—it is easier to feel like a brother toward John Smith than to combine brotherly action toward him with the processes of getting my daily bread. The reason for this is that I can, in thought, put John Smith in other conditions in which brotherly actions will be most natural, and thus arouse the emotion that would accompany such action. But to change actual conditions, so that my own immediate struggle for existence will involve consideration for him, may be the work of generations yet it would be false to call this a purely emotional attitude.

It is the beginning of the reorganization of social conditions. It marks the difference between the barbarian's assumption that every stranger is an enemy, and the civilized man's assumption that every enemy is a possible friend. The result of this is that the civilized man will tend to emphasize what looks toward friendship, and will thus be taking a long step toward doing away with enmity. But, as long as this cannot be done in detail, the tendency is to abstract from the refractory elements of the situation, and conceive a more or less ideal one, in which immediate action will be essentially brotherly. Of course, the details of such a situation are apt to be hazy or very unreal, but the emotional accompaniments of the conceived actions may be very pronounced. E.g., in the apocalyptic vision of the New Jerusalem the demand for the statement of the details of actions, flowing from natural human impulses, in this ideal condition, is lost sight of in the wealth of emotional expression.

There are several results which this emotional expression may have. Representing a larger act which cannot yet be realized as a whole, it may emphasize those elements which are symbolic of the whole and heighten their subjective value. E.g., when the political and social conditions of Christendom made the treatment of all men as brothers and equals an impossibility, alms-giving, symbolizing in some sense this ideal, received an emotional content and gained a subjective value for the individual, which today passes over into the effort to make men commercially independent, and so quicken our social relations that the brotherhood of man may be a matter of daily conduct. Upon the actual social value of these symbolic acts for the community will depend in part the healthfulness or disintegrating character of the emotional content as a whole. If the emotion can pass over into action, then the ritual and all that goes with it does not exist for the sake of arousing the emotion. When this is the case, a sentimentalism is the result which cannot be formally distinguished from self-indulgence, and the question arises, whether there are conditions under which this use of various stimuli, for the sake of the emotions they arouse, has a value for the community. E.g., has the technique which was worked out within the cloisters of the medieval period, for producing states of religious ecstasy, and all that has served for similar purposes during that period and since then, represented any organic social end?

I think such an end is served in keeping valuable ritualistic and symbolic processes from becoming dead services. Many ancient rituals tended to become orgiastic. There is much evidence to show that the burst of religious feeling in Greece, represented by the Dionysic and Orphic cults and others of allied nature, was an emotional reaction against those which had lost their connection with the fundamental life processes from which they sprung. They served to bridge over the distance between the original primitive cults and the more spiritual ones of the developed city life of Greece. The ritual of the Catholic Church, which was developed during a period when men expected an early end of the world and was adapted to the keeping of this in consciousness, was reinforced at intervals by outburst of religious fervor which, while affecting conduct but slightly, if at all, certainly served a most important purpose by preserving a vivid subjective feeling of the reality of the ideas that were involved in the Christian Church. For the Christian ideal of conduct called for a morality which, in the medieval period, could only be realized by withdrawing from the world. The very organization of society made its positive enforcement in the midst of active life an impossibility. The natural tendency was to make out of the ritualistic ordinances of the Church ceremonies which, mediating between the actual possibility and the ideal demand, would soon negate the very meaning of the demand. Such tendencies we find in the institutions of Penance, the dogma of Purgatory, and in the pardoning and dispensing power of the Church. These reinforcements freed for the time being the ideals of Christianity from this benumbing and legalizing ritual of Roman Catholicism. Furthermore, they not only brought these again vividly to consciousness, but as well prepared the way for their fuller realization—in so far as better social conditions made this possible. For while such an emotional outburst, answering to what we may term social stimulants, does not carry with it the intellectual recognition of the means by which the higher activity may be carried out, it serves the purpose of breaking down the conventional valuations and judgements and so opens the way for what is ready to come to expression.

We can see this in the function which the building of air-castles may have in the life of a maturing child. This building of air-castles—being the enjoyment of the results of actions which are only suggested in consciousness—is of the same nature, if on a lower scale, as this type of religious emotion. But, instead of working out the means for the realization of these ideals, they rather paralyze action, for the attention is occupied with the emotional resultant rather than the action itself. Still the dissatisfaction with the immediate surroundings and the broadening of the horizon beyond conventional landmarks may be of distinct advantage to the maturing individual. We have another illustration of this in the reforms that frequently follow upon the emotional outbursts called conversions in the life of the individual. The emotion seems to clear the ground for activities which have been clogged and rendered futile by various conventions and the results of past conduct.

To explain this power of the emotion, we must recur to the statement made earlier that it is much easier to imagine situations in which one feels as a brother toward John Smith than to produce the situation in actual life. This imagining is but an abstraction from refractory elements in the surrounding conditions. I overlook the business rivalry between myself and my competitor if I meet him in a foreign land. The ocean has for the time being done what a prayer meeting or a dream of a Utopian state could do for me at home But the ultimate effect of such an abstraction will depend upon the vitality of the resistances which are abstracted from. For the child who is about to go from home to seek his fortune the day-dream helps to sever ties already parting. The gambler, who at the bottom has the instincts of a business-man, under the influences of the revival meeting, abstracts from the environment that represents his pursuit of chance, and so gives the healthier side of his nature an opportunity to come to expression. While the emotion achieved in this way does not itself forward action, the abstraction which is necessary to obtain it may be, under certain circumstances, of real reconstructive value. The burst of religious emotion during and following the period of the Reformation set free social and political activities that were ready to come to expression. The Methodist revivals at the beginning of this century were the precursors of the great movements of reform that have characterized its whole course.

The implication in what we have said is that the demand for a stimulant, whether institutional or physical, is always found in the insufficiency of the present activity. The hedonistic assumption would be that there was not sufficient emotional element—to wit, pleasure—connected with it. The difficulty with this statement lies in determining what is meant by sufficient. From the consistent hedonistic standpoint one always wants pleasure—unless he has been actually satiated. The tendency would be to compare the activity of daily work, for example, with that of drinking. With the latter would be connected more pleasure than with the former, therefore that would be the choice. But, as we have already seen, this denies the very nature of this emotional element. The latter belongs to entire acts, not to that of drinking which simply succeeds in bringing out their emotional resultant.

Part II

The Beginning of the Social Act

6

The Problem of Comparative Psychology[1]

A great part of our more recent psychology is functional. This characteristic has manifested itself in two phases of psychological theory. In physiological psychology the attempt is made to parallel so-called psychical phenomena with physiological processes. As the statement of the latter is largely functional, and the physiological psychologist assumes a complete parallelism of all psychical phenomena with physical correspondents, there is a strong tendency to give a functional statement to psychical life. This may be the case even when the psychologist has no such purpose in mind. Again, from the stand point of introspection we have advanced to the doctrine that our ideas are all motor in their nature, i.e., that they tend in some way to realize themselves in overt action. The influence of this doctrine is to interpret the idea in terms of conduct. Here come in the theories of the will which abolish the gap between the intellect and volition, which do away with the abstract thought or idea as separate from action, and see in the volitional process but the realization of the ideal involved in thought or idea. Here also belong the theories of the emotion which connect them on the one side with physical attitudes that are the expression of ideas and on the other with physiological processes by which the idea passes into overt action.

This tendency of psychological theory has great import for the other branches of philosophical discipline. I have already attempted to point out some of the possibilities it carries with it for the general theory of thought.[2] In this article I wish to make some allied suggestions with reference to Comparative Psychology.

Professor [William] James[3] refers to the whole nervous system, including the hemispheres, as an organized set of paths. These paths connect sense-organs, contractile muscles, and secretive glands with the nerve centers which are the storehouses of nervous energy. That which traverses these paths can be nothing but an expression of nervous energy. Within the physiological system the expression of this energy can be nothing but the various movements of the body and the inner nutritive circulatory, excretory, and reproductive processes which make these motions of the body possible and preserve the form and the species. Without discussing, then, the value and import of psychical phenomena independent of the physical organism, this conception of the nervous system, plus a parallelistic doctrine, carries with it the conception of a complete statement of all so-called psychical phenomena in terms of overt movements either carried out or inhibited within the system. Such movements would all have a place in a general or comparative physiology, and the assumptions of functional psychology imply that we would also be comparing movements, which correspond at least to all our so-called psychical experience, with movements in the lower forms which would represent whatever psychical experience they may have.

A comparative psychology would result in which the corresponding phenomena would always be present. If comparative psychology means the comparison of the psychical phenomena of man with the same in the lower animals, no such presence of corresponding elements can be assumed; It may be said that we are already interpreting the overt conduct of the animal forms through our own, and only after this comparison make the legitimate inferences to the psychical states behind these overt acts. But as long as we insist on continually cashing our checks drawn on the psychical phase of experience by the overt act, we are subject to an unavoidable error. The abstraction we make of the psychical from the physical is applicable, probably, if not certainly, to our type of intelligence alone. There is in all probability such a qualitative difference between the consciousness of man and what may be ascribed to a lower animal that the results we get for comparison are, on the side of the lower animal, hopelessly uncertain.

I will refer to two methods which have been suggested, one that represented by the chart at the beginning of [George John] Romanes.[4] Here we find a series of so-called "products of intellectual development," or, in other words, psychical phenomena. These begin with nervous adjustments with which consciousness is supposed to appear. Then follow pleasures and pains, memory, primary instincts, association by contiguity, recognition of offspring, secondary instincts, association by similarity, reason, recognition of persons, communication of ideas, recognition of pictures, understanding of words, dreaming, understanding of mechanisms, use of tools, indefinite morality. To these psychical states are paralleled in a so-called psychological series Coelenterata, Echinodermata, larvae of Insects, Annelida, Mollusca, Insects and Spiders, Fish and Batracia, Higher Crustaca, Reptiles and Cephalopeda, Hymenoptera, Birds, Carnivora, Rodents and Ruminants, Monkeys and Elephants, Anthropoid Apes and Dogs.

Here we have a series of faculties that are supposed to appear in the order of the animals given. The mere examination of these faculties or, if one prefers, these stages of psychical experience shows that there is no psychical principle by which these stages succeed each other, and that so far as they can be co-ordinated it is by criteria of overt action, although the content is supposed to be psychical. There is no inner reason for the succession of recognition of offspring and secondary instincts to association by contiguity followed by association by similarity and reason. There are overt expressions of intelligence which are perhaps suggested by these, but an interpretation in psychical terms that imply ideas associated by contiguity in one animal and those associated by similarity in another is hopelessly futile.

Professor [Conway] Lloyd Morgan [1894] attacks the problem with more feeling for method. Speaking of the study of other minds than our own as a basis for comparative psychology, he says:

> Its conclusions are reached not by a simply inductive process as in Chemistry or Physics, in Astronomy, Geology, Biology, or other purely objective sciences, but by a doubly inductive process....First, the psychologist has to reach, through induction, the laws of mind as revealed to him in his own conscious experience.... This is the one inductive process. The other is more objective. The facts to be observed are external phenomena, physical occurrences in the objective world....Both indications, subjective and objective, are necessary....And then, finally, the objective manifestations in conduct and activity have to be interpreted in terms of subjective experience. The inductions reached by the one method have to be explained in the light of inductions reached by the other method.[5]

The meaning of this is that we cannot estimate the intelligence of lower forms without constantly presenting each act of another individual in terms of our own psychical consciousness. Not only must we recognize the overt actions as purposive and adapted to produce a certain result, but we must also be ready to present as counterparts of these the states of inner consciousness of the individual before we can compare this individual with ourselves or another. If our scientific method requires this unremitting presentation in terms of psychical consciousness[,] it is evidently impossible to pursue a comparison of our own intelligence with that of lower forms. We cannot reproduce such states of consciousness from lower animals, and it is it a contradiction in terms to call such vague guessing a scientific method.

If there is to be a comparative science at all, there must be comparable terms, and the comparison must confine itself so far as it can hope to be scientific to such terms. If we can express our own intelligence in terms of overt action, and these acts can be compared with those of lower form, and we can keep within this field, such a science is possible. Afterwards we can draw what conclusions we may in regard to the point at which consciousness first appears, its content in the different forms, and the curve of its evolution, but these speculations will be outside the actual comparisons with which this discipline deals.

The comparable objects would be the acts of animal forms. The definition of the object, however, would be taken from our own experience—not from the so-called psychical content of the act, but from the organization of this conduct which leads us to select out and hold together certain motions, and call them acts. We may find out what an overt act is in our own experience. We may find similar acts in the life-processes of other forms and we may compare them. The first task, then, of the science is the definition of the act.

The attack upon this problem can be made from the vantage ground of our own experience. When one acts overtly he moves toward a recognized distant object and obtains contact with this object. In most of our acts this contact means manipulation of some sort. This exhausts the possibilities of our movements. We have distance senses which put us into relation with objects outside our physical selves; we have organs of locomotion which, acting under the direction of the distance senses, bring us to these objects or carry us away from them toward others. Our contact with the object may represent the food or reproductive processes, but even in these cases manipulation precedes, while by far the larger part of our own contact experience is a manipulation of some sort which serves more distant ends. These more distant ends, however, are but repetitions of the same type of act.[6]

But another demand will be made upon such a conception of the act beside its complete applicability to human experience and to the life of lower forms: it is that we should be able to express by it different degrees of intelligence. It is a simple matter to show that in a certain sense the physiological processes of all forms of animal life are and must be the same. Ingestion, digestion, assimilation, respiration, with expenditure of the energy gained by these processes in getting more food, maintaining the requisite animal warmth, and finally reproducing the form,—these processes are at bottom identical in all animal and, indeed, in all but one phase of vegetable life. In the higher forms there is an indefinite complication of the process, but it is not possible to grade intelligence simply by the mere complexity of physiological processes taken by themselves. We inevitably take other factors into account, such as adaptability, together with what, goes under the term of choice. The criterion which is applied unconsciously by all observers of animals has been stated by Romanes in the question, "Does the organism learn to make new adjustments or to modify old ones, in accordance with the results of its own individual experience?"[7] This individual use of experience is accepted by [C.] Lloyd Morgan[8] as the criterion of the effective presence of consciousness, or what we consider intelligence akin to our own. This capacity to make use of the past and create afresh, this power to adapt and choose, must be capable of expression in terms of the act if it is to serve the purpose of interpreting the evolution of intelligence. It is not simply control over the environment that is involved in the expression of intelligence, for this is found in vegetable life and in a high degree among forms which stand comparatively low in the scale. Parasites represent a complete adaptation to, and for their purposes, control over their environments. What is involved is this individual attack upon the problem of control, that is implied in the use of experience, or choice. The conception is one, of course, that calls for an elaborate psychological analysis, but as long as the content is one which is familiar to every one who compares intelligence in animal forms, this may be omitted here, provided it can be shown that what is essential to it is stated in terms of the act. We must define individual control over experience—this

power of adaptation, connating choice, in a formula of the movement toward a recognized object leading to contact-control.

It is symbolism that renders this possible if we look at the problem from the standpoint of consciousness. It is in a symbolic presentation that puts our experience under our control. It is in the form
of thought that is essentially symbolic that we are able to analyze,
reconstruct, and thus adapt experience in individual ways. It is symbolic thought, that makes self-consciousness possible, because it is
only in this form that it is at the disposal of the individual as individual. Experience that is deep-bedded in subconscious habits, that
is never separated from the objects of action, cannot belong to the
individual in the passing moment of his ephemeral existence. In the
world of instinct and unquestioned objective validity the individual
has nothing that is his own. He but represents the species. He belongs to experience, not experience to him. The possible abstract-
ness of consciousness is in direct proportion to the concreteness of
the individual. The problem is, therefore, to express symbolism in
the formula.

Now, there are many ways in which one phase of an overt act
stands for another. The line of vision represents the line of steps by
which we approach the object. The pull on one side of us represents
that on the other in the balance maintained by opposing muscle, and
looking stands for possible handling, etc., etc. In physiological terms,
one aspect of these processes list be represented in the response of
the other, and in so far as we conceive of such activities being expressed in consciousness there must be a feeling of correspondence
or immediate translation of the value of the one phase into the other.
But this does not involve consciousness of the symbolic character of
any one value. To put it in somewhat different form, in order that
anything may leave symbolic value, we must be able to dispense
with it for immediate action, If, for example, the value for the contact senses which the object of vision has were to be abstracted for
symbolic purposes, we could not use this for immediate control of
conduct. Different colorings and shadings and seen dimensions at
different distances mean the solidity and dimensions which the object will leave when we grapple with it. That we may assign conscious symbolic value to this seen content would mean that we no
longer instinctively reach for and manipulate the object. If it is symbolic of something, it no longer is that something, but if what we see

is not presented as existing m contact terms we cannot possibly act with reference to it. Otherwise there would be no difference between our attitude toward an admirable picture of an object and the object represented by the picture. That any content may become symbolic it must resign its value for immediate action.

At no point, then, within the act in its simplest terms, could this symbolism be found. For the lowest terms to which we can reduce our world involves the elements of relation to a distance sense, approximation, and contact. There can exist for us no world in three-dimensional space without these elements. In other words, there could be no object of physical perception without a complete act. But no analysis can carry us beyond an object. If we analyze an object into elements, these elements must be objects or they could not be parts of an objective world.[9] The reality of a physical object—the lowest term to which the physical world could be reduced—involves an act. Within this act in it's simplest terms symbolism could not appear. If this statement is to provide for symbolism and the type of intelligence which this makes possible, it must indicate an involution of activity in which one act or corresponding object stands for another.

Within the act itself sight may not symbolize contact, for then sight would not involve reaching and grasping—in other words, the world would become a picture without a canvas or a frame. Of course, this act must be stated in some way in terms of the environment. Seeing, walking, devouring are all movements whose value and content is found in what is seen or trodden on or torn in pieces and devoured. If the act is to stand out by itself it must be in terms of an environment that definitely answers to these processes. But this environment must here serve not as occasion for the expression of immediate impulses, but as possible occasion for an act which does not come to immediate expression. An act, then, or the object standing for an act, must represent some other act or object.

In this way the immediate situation with the impulses it sets free may through its objects be compared with an environment or objective situation that stands for another act. For example, a path representing locomotion toward a distant goal, when interrupted by a chasm, may be set over against a board which means bridging the chasm. The chasm means a jump, the board means lifting, placing, walking. Immediate impulse leads up to the spring. Through the board we may compare activities it calls forth with the instinctive but inhibited jump. The problem narrows itself to this: When can the object serve the form not simply as occasion for immediate action but also as a means of adjusting and adapting different impulses? This, it seems to me, could not take place until the relation toward the environment meant direct reconstruction, not simply mediation of the present impulse. If the form can make another situation, it can give the occasion for another act, and the elements out of which this can arise become symbols of this act.

Direct control over environment—manipulation—gives the possibility of symbolism. The power of control over the objects which through the various distance-senses set free our impulses, is also the power of control over the impulses themselves and the past experience they embody. With the power to construct that object comes to the individual the power to adapt and use the experience those objects represent. This primitive act, illustrated in sight, movement toward, and seizure of the distant object, brings with it the possibility of reason, or effective consciousness, or choice, or use of past experience for the immediate individual, when manipulation enables it to construct the object to which it responds. When the animal is able to construct the stimulus that brings his inherited and acquired habits to expression he has control over these impulses and their habitual expressions. The construction of the stimulus brings with it the power of adaptation and change. Introspection reveals that we have no power of immediate conscious change in the contraction of the muscle. It is assumed that our consciousness does not accompany the efferent nerve currents at all. On the contrary, our consciousness of an activity appears only when nerve currents [are sent] from the contracting muscles. Only indirectly can we control our movements, and this indirect control is found in selection of the stimulus which sets the impulse free. This control becomes most perfect when manipulation can itself construct the situation out of which the action arises.

We can illustrate the value of this by the mental image. The working image is one that arises through the conflict between the tendencies to action and the inhibition of these tendencies by the situation itself. Thus, the image of a house we are seeking arises when we are brought up before the wrong edifice. With great clearness the stimulus which is needed to give expression to the inhibited impulses

stand out before us. A successful working image of this house and
its surroundings is one which passes into the present experience,
interpreting and filling it out so that it becomes not simply the house
we seek but a locality with definite relation to the desired spot. The
psychological process by which this image that is merely the result
of the inhibition of the impulses becomes the working image is somewhat as follows: The image may readily merge into the present situation, interpreting it as indicated above, or this may be impossible
without a reconstruction. For example, one may be so turned about
as regards the locality that the present surroundings are out of all
immediate relation to the place expected and presented as an image.
An orientation by the points of the compass and other fixed relations becomes necessary.

What is essential for such a reconstruction is that there should be
in consciousness a *schema* to which these localities can be referred.
It is in this field that the common element is found out of which
adaptation is possible. This, of course, is the reasoning process, that
finds a universal by means of which the conflicting phrases of experience may be harmonized. Psychologically we have the two tendencies—one the movement along this path toward an expected
house, and the opposing tendencies arising from the presence of the
other objects. The strange locality and the image of the house will
not merge into each other, to serve as stimulus for immediate conduct. The conflict between the two or more impulses, that of entering the edifice present—being a part of the whole movement up to
the point at which we find that it is not the house expected—and that
of moving from it or by it, using it as a negative landmark of the
desired goal, this conflict robs the objects about of their content and
value as stimuli for mediating the present impulses.

In terms of the act the recognition of the distant object and movement have been present, but the contacts which consummate the act
are lacking. On the other hand, the tendencies to carry out these
contact processes are inhibited when they are all ready for expression. The ground for the inhibition is the inappropriateness of the
immediate contacts. Within the immediate act, which is that of reaching a particular object, any other object is but a stimulus for the
direction of approach toward the object. There is, then, a conflict
between two processes: that of attempted contact or manipulation
and that of farther procedure. The object represents two conflicting

phases of the act. The conflict defines the two tendencies over against each other. It is the inter-relation of these tendencies which is of importance. The object may fall readily into the place of a landmark—the error be corrected, and the movement toward the real goal be taken up again. In this case what may be called the orientation has been perfected. The definiteness of the contact values in their relation to the ground to be passed over simply organizes more perfectly the field of approach. But in case the object refuses to take its place as landmark, and the individual is at a loss to place it within the field of approach, these inhibited contact processes still seek expression. If the tendencies to contact expression cannot merge into the field of approach to the more distant goal—and therefore the tendencies to movement toward a distant goal are inhibited—there will be the opposite possibility of the merging of the process of approach into those of contact, i.e., regarding the objects about not as landmarks that as objects of contact. The possibility will depend first of all upon the applicability of contact values to the approach values, and second, upon the functional value of such a merging to the form.

There can be no question that the approach value—the landmark—is applicable to the contact value. What we may handle and manipulate can become an object for determination of movement, provided the object has any place in the field of approach. Illustration of this is found in the series of provisional goals into which a long journey is divided. We move toward an object seen in the distance, and this object has the value for the time being of the goal. Approach to it, however immediate, robs it of the character and a farther goal takes its place. Indeed, we may say that no object could be a goal which could not also be an object in the field of approach. There is it universality about the landmark that can cover practically every object which might also be a goal. But that an object should be a goal implies that it is of functional importance in contact processes. The prominent values that go with contact in lower forms are the ingestive and reproductive processes. These are specialized and not capable of application to mere objects of orientation by sight. It is suggestive of this that, for these forms, mediate goals are not so largely determined by sight as by smell—for smelling is the projection of the process of eating, and in no small degree of reproduction. The sense of smell, therefore, is in a certain sense a means of generalization through which what is only a part of the field of approach may be here also a goal value. This is not so important to birds, who are able to keep within sight of their ultimate goals to a much greater degree than land animals. It is also evident that the capacity for attachment on the part of an animal depends upon his ability to give to mediate objects—such as a master—goal values. A dog without a sense of smell would not only be helpless but heartless.

But the sense of smell is capable of only restricted use, because of its lack of connection with other objects than those more or less referable to the eating and reproductive processes, and because it gives little reconstructive power—power to construct a stimulus appropriate for the interrupted activity. On the other hand, the process of manipulation is applicable within a comparatively wide field. Take the map, for example, as an illustration. By constructing this symbolic presentation of the field of approach—that is, by presenting through the band to the eye the relation of the objects about to the image of the stimulus needed for the realization of the act—it is possible to work backwards from the required object to the present situation, and thus reconstruct the field of approach, so that present objects serve as landmarks for the distant goal.

The function which manipulation serves here is that of completing the statement suggested in the image of the distant goal—enabling us to start from that and thus seek out the appropriate means, which may be finally connected with the actually present environment. Such a process as this does not necessarily involve the actual drawing of the map. The tactual images of other objects are associated with the goal image. It is evident that this would not be possible, if the contact values of these other objects existed for the form only as satisfaction of actual wants, such as food or protection. They could then be only capable of presentation as ends, not as means, except in the slight degree indicated above. But if they are present as objects which we can feel and handle, as well as final satisfactions of organic wants, they can be freed from their value as ends and become means. Manipulation involves not simply the handling of the object but its possible contact presentation as mental image, and, of course, includes not simply those objects which can be lifted and manipulated by the hands, but the entire actual and possible feeling over [sic] of an object, all of that phase of tactual experience which comes through the muscular reaction upon the object, the joint sense, and the more or less inhibited tendencies to carry out these processes.

Let me repeat that only when the act of sensing the distant object and approaching it can be provisionally completed by contact reactions of manipulation can the experience attain to the value of an object, which may be used as a symbol. As soon as this is possible, objects which could not otherwise be freed from the particular act may be associated with an indefinite number of goals and attain, therefore, the mediate goal value which enables us to indefinitely complicate our activity.

It is possible to answer the questions suggested above in the affirmative. All objects that are presented in terms of manipulation are first of all goal objects for the primitive act. In so far, therefore, as any object in, the field of approach may be presented in terms of manipulation it may become a goal object. It is possible, therefore, to allow the inhibited tendency to contact processes which appear, for example, when we have reached a false goal, to extend itself to all the surrounding objects. As we saw in a case of immediate and successful orientation the false goal would at once become another object in the field of approach toward the true but still distant goal. In this case the goal object falls within the processes of approximation. The other case suggested was that in which the goal object refuses to merge in the field of approach. We have just seen that, for a form which has powers of manipulation, it is possible to merge objects in the field of approach in the contact activities even when these are inhibited. Such a possibility would not belong to a form which has no universal powers of manipulation. The second question was in reference to the functional value of this extension of the contact values to the field of approach. We have seen that this value is found in the reconstruction of the stimulus which gives control over the impulses which the stimuli set free. Thus the power of presenting the field of approach in contact terms brings with it that of constructing a map, or orienting ourselves by the use of symbolic contact elements.

We may find, then, in the act provisionally completed by manipulation, and the objects for which these acts stand, the possibility of symbolism and all that goes with it in the estimation of intelligence, and we may apply this without necessarily going back of the act to the assumed consciousness of the form.

I have not attempted to give an exhaustive analysis of the act. What I have attempted to show is that all our overt processes and the image of such processes may be reduced to a series of acts which consists in sensing the distant object, approach to it, and contact use of it; that this is applicable to all animal forms, and finally, that the peculiar type of intelligence which we find in ourselves, and which has its basis in a symbolic presentation of our world, can be expressed in terms of this act. We may then compare ourselves with other forms in terms of the act, and in so far there arises the possibility of a comparative science of intelligence which admits of whatever interpretation is possible in terms of our own psychology.

I shall attempt in a later article to show that our control over the physical environment may be stated in these terms.

7

Concerning Animal Perception

I wish to call attention to a phase of animal psychology which has received, it seems to me, but inadequate treatment. This inadequacy is evident not only in the general psychologies, but also in special experimental investigations of animal intelligence. The difficulty gathers about the doctrine of perception, and is due in part to the incomplete character of the theory of perception in human psychology, and in part to a failure to analyze sufficiently the conditions of possible perception in lower animal forms.

Can we draw a line between perception and higher cognitive processes, leaving below the line a cognition which is not rational though intelligent, such as characterizes the adaptations of a crab or a rat, and placing above the line all the consciousness of relation which makes human intelligence rational? Do our own predominately perceptive processes, such as those of rapidly climbing a steep, rocky cliff, or playing a game of tennis, where we are seemingly unconscious of anything except the physical environment and our reactions thereto, differ qualitatively from the more abstract processes in which we consciously deal in symbols and isolate the relations of things?

If these discursive processes are mere developments of contents which are implicitly present in perceptual consciousness, is there any definite line which can be drawn between the intelligence of man and that of the lower forms, unless we deny them the form of consciousness which we call perceptual in ourselves? [L.T.] Hobhouse,[2] for example, assumes that the cat, the dog and the monkey, which he observed had a "feeling" for relations which enabled them to learn by experience, without the ability to isolate the relations as elements in thought.

[G.I.] Stout[3] would grant to the chick that learns to reject a cinnabar caterpillar, an "apprehension of meaning or significance," which would come to the same thing. On the other hand, [Edward Lee] Thorndike[4] explains such learning by experience on the part of lower animals through the association of an "impulse" with a stimulus, which seems to imply a qualitatively different state of consciousness from that which would ordinarily be called perceptual in human experience. He undertakes to illustrate this by phases of human consciousness in which even perception would be reduced to a minimum. This latter illustration indicates a possibility of discrimination which seems to me to have been but inadequately recognized. In learning to play billiards or tennis, we are moving in a perceptual world, but the process of improvement takes place largely below even the perceptual level. We make certain movements which are more successful than others, and these persist. We are largely conscious only of the selection which has already begun. We emphasize this and control to some extent the conditions under which the selection takes place, but the actual assumption of the better attitude, the actual selection of the stroke, lies below even this level of consciousness.

Thorndike calls this selection a process of stamping in [sic] by the pleasure coming with success. This explanation, however, calls for its own explanation and ascribes active control to states of pleasure and pain, which is by no means proved and opens up another field of dubious animal psychology. Thorndike calls the process of improvement an association of an impulse and a stimulus, which lies quite outside of associations of ideas. The phrase is perhaps a vague one, that calls for further specification, but it answers to a large number of instances which are commonly conceived of as perceptions by the animal psychologists, although it is to be presumed that Thorndike himself assumes that these animals move in a perceptual world. The instances to which I refer may be well illustrated by the action of the chick in rejecting the cinnabar caterpillar or the orange peel. Is there a revival of the past experiences which leads the chick to reject these disagreeable objects; or may we assume that the impulse to reject has become associated with this particular stimulus, without any intervening reintegrated psychoses?

This question is closely allied to that which arises with reference to the plasticity of the young form and the manner in which it acquires the specific habits which are not found performed in its nervous system. A chick learns to make use of the impulse to hide when a hawk sails overhead. A young fox learns to run away from the odor of man. The process of hiding and running away are indeed performed in these young animals. It is the association of the instinctive action with determinate stimuli which is acquired. What seems to take place is this: The animal tastes a disagreeable morsel when it instinctively strikes at a moving object before it. The action of the flavor of the morsel upon the organs of taste sets free an equally instinctive reaction of rejecting the morsel. At the same time, the chick eyes the caterpillar under the excitement of the disagreeable experience. Now, the caterpillar hereafter to be avoided must be different from a mere moving object, such as would have called forth the reaction of pecking. It is fair to assume that the condition for this discrimination made by the chick lies in the different reaction which it has called forth. The mere reintegration of the experience would not protect the chick. Either the chick would peck again, since presumably the same bad taste and same rejection would follow, simply reinforced by the revival of the past experience, and this would bring about no improvement in adaptation; or else the past experience would be revived with the appearance of the old stimulus. This stimulus was not a caterpillar with certain markings, but a moving object within reach. The revival of the experience with this generalized stimulus to which, as [C.] Lloyd Morgan's [1894] experiments show, the chick reacts, would lead to the rejection, not of cinnabar caterpillars alone, but of all moving objects within reach. The ability to distinguish between stimuli which had been identical in their value before arises together with the new reaction, that of rejection. The meaning of the plasticity of the young form seems to be that there exist in the form instinctive reactions which have not as yet determined external stimuli. Through the experience of the animal the appropriate stimuli are determined. One condition, at any rate, is found in the new visual or olfactory experience which arises when for any reason, this new reaction takes place. A dog's shrinking from the sight of the whip involves not simply the revival of the painful experience of the flogging; it involves his reacting to characteristics in the sight of the whip which led to no reaction at first. It is not, then, so much the association of an old visual or olfactory experience with the impulse, as the arising of a new visual or olfactory experience which now becomes the stimulus for the particular impulse or reaction. If there be association of ideal contents, it is between this new visual or olfactory experience and the old experience which had not as yet been discriminated; of this association, Mr. Thorndike[5] remarks, we have little or no evidence. What we must assume, in what is implied above, is that the animal gets the new visual or olfactory experience because it is carrying out a new reaction; that the ground for discrimination in sensation lies in the difference of reaction to that which is sensed, an assumption that is reinforced by the recognition that the process of sensing is controlled and directed by the reaction to the stimulus.

Now, what is implied in perception is the association of the new sensory experience with the old. If the chick perceives a caterpillar as a "thing," he may associate the former experience of pecking at a thing with the new experience of rejecting the peculiarly marked thing. But evidence for such an association in the case of the chick certainly is lacking. What has appeared in its conduct is a new stimulus of a visual character for a performed reaction, which up to this and other like experiences had no determined visual stimulus.

The question then arises, what are the conditions for the appearance of this permanent core to which varying sensory elements may be associated? It is impossible to appeal directly to the introspective analysis of human perception. We cannot get inside the consciousness of the lower forms. It is, however, possible to find in our own experience of physical objects what constitutes this core which endows it with its Thinghood [sic], and investigate the conduct and sensory equipment of these forms, with a view to determining whether their experience can also contain this identical core to which varying phases of the same object can be referred. Stout[6] finds this core in what he terms "manipulation," understanding by this any contact experiences which arise as the result of visual stimuli, such as the hearing, scratching, pulling, shoving, as well as our actual handling of what we see. This he illustrates by the visual experience of a hole to which an animal is fleeing and which answers to an experience of contact, that enables the animal to determine whether the opening is passable.

If this distinction be carried out somewhat further, we find that the sensory experiences of animal life may be divided into two categories: those that come through what may be called the distance sense organs, the visual, olfactory and auditory senses, and those that come through the contact sensations. The distinction suggested by Stout's use of the term "manipulation" is that intelligent conduct, when it reaches the stage of perception, implies a reference of what comes through the distance sensations to contact sensation. There is perhaps nothing inherent in contact experiences which accounts for their being the substantial element in perception—that to which, so far as physical, i.e., perceptual, experience goes, all other experience is referred. Visual discriminations are much finer and more accurate than those of manipulation. The auditory and olfactory experience are richer in emotional valuations. But it remains true that our perception of physical objects always refers color, sound, odor, to a possibly handled substrate, a fact which was of course long ago recognized in the distinction between the so-called primary and secondary senses.

The ground of this is readily found in the nature of animal conduct, which, in so far as it is overt, can be resolved into movements, stimulated by the distance senses, ending up in the attainment or avoidance of certain contacts. Overt food, protective, reproductive, fighting processes, all are made up of such movements toward or away from possible contacts, and the success of the conduct depends upon the accuracy with which the distance stimulation leads up to appropriate contacts. Consciously intelligent conduct within the perceptual field lies in the estimate of the sort of contact to which distance sensory stimulates the animal form, that is the conscious reference of experience resulting from the stimulation of the eye, the ear, the olfactory tracts, even the skin, by the movement of the air, etc., to the contacts which this stimulation tends to bring about.

The vast importance of the human hand for perception becomes evident when we recognize how it answers to the eye, especially among the distance senses. The development of space perception follow in normal individuals upon the interaction of the eye and the hand, and this interaction works a continual meeting of the discriminations of the eye by those of the skin, mediated through the manipulating hand. It is this contact experience which gives the identical core to which the contents coming from the distance senses are referred in the so-called process of complication. It is this core which answers to varying experiences while it remains the same. It is this core which is a *conditio sine qua non* [an indispensable condition] of our perception of physical objects. Of course this content of contact experience is supplied by the process of association or complication out of past experience in most of our perceptions. The objects about us look hard or soft, large or small. But the reference is always there.

There are two respects in which the contact experiences of lower animal forms are inferior to those of man for the purposes of perception. The organs of manipulation are not as well adapted in form and function for manipulation itself, and, in the second place, the contact experiences of lower animals are, to a large extent, determined, not by the process of manipulation, but are so immediately a part of eating, fighting, repose, etc., that it is hard to believe that a consciousness of a "thing" can be segregated from these instinctive activities.

To develop this second point a little further, we need only to recall what has been brought out by Dewey[7] and Stout[8] that perception involves a continued control of such an organ as that of vision by such an organ as that of the hand, and *vice versa*. We look because we handle, and we are able to handle because we look. Attention consists in this mutual relationship of control between the processes of stimulation and response, each directing the other. But while this control is essential to perception, perception itself is neither eating, fighting, nor any other of the organic activities which commence overtly with stimulation and end with the response. On the contrary, perception lies within these activities, and represents a part of the mechanism by which these activities are carried out in highly organized forms. Perception is a process of mediation within the act; and that form of mediation by which the possible contact value of the distance stimulation appears with that stimulation, in other words, a mediation by which we are conscious of physical things. The actual eating, fighting or resting, etc., are not mediations within the act, but the culminations of the acts themselves. We could not perceive bread as a physical thing if that cognitive state grew out of the presentation of the mastication and taste which constitute eating. We perceive *what* we masticate, *what* we taste, etc., except in so far as we may perceive, through their movements, our various organs, as things.

The great importance of the human hand for perception lies in the fact that it is essentially mediatory within the organic acts out of which the physiological process of life is made up. The presentation of a physical thing which must be made up out of the contacts necessary to the actual processes of eating or those of locomotion cannot offer as fruitful a field for the growth of perception as those which are based upon the mediations of the hand within the act. And the contents of contact experience which a mouth or the paws can present must be very inadequate, for just that function of correspondence between the elements of the retinal and the tactual experience out of which the physical world of normal perception arises.

To assume that a chick can find in the contact of its bill, together with those of its feet, the materials that answer to the perception of a physical thing is almost inconceivable. Even the cat and the dog must find in their paws or mouths, fashioned seemingly for the purposes, not of "feeling things," but of locomotion or tearing and masticating, but a minimum of that material which goes into the structure of our perceptions. In the case of the monkey the question arises whether the function of locomotion is so dominant in use of the so-called hands that that of "feeling" can be isolated out of the monkey's contact experiences to build up perception.

Finally, to recur to the difficulties inherent in the doctrine of perception referred to at the opening of this paper, the assumption of a perception of things, that is, of what is mediatory in experience, carries with it the essence certainly of reasoning, i.e., the conscious use of something—a certain type of experience—for something else, another type of experience. Every perceived thing is in so far as perceived a recognized means to possible ends, and there can be no hard and fast line drawn between such perceptual consciousness and the more abstracted processes of so-called reasoning. Any form that perceives is in so far carrying on a process of conscious mediation within its act and conscious mediation is ratiocination.

8

On Perception and Imitation[1]

Mr. [Leon Trelawney] Hobhouse, in speaking of the possibility of imitation in animal behavior, remarks: "What has first to be settled is the possibility of a still simpler mental act—learning by the perception of an event and its consequence—when that consequence directly affects the learner."[2] Giving the results of his own experiments, he concludes that, "Whether by the perception of what was done by another, or by noting the results of their own actions, it seems fair to say that what the animal learnt to do was, in some instances, though not in all, to effect a certain perceptual change as a step to procuring food."[3] There is no question, then, that Hobhouse in his somewhat liberal interpretation of animal intelligence recognizes learning by a perception of an event and its consequence in animal behavior, and therefore that the basis for possible imitation is also there. Indeed, in his account of the monkey upon which he experimented he definitely ascribes certain achievements to the influence of imitation. I am not interested in criticizing Hobhouse's results, though one cannot but feel that he failed to recognize the importance of the past training which these apes had had, and that he took the data given him by the keepers in the Bel Vue Gardens in Manchester with too little criticism.

It is rather the bearing of the doctrine of perception upon imitation to which I wish to call attention in the few words which I have to say. Mr. Hobhouse follows the growth of perception from mere stimulation with purely instinctive response, to stimulation which has assimilated a certain character out of the active content of the experience, on to the perception of objects in what he calls concrete experience and practical judgment. In this latter stage the "character," which for example we find in our own immediate perceptions of distance, has developed into a consciousness of relation. There is not as yet the simultaneous presence of both terms in the relation as parts of a whole and yet separate from each other which character- izes a more reflective consciousness, but the experience is con- sciously controlled by a content in which both elements are felt.

The problem in animal psychology is to find out in what way consciousness of the consequences of an act may get into the stimu- lation that leads to the act. The steps in Hobhouse's treatment are unconscious assimilation of the affective nature of the consequence— its agreeableness or disagreeableness—the assimilation of a certain character of the consequence, a character which has a felt intellec- tual content, not simply an affective one; and finally such a con- sciousness of the consequence that it can conceivably control im- mediate reactions, that is a working consciousness of relations— a working, not a discurie [sic] consciousness.

This type of animal psychology, which in its fundamental tech- nique is not different from that of [Conway] Lloyd Morgan's [1894], is after all at the mercy of a logical analysis. The consciousness of relations, which is the essence of reason, is identified, by our *own* introspection, with the feeling of characters and affective states where these have in them the implicit relation. The behavior of animals seems to justify us in ascribing such feelings to their consciousness, as effective contents.

It is refreshing to turn to Mr. [Edward Lee] Thorndike's [1898, 1901] analysis, where one finds intellectual states of consciousness used as little as possible in the explanation of animal behavior. Mr. Thorndike suggests that in the place of the association of ideas, or of any states of consciousness as such, we may explain most instances of the learning of animals, by the association of an impulse with a stimulus. The cement for this association the author still finds in pleasure and pain, but the association is one that lies not between watered down logical elements, but between the stimulation and the whole act of the animal. By a system of trial and error the different impulses of the animal are provided with appropriate stimuli.

Of course, Mr. Thorndike does not imply that this is the only method of explaining all animal behavior, but he insists that this method of explanation of animals' learning tricks should be used where possible.

The association of a complete impulse with a sense-stimulus leaves no room for imitation in the sense in which Hobhouse uses the term.

There could be mimicry and automatic imitation, because both of these imply simply that impulses to instinctive reaction are mediated by certain stimuli that mediate like impulses in other forms. Mr. Thorndike leaves us somewhat in the dark as to the exact nature of the impulse. My understanding of his use of the term is that of an activity which goes off under stimulation without cognitive control, that is without conscious analysis of the stimulus. The means of stamping in this relation between an impulse and a particular stimulus is, as has been said, the pleasure or pain that accompanies the experience.

Where Mr. Thorndike can explain animal conduct by this formula, he finds no evidence of imitation on the part of the animals, that is, of imitation which, to use his own phrase would [be] an "associative transference of the self."

So far as this formula can be used to explain animal behavior it would be out of place, as well, to use the term *perception* for the consciousness of the stimulation and its relation to the impulse which it mediates, but the formula gives us a basis, on the other hand, for a psychological in the place of a logical analysis of perception.

The other type of theory imply that there are certain states of consciousness there, due to stimulation of sense organs and organic tracts, which have in themselves possible cognitive values, that the animal learns by associating these contents with the execution of the act and its consequences. (The term "association" is used in the general sense, including assimilation and fusion.)

If we start from he point of view represented by Mr. Thorndike's formula we can ask what are the conditions under which a cognitive, that is a control, element would arise within the act and so get the conditions for the appearance and growth of perception. We would look for these elements in so far as not only the stimulation but also the response in its relation to the stimulus could be conceived of being present in the consciousness of the form. In other words, we would take the functionalist's point of view and recognize no contents in animal consciousness whose function was not the ground of their existence.

To give a concrete illustration: if a monkey is offered a stick with which to push a banana within his reach, we imply that he perceives the stick as a possible tool, and this perception implies that the sensing of the stick awakens the tendency to respond, that the tendency to grasp and move the stick reacts back upon the sensing of it. These two processes control each other. The visual process awakens the impulse to seize and manipulate, the tendency to seize and manipulate keeps the sensing to those features of the stimulation which mediate the impulse. Those who have watched animals or who are familiar with recent observations of animal conduct will recognize that evidence of this sort of relation between the stimulation and response is just what is lacking. The stimulation calls forth, it may be, well-directed and even complicated responses, but there is little evidence that the tendency to respond is there to hold the eye to the object or what is done with it.

This amounts to saying that the ground for the selective character of perception lies in the inter-relation of the response and the stimulus, and when we say that it is impossible to get an animal's attention we imply that the inhibited tendency to respond is not there to hold the eye to what we are presenting to his vision.

If we ask now what type of behavior will indicate such possible perception in the conduct of lower animals, the reply will be, where we find intermediate acts which must be adapted to final results. In such cases, if the response and its stimulus can be both present in terms of mutual control these intermediate acts can serve to mediate the final act, and would represent in a possible consciousness just the contents which are called for in perception. On the other hand, many complicated acts take place in the experience of animal forms where each step simply provides the stimulus for a succeeding step, and in which there would be no necessity of the preceding act being present in its inhibited tendencies. The first step need not even lead up to a unique stimulus. After the completion of the first step the organism may be ready to respond to a number of different stimuli, e.g., a cat seeking to reach its feeding place and finding a door shut may respond to the stimuli which take it about by another path without necessarily having a perception of the house as a whole.

If, however, the ape whose behavior Mr. Hobhouse describes adapted its throwing of its blanket so as to bring in the banana without training and not by a purely accidental throw, its consciousness of the blanket would certainly have the same character as our own perceptions, that is, there would arise certain sensuous contents which would be sensed with the unity of the act which it mediates, while the kinesthetic contents, which the inhibition of the tendencies to react supplies, would provide the material out of which the consciousness of a physical object arises, and the adaptation of the process to the later act would carry with it the crude relational content out of which the meaning of the percept springs.

There is a further consideration that deserves attention here. What type of physical reaction lends itself to this mediating experience out of which perception may arise? If one passes in review the tricks and test acts which the comparative psychologist uses in his observation of animals, he finds two general types: those of the maze, and those which require some sort of manipulation that must precede the final act, e.g., the opening of a door by various devices, the use of a stick, *etc.* The first type has served to indicate the comparative case with which a series of acts may be built up, each providing the stimulus for the succeeding step, without the necessity of implying any perceptual process. The second type is of interest because it suggests the fact that our own *perceptions* consist so largely in the interpretation of what comes through the eye, the ear, and other distance sensations, through the suggested kinesthetic experience of possible contact. This fact, which lies at the basis of the older distinction between the primary and secondary sensations, and finds further expression in the inevitable presentation of the outer world in terms of solid matter, i.e., in the imagery of actual manipulations, this fact suggests that a rich kinesthetic experience in manipulation may be almost a pre-condition of perception, that is, that the sort of mediate experience in which stimulus and response would mutually control each other in the adaptation of one act to another could hardly arise before the primate with his highly sensitive flexible hand.

If we accept this or an analogous definition of perception, it would follow that imitation could not arise as a conscious phenomenon before such mediate acts appeared. One cannot have imitation in this sense without perception, and given perception it is hard to see how imitation can lag far behind.

A crucial test for the presence of imitation would be something like the following: Make sure that the animal has a series of acts well co-ordinated which lead up to a final act. If, then, it will vary this final act while keeping control over the mediate processes, after seeing the variation carried out by the observer, it would be difficult to deny the animal the power to perceive and to imitate. If, for example, to open a door a latch must be lifted and a plug pulled out, and the observer should push in the plug instead of pulling it out, and the animal should lift the latch and then push in the plug, there would probably exist no doubt in the observer's mind that his subject was imitating.

9

The Relation of the Embryological Development to Education[1]

One of the ideas that is most commonly connected with the name of John Fiske [1893] is that of the primary social importance of infancy. He has worked out in some detail the value of the long dependence of the child form upon the parent forms in the evolution of society. He has shown that no animal which had so long a period of dependence could possibly have survived, unless he grew up within a community in which all the essentials of our social relations were at least implicitly contained. From this conclusion he has drawn the further one that the passage from the period of short infancy to that of so long a one as that of the human child could only have taken place gradually, i.e., only so fast as the family involving the whole social organism developed to protect the infant form. Mr. Fiske has also pointed out what has often enough been noticed, that this long period of protected infancy was particularly favorable for the development of higher intelligence. For, during this stage it is possible for the child to form a large number of important and highly valuable habits that are of great service to him later, but which he would have no opportunity of forming if he had been obliged from the first to adapt himself to the immediate environment in which he found himself, and to support himself. For a highly complicated intelligence such as that of man it is necessary that a long period should be allowed the developing form to make the nerve co-ordination or idea association which are the basis of all intelligence. The importance of infancy, then, and by infancy we understand the whole period of dependence, lasting in the human child till nearly twenty-five—both for society and for the child has been fully recognized. It is to another phase of this period of infancy that I would call your attention in these two lectures. I shall try to indicate in a very general way what is nature's answer to the question, "How should this period of infancy be spent?" It is of the utmost importance for us to recognize in the first place that in education we are but supplying certain of the conditions what should surround the developing form. The family and society that receives the child into itself for further evolution is doing nothing that is essentially different from the mother form that supplies within itself the favorable conditions within which the embryonic form may grow to greater maturity. From the beginning of the development of the embryo till the mature individual takes his place within the social organism there has been no essential break in the process of growth. There have been critical periods such as that of birth, at which the immediate conditions which have surrounded the child have changed and new organs, which have reached comparative maturity, come into play: But there is no essential difference between the calling into play the lungs and new tracts of the brain, and this can, with reference to many tracts, only take place long after the birth of the child. But during the period of embryological growth the problem is, although tremendously complicated, still infinitely simpler than when the child comes into the midst of a community; at least it seems possible to gain some general conception of the conditions under which this development is carried out. If we can find out such general principles, it is but fair to assume that they will apply to the whole period of infancy, i.e., that they will give the fundamental principles for the education. For education represents simply our conscious effort to fulfil the conditions which it is incumbent upon us to fulfill as part of the environment of the developing child. The whole society, as far as it comes in contact with the child, takes the place which the surrounding mother form takes with reference to the embryo. The whole trend of biological thought is at present toward recognizing a structure within the cells from which the embryo arises. It is in this structure that we must seek largely for the explanation of heredity. The facts of rejuvenation, of substitution of one portion of the form for another seem to indicate that there is such a determining structure within all the cells of the developing form, at least at early stages of its growth, that only the opportunity is needed or the stimulus, and any of these cells could develop into the appropriate organ. When, however, the organ has become differentiated the cells that compose it could not take upon themselves the functions of another nor pass over into the structure of another organ. That is, the question as to what organ should develop or where or when seems to depend upon the surrounding conditions. Now, it is to this that is due the advantage which the higher forms have over the lower of the keeping the embryonic cells a much longer time undifferentiated. Differentiation always takes place with reference to use. To differentiate the cells early into organs, then, would mean an adaptation to a correspondingly early stage of life. As we all know, the developing forms pass through stages of growth which correspond to the great divisions of the animal kingdom below us. Early differentiation would then mean adaptation to use within the conditions represented by the environments of these lower forms. The higher forms, then, can keep the cells largely undifferentiated during the periods corresponding to these lower forms. The lack of the necessity of self-maintenance, of the necessity of use, enables the cells to remain partially undifferentiated and leaves them free to differentiate under the conditions that correspond to the higher forms of life.

We have an excellent example of this in the distinction between the larval and the embryonic forms. Larval development involves very early adaptation to fixed conditions necessitating self-maintenance of the larva. When the differentiation has once taken place the opportunities for higher development to any great degree are removed. By removing them from the developing embryo the necessity of conforming to early conditions of life, of differentiating its cells into organs such as would be necessary for self-maintenance in these lower stages of growth, nature has given the form the opportunity of reaching a higher stage within which to attain its full growth. But there is another set of conditions that have to be taken into account here, beside the primitive structure that we are forced to assume belongs to the original germ plasm out of which the embryo arises. These set of conditions is the immediate environment within which these developing cells live and grow. This environment is the blood of the mother form, from which the embryonic cells get all their nourishment and stimulus for development. To comprehend the importance of this medium within which these cells live we must remember that all living forms are and remain water forms. All live cells in the human body are as really bathed in a liquid medium as those of the unicellular animalculae from which all life has ascended. We may say, then, that the chief problem of the multicellular form is to provide a concentrated medium within which the unnumbered cells that make it up may find the requisite nourishment and which at the same time can carry off the deleterious waste products. We know how complicated a set of organs it requires to keep this medium in proper condition. We know also that the blood of all animal forms is different from that of other types, though as yet our knowledge of the chemistry of the blood is so slight that we cannot determine what the value of these differences are. Our higher pathology has taught us that many diseases which we have traced heretofore to separate organs is to be traced now to the blood. We know, for example, that very many mental derangements undoubtedly go back to subtle changes in the blood that our methods as yet are not able to detect. The character of the blood and its constituents is a complete counterpart of the life process of the form in which it is found. Every new organ or every greater complication of organ must find its counterpart in the blood that must now supply it with nourishment and carry away the waste product that, unless properly cared for, becomes just so much poison for the system. The tremendous drain upon the nutritive system that is involved in the supply to the central nervous system of a human individual must be met by a blood which can carry within it the rich elements that the brain and spinal column need to repair their waste. We have, then, for the sake of the blood a digestive apparatus to prepare the crude nourishment for its peculiar medium, a heart to pump it about to the farthermost capillary of the body, within the blood peculiar corpuscles to carry about the requisite oxygen, and then a whole series of excretory organs to take out the poisons that are thrown out by the cells as they select for their purposes the particular elements that the blood carries for them. The blood, then, of a highly developed form must be an exact index of the complexity of its life and the position it occupies on the ladder of evolution. The entire life process of the form to its last iota is reflected in the blood and its changes.

Now, the blood forms the environment of the developing embryo. The larva to which we referred earlier is not only thrown out into the world of waters to support itself, but the environment that it finds about it both requires a rapid and fixed differentiation of parts and offers not stimulus nor conditions for higher development.

The three great factors, then, which we find going to make up possibility of development of the embryo are an intercellular structure, which in some degree represents the form into which the embryo will, under favorable circumstances, develop, a protracted state within which the cells remain comparatively undifferentiated waiting for the conditions answering to their place in the scale of beings and the constant presence of a medium which, while it does not require of the embryo the complete development of the parent form, still keeps its subject constantly to the full life process of the parent form. So far as we can trace the rise and growth of the organs within the embryonic period they represent simply the principle of unequal growth and the division of labor arising from formation of the organs into that which eventually gives rise to the differentiation of their cells. That is, we must assume that the cells of the embryo all possess a structure which allows of the development of the appropriate organs of the human form under the proper conditions, but that the stimulus to the formation of the separate organ is one of nourishment leading to the unequal development of certain cells. This stimulus would come, then, from the blood of the parent form which, representing as it does, the complete life process of the species, is able to provide in succession the stimuli necessary for the development of all the organs as respects their extent and content.

We get, then, as the principle of embryonic development the constant presence of the entire life process acting through the blood as the stimulus to further growth without the necessity of self-maintenance and the consequent too early differentiation. Whatever the cause of the development of the parent form may have been, whether it is the result of a fight for existence or not, in the embryonic form we find the opposite conditions present. Instead of forces of life and death acting upon the form to complete differentiation of organs we find a prolongation of the period of undifferentiation, and instead of want the struggle for existence driving the form to the working out of new, higher, and more perfect organization we find unstinted abundance of food. In a word, the stimulus to development is not want but surplus. Embryonic growth represents on the one side probably a cellular structure that responds to favorable conditions for growth and on the other conditions in the surrounding medium which represent not the successive stages of evolution of the lower forms, but all the complexity and richness of the fully developed parent form.

There is no reason to assume that the infant form, when it comes into the larger social world that receives it, is to develop upon a different principle from that which governed its growth during this earlier stage. It seems to me that the defects of education come back to the substitution of opposite principles to those indicated in the first stage of the growth of the individual.

The growth of the child after birth may be for convenience divided into three great parts. First comes the simple increase of the child to normal size of the adult form. There can be no question that the same principle should apply here as in the embryonic growth. There should be abundance of nourishment and sufficient sleep to enable the child to give the larger part of his vitality to the demands of simple growth, and the conditions under which this should reach the child, the social conditions which surround him, should not be stimulating but quieting. The child in his early years especially needs not the stimulus of excitement and exercise so much as that of food and sleep. What we need to recognize is that these are stimuli to the normally developing organism. The second to which I shall refer is the development of the sexual system at the period of adolescence. Here, especially, the failure of our education to follow out the principles of embryonic growth has led to most serious results. Our aim has been largely in the past to remove the whole fact of reproduction from the child's life, even after the age of adolescence, and this is just the opposite of what takes place in the growth before birth. Here proper development follows when even upon the undeveloped form the whole of the influences of life are brought to bear and left to operate as far as they can. The natural interpretation of this in the case before us is to recognize the child's natural interest in reproduction as an essential part of life. A child who has learned in nature what the meaning of reproduction is before the age of adolescence has the basis upon which to recognize the proper use of his own functions. By shutting the child out from the facts of reproduction we are not allowing the essential relations of life to reproduction to become a part of the child's consciousness. For nature's teaching is that these relations must be set up before the function comes to full expression. She keeps the whole influences involved in the blood of the parent from at work upon the embryo during its whole growth, with the result that all the development is constantly under the influence of the entire life process and no organ comes to operation without finding itself in intimate harmony with the whole organism. A child's interest in the facts of reproduction before adolescence represents just such a relating of the sexual function to the whole of his life activities, and the result should be that when this function is matured his ideas with reference to it would be not confined simply to its immediate exercise but would include the bearing of it upon all life. Instead of allowing nature to gradually make the central life fact of reproduction an integral part of the whole conception and giving it all the meaning and dignity that belongs to life as a whole, we suppress this relationship in the child's mind until he is occupied suddenly and without preparation with his purely personal relation to it. Nature does not bring one organ to maturity except so far as the whole system responds to its exercise. She keeps the entire life process at work upon all parts and during all stages of development. This brings us to the third essential fact in the development of the child. This the so-called mental development, or on the physiological side, the growth of the brain co-ordination.

How should the intelligence of the child grow? By the acquirement of separate facilities such as the use of number, of language, etc., irrespective of their relation to his immediate consciousness, or should he be continually aware of the bearing of all that he learns upon that which makes up the interest of his own life. The attitude that has been the dominant one in the past has assumed that, because the skill that the child was acquiring was to be used in adult life in occupations that have no meaning for him now, he should be taught the abstract techniques. The little child can have no conception of the double-entry bookkeeping in which he is to use his facility in adding. The only thing we can do now is to teach him to add and then, when his intelligence is sufficiently advanced to enable him to appreciate the bearings of adding, he will be able to relate it to the whole of his business activity. In a word, this trains separate brain tracts by themselves irrespective of the relations of these tracts to the activity of the brain as a whole. This method, then, is at variance with the principle of development which we have seen to be that in the growth of the embryo. No organic facility is gained here except as it is adequately related to the whole system at the time of its development. Nature develops a facility for future use by making it at each stage of its development a natural part of the whole.

We may then start out with the assumption that a child's interest is always adequate to any task that comes in the right form and with the requisite relationship to the whole of his life. Double-entry book-keeping has no meaning to the seven-year-old child, but the use of tools in building boxes whose sides have a given relation to each other has an intense interest to him. He is constantly interested doing a multitude of things, and these actions all have an essential relation to each other. It is possible to arouse the interest that belongs to the whole of any activity in any of its parts, so that it is possible to give him in this way any necessary facility by finding its place in these activities. But the most serious failure in our system of education does not consist so much in giving techniques apart from their meaning in the immediate activity of the child, but in losing in this and analogous ways the feeling of the child for life as a whole. A child can be kept just as really under the stimulus of life as a whole as during the prenatal period. He has a peculiar interest for the whys and wherefores, that is, for the relations of things as a whole. By neglecting this we are sacrificing the central ethical element of his life. Because he is able to feel the connections of all that has a bearing upon him if brought to bear upon him in the right way, that he suffers when he comes in contact with that which is for him perfectly arbitrary. We lose the ethical hold upon him by breaking up the unity of his life. Of course, it is not meant by this that he can appreciate the whole bearing of his actions, but that life as a process of getting and eating food, of building and living in houses, of buying and selling things of value, etc., etc., are of interest to him as a whole if he will only let them be so. All his plays reveal this, his constant questions why things are done in this or that way are instinct with this feeling. Life normally acts upon him as a whole. Of course, this seems to him as yet as play. But play is the normal activity of the child. Education must come to him through the regulation and direction of the play activity. But not only is this isolation of separate facilities which we try to give the child at variance with nature's method of letting life as a whole act upon him, but it also is deleterious because it aims at early differentiation when the advantage of the child's position as respects lower forms lies in the fact of the possibility of leaving the differentiation to take place later under more favorable circumstances for the adult activity. The growth of intelligence in the child, as we have seen, represents the formation of co-ordinations in the central nervous system. The paths that are formed are the lines of least resistance form that time on. Differentiation here means the fixing of these paths by constant drilling, so that the nervous energy will always flow over these lines more readily than over others. The error arises from overlooking the fact that the motives that we bring to bear upon the child to force him, for instance to study an arithmetic lesson that has no meaning to him, represent such fixed paths just as much as the processes of adding and multiplying. Now, I take it that intelligence will become higher in proportion as the steps in an act follow the one upon the other from the sense of their intrinsic relation to each other within the whole act. It is only so far as the individual feels the bearing of each element in the act upon the whole that he is intelligent in its execution. The man who must stop in the midst of his activity to get the motive power for the next step outside of his interest in what he is doing may possibly get to the goal he set out to reach, but the act lacks just that subordination of all the means to the end—the direction of every step by the view of the goal in advance—which is the very essence of intelligence.

Now, it is the peculiarity of the play activity that it keeps the relation of means to end—the government of the entire act by the end—in view always unbroken, and it does this without fixing the process or, in other words, without differentiating the different tracts of the nervous system into organs adapted to the early and imperfect stage of development of the child. The child is always interested in doing something in which the ground for each step lies in the end to be accomplished. This activity may be very imperfect and the end in view seemingly very slight and trivial, but it is a subordination of means to ends that lays all of it within the comprehension and interest of the child. On the other hand, the associations that are formed here, and the brain co-ordinations, lie, as it were, on the surface. That is, the child is not obliged to say to himself I must play in this way or that in order to get bread for my mouth, nor should he be obliged to say I must play in this way or that in order to avoid punishment or win the approval of parents or teachers that is essential to his comfort. The child should not be obliged to relate his actions to the immediate problem of his own existence. To force this upon the child is to take away from the advantage that should accrue to him from his dependence. It compels a complete differentiation of his brain organs with reference to his present incomplete development. Now, this is just what is done when a child is set at tasks which have no meaning for him, which cannot be spontaneous,—and when he gets motive power by rewards and punishments that push upon his consciousness the immediate problem of his own existence. The evil effects of such a too early differentiation are not lacking. The child becomes dependent upon these motives. He loses power to relate these activities to an ultimate end in which he is interested, because the paths which connect the act with the reward or punishment have been made the dominant ones in his life. This has been well expressed by Professor Dewey in terms of a psychological fallacy: one thinks he is trying to fix the child's attention upon the object or end while in reality he must be fixing the attention upon the reward or punishment that keeps him at work. We all resent the unnatural course of forcing a child to take upon himself the responsibility of maintaining himself, of earning his own bread. We feel that this is taking away from him the benefit of his childhood. But so far as the development is concerned it is a matter of indifference whether the appeal is made to the child's empty stomach or his quivering back, to the satisfaction of keeping the wolf from the door or that of getting the approval of those whose approval is made as essential to his comfort as bodily necessities. There is, however, the advantage in the former case that the child can feel the meaning of what he is doing, while he has to be satisfied in the latter case by the assurance that he is too young to comprehend why he must perform these tasks.

A child's activities should always reflect the intelligent character of human life as a whole. They should never spring from the necessity of adapting himself to the stern requirements of immediate necessity. For this means the differentiation of his higher brain function at an early incomplete stage of development.

In general, this embryonic development gives us the above principles to govern the further stage of infancy after birth. The stimulus in education should be found in plenty, not in want, or expressed psychologically in interest, not in distress. Life should always be made to appeal to the child as a rational whole that falls within the scope of his comprehension. His child activities, i.e., play activities[,] should remain spontaneous and as yet without forced connection with the problem of an endurable life.

10

The Child and His Environment[1]

It is easy to arouse a child's interest. It is not difficult when one has the knack to interest the children,—when one makes this the real end of work in the schoolroom. It is not impossible to make the subjects and methods appeal to the child's interest from the start, and to maintain this. But it is perhaps as yet by no means a solved problem,—the securing of such control over his work that exactness of detail may be secured when one depends upon his interest instead of a school discipline.

This is easily explained; the spontaneous acts of the child are disjointed. The play acts have an undoubted connection and interrelation among each other. The anthropologist and comparative psychologist can trace in them the different phases of the primitive acts by which man has maintained himself on the earth, and can show that our most complicated activities are but evolutions of these simple games. They have the unity of the life process that lies behind and beneath them, but this unity is not all recognized by the young child. The hunting game has no necessary connections with eating. Play battles no relations to dependence, nor marriages, funerals, sickness, etc., with any of the social results that flow from these in adult life. It is the game that absorbs the attention and the result is of the very slightest importance.

Now, just because the results, the products, are of no importance, the necessary relations between the plays which the student can find out, are not present to the child's consciousness.

In all of our adult activities it is the product of one that connects it with another. The product of the mechanic's skill is that which relates his art to that of the other workmen who use it in their succeeding labor, upon the manufactured object, and finally to the use which is made of it by the purchasing public who pay his wages. The

83

product must be such that it will be the starting point and basis for that which follows. The steel tubing must answer the demands for strength and lightness which make it the proper material from which and out of which the bicycle maker can work.

The bookkeeper must produce a statement of the financial situation of the firm, which may be made the starting point for, and basis upon which its investments and ventures may be undertaken.

The products are the connecting links between the different stages of a whole activity. They are statements of the whole act at each step in the process, and so, as representing the whole, they control and criticize it. The steel tubing represents to its manufacturer wheeling in terms of the greatest strength and elasticity, combined with the least weight and resistance. He must be able to see the ultimate act in his product or he is without direction or control, and he must see it in terms of the process which follows upon this product. That is, the product must be the immediate stimulus for the next following act, and the interest in this, as well as that in the whole, will evince itself in the exactness and nicety with which the product is brought forth.

The child with next to no interest in the product has no connecting link between the different phases of his acts, and is therefore, without control over these spontaneous acts, at least within themselves. His acts are isolated. He is interested in the activity, and when this ceases, it leads on consciously to nothing else.

The delight of the child in his box of tools generally does not go beyond sawing, hammering, planing and boring. A countless series of unconnected acts follow upon each other, and there is no criterion by which to test their success or failure. Point out the crooked line the saw has followed, and urge him to saw straight, and he fails to understand you really, for what he wants to do is to saw, not to produce a straight edge. Or, if he is a step farther, and is making a box; he is interested in making it, not in the use to which it can be put, and it is almost impossible to get him beyond this imperfect process. He is satisfied in doing it, and none of the uses can compare with this in interest.

How, then, is quality to be got into his work? Discipline of one sort or another may do it. In the words of the illustrious Abbot, his tools may be given to him only as he has schooled himself to use each exactly. The straight line, the tight joint, the immaculate sur-

face, may be made by a teacher's or a parent's influence, the end
which controls his activity. Can it be got otherwise?

As long as number cannot mean business, nor language effective expression, how can you supply the control which the whole
exercises over the part, except by carrying that whole in your thought,
criticizing from this standpoint, and making his dependence upon
you the means of making this criticism effective?

It is a very weak and insistent problem, for our psychology
forbids us the use of a discipline that comes back to the appeal in
one form or another to the comfort or discomfort of the child, his
pleasure or pain. A result attained by this means must be very indirect, and therefore at great and unnecessary expense. It must set up
connection in the child's mind and central nervous system which
requires a certain amount of violence at first and must be discarded
later if he is to use his acquired capacities to good advantage.

A child's brain is not an open country within which the pedagogue, like the manager of a telegraph company, may set up and
take down wires at pleasure. A habit that has connected work in
school with its comforts and discomforts as motives cannot be dropped
at once thereafter, to be replaced through the essential relations represented by an interest in the product.

If we turn to brain development we find the same conditions. Tracts in the child's brain develop from undifferentiated nerve
cells one after the other. There is seemingly here the same isolated
series of activities, and the ultimate controlling intercommunication
between all comes only later. Leaving each set of arcs to develop by
itself seems to carry with it the same imperfection, for the fineness
of perception and reaction can only come under the direction of the
complete coordination. This gives the ultimate meaning to each
stimulus and the grounds for discriminating between valuable and
valueless stimuli. For the kitten any moving object calls forth the
spring and the clutch; for the full-grown cat these follow only upon
stimuli that nose and feeling and eye detect and judge with reference to food and its use. We cannot as yet follow out the training of
the young animal, for training it certainly has in its play acts.

But it is safe to assume two things in regard to it. First, its
environment represents in a real sense the whole life process of the
form even before it is forced to be dependent upon it. The smell of
prey, movements of the parent forms, the chase after indifferent

moving objects, all together with many other elements constantly present to its senses, give opportunity to all its activities to develop as fast as growth makes this possible.

All the essential phases of the ultimate life process are present to the young, so that the connections between the different brain tracts, which represent its different acts may be made and naturally will be made as fast as this is possible.

The more we study the growth of the embryo and the infant, the more do we find that the relationship of environment to the developing form seems to be that of opportunity. The great advantage of intra-uterine growth seems to be that of the absence of the necessity of differentiating at an early stage,—the possibility of growing surrounded by the nutrient fluids of the adult parent form without the necessity of struggling for appropriate nourishment, and thus becoming fixed before its highest possibilities of growth were reached.

There is no evidence of any other influence exercised by the mother upon the unborn child except that of providing a highly organized nutriment that answers the demands of the fully developed adult. And the relationship of the environment to the infant is, or should be, the same. Surroundings which represent the results of adult activities are placed at the disposal of the child without effort on his part. All that is then within him, at least up to the level of this adult life, may come to unhampered expression before he is thrown upon his own resources and compelled to fix himself and his habits by the fight for good and life.

There is here not only opportunity for unhampered growth, but also these opportunities represent the entire life of the form. The blood of the parent form is an epitome in the nutriment gases and salts it carries of the whole adult organism. Though one organ or set of organs may grow at one time, and another at another, there is present the stimulus for growth of those as yet quiescent. When, then, the balance between all the organs is threatened by the overdevelopment of one set, the appropriate stimulus for the growth of the rest lies ready to call them forth.

One may say, then, that the whole life process lies behind the isolated appearance of the successive activities, acting as a neverfailing source and direction as soon as the appearance of other sides are needed to make development symmetrical.

And in the infant life the child is surrounded by the full life of the parent form. When the developing speech centers have responded to the surrounding atmosphere, vibrating with the spoken language of the family, the connections between ear, throat, on one side, and the eye, hand, and foot on the other, are all ready to be called out by the use which language serves in the home, in getting, and manipulating what lies within the range of the eye, the foot, and the hand. As fast as the organs and their activities appear, they find the stimuli which lead to their being co-ordinated in the full life process of the parent forms.

It should, then, be one of the most persistent aims of education to provide for the child such an environment as this. There should be about him constantly a life which can unfailingly supply the unity which the more or less isolated appearance of difference powers in the child looks.

It is characteristic of the modern family and school that it fails signally in this function. The absence of the child from the immediate providing and preparation of food, from the care of the home and use of the soil, which complicated conditions[;] servants and city life bring with them, leave many a child's hunting, fashioning, ordering and social plays without the essential connection with the adult life behind, that should give them meaning and interrelation. They are mere isolated plays. They cannot become a part of the real life of the home. The appeal of the child to help goes only too often without response, and yet out of this could grow a feeling for the connections of things which bring a natural control that is not arbitrary, but an expression of the deepening growth of the child's nature.

On the other hand, forcing the child into the work of an adult when the full meaning of this cannot be present, when only a very few things can be done, and these to the exclusion of the other powers, that should be evolving in their turn, is to deprive the child of every advantage of not being forced to differentiate too early. It is like forcing him to pass through a larval period when he is in a sense dependent for his comfort and life upon his own exertions.

The most glaring case of this separation of the child from the full family life is to be found in his exclusion from the meaning of the facts of sex, as this side of his nature develops. One of the most profound connections which more than any other organizes life as a whole, he is shut off from, while the consciousness of the isolated processes becomes almost overwhelming.

In many respects the organization of our material comfort, of the reconstruction of the home, is making this separation of the child's isolated activities from [the] unifying life of the home for the time being necessary, but here the school should come in. The simple processes of home-making, the getting and use of food, the appearance and growth of new life should be a surrounding matrix within which the different powers of the child may find not only abundant stimulus, but the interconnection and co-ordination which carry with them the control that the whole exercises over the part.

Our present working hypothesis[2] of education is that the whole can be present only in the thought of the teacher, and can be awakened in the child alone when he has passed beyond his childhood into adult life. There is here the assertion of a necessary isolation of child activity, not only as regards this spontaneous play, but also as regards his acts when consciously ordered and directed by the family and the school.

Over against this we may place the hypothesis just worked out, of a unifying and relating life in the family and the school, with stimuli ready to call out the immediate connection between the different spontaneous acts of the child with each other, and the life that lies behind them.

The Kindergarten which has responded largely to the demand for a school which shall do for the child what home should do, seems to me to have failed here. It has set up symbolism instead of the reality. It has fallen under the same conception as that which has lain behind the public school,—that it is of an adult life which must organize the play acts of the child outside his consciousness. It is one thing to let a child feel the connection between what he does and the life that lies behind and around him. It is another to emphasize one side of his own play, and to make it symbolic of the whole which lies quite beyond him. The child who cooks in the kitchen with his mother gets a connection between his playing at keeping house and the reality that is fundamental, but the boy that flaps his arms as wings and hops after imaginary food for imaginary birds is symbolizing essential life processes to his teacher. I doubt if he is to himself.

It belongs to the school, then, as filling out and perfecting the social and material environment which should surround the child, to present real life processes in planting and gathering food, in cooking and making it ready, in building and decorating, in buying and selling, etc., within which not only the spontaneous acts of the children fall, but which will relate them and give, in the realities children recognize and respect, a control over their acts which must otherwise be absent.

There is a second phase of child life which also helps to solve the question we have started. The different brain tracts come to development, as we have seen, in a more or less isolated way, and one result of this is that the child's consciousness is for the time being quite swallowed up in the activity this represents. This law of unequal growth, which finds expression in the whole development of the child from the beginning, seems to be an arrangement by which nature may concentrate her effort now on one side and now on the other. The isolation is not simply a lack of connection between different activities, it is merging of all the life and energy in one act with a correspondingly rapid development. It is in this complete absorption in that which immediately is being done that lies the sui-generic charm of childhood. When we have lost sight of the end and purpose of our life in the midst of consciousness of how we should live, we look back with profound appreciation and longing to the time when we were completely swallowed up in what we were doing with an intense interest that knew nothing beyond.

This shows itself not only in the so-called games of childhood,— it is just as evident in acquiring of command over language and number, or, in general, over any new capacity which has just shown itself. The child who is just learning to talk, chatters incessantly, sense and nonsense, makes words and jingles, give himself up completely to the mere use of the vocal organs and their effect upon the ear. The boy who has learned to count, counts any and everything, revels in continuous number with no thought of result or product. In the collecting age, buttons, stamps, eggs, woods,— anything may serve for this embryonic scientific observation and systematization.

There is a period then with every budding faculty when it will absorb the whole interest and attention of the child if it be not forced before its time, or compelled to do adult work before it has its growth. Long multiplications, rhythmic tables, divisions that come out beautifully even, fractional relationships when they can be approached as relations of wholes, are play in the full sense of the word.

In the same way the creative faculties of imagination run riot when the child awakes to the possibilities of making his own selections and combinations instead of following dumbly the eye and ear. Later comes the logical stage in which he becomes conscious of his power to use the necessary connections of things and ideas; the philosophic age in which he takes the world to pieces like a machine, and is absorbed in trying to put it together again to suit his own wishes and the yearning of his own soul. At this period it is possible to direct and draw out in detail the techniques of these powers with no unnatural stimulus or disciplinary sanction.

In some of the schools of this city number has been given to the child in such a way as to take advantage of this natural absorbing interest in the technique for its own sake. It has been studied in blocks which at once represented to the eyes various multiples of each other, and out of the relations of these blocks has sprung up a regular play in fractions, in which the child often outstrips the adult who has gained his technique in the abstract routine fashion. It is a play that has as much fascination as cards or dominoes.

The control here over the activity is not so much a conscious or unconscious relating of the part to the whole, as in the perfect freedom of movement that makes it possible to bring all the fundamental phases of the technique to expression. There is no time at which a child is more conscious of emphasis and vowel values than when he is getting control over the language he hears about him. He may be able to copy the manners of speech of all with whom he comes in contact. He is full of correction of others' pronunciation. He can pick up several languages or dialects and keep them remarkably distinct. It is then that correct pronunciation and enunciation can be given without an effort, by merely playing with him at his word game.

The principle of use of these periods, however, cannot be the arbitrary use of the power. There is underneath even such, for the time, isolated growth, the essential connection with the organism behind. What is to be sought is not abstract, but a free power that is able to reach untrammeled expression. Under what seems most arbitrary in the child's expression there lies the law of his nature. What the school can do is only to draw this out, give the room within which to disport itself, and the means which it naturally makes use of.

On the other hand, it is equally evident that the development of one side in accordance with this law of unequal growth at last furnishes the ground for the development of others and the relationship of that which has been gained to the whole nature.

The interest in the technique, for itself, is gone, but there remains the power which can be now used in that which the child does. The further education of the capacity must then be found in accepting the child's interest in the larger act, and letting him use and relate what he has gained in reaching the more distant end. It is in this change of base in the growth of the child that I think the so-called different plateaus consist. We reach a stopping point in a child's development along a particular line, not because this power becomes dormant, but because his interest involves the *use* of the technique instead of its gymnastic exercise.

The same recognition explains the seeming increase in knowledge after a period of quiescence, even when one had dropped a problem perhaps as insoluble. The isolated development could go no further, but in the growth of other sides of the nature and the consequent relationships of that are acquired to the rest of our conscious world, come out meanings and capacities of which we were unconscious before. It is at this point, then, that the relationship between the isolated play act and the real life behind it can come to consciousness, organize it, and thus give the control we are seeking.

It is then that we find the child rejoicing so in doing something, helping some one, making something that has real value.

But if we continue the more technical development with reference to an adult activity that lies far beyond any immediate relationship to his real world, the interest is gone, and the life of the child cannot be deepened and rounded out upon his own plane. We have lost contact with him, have deprived him of nature's unifying and supporting environment. This should have taken him up and out of its boundless wealth have given him feeling of the reality of what he was doing and could do. But it is not simply the loss of reality and its consequent control we are interfering with the rhythmic development of his nature, out of the developed technique has arisen the stimulus for the growth of the other sides of the child. In putting it to use is found the channel through which comes new nutriment for his evolution and the regaining of the balance which is necessary if the child is to grow in the consciousness of being a real part of the world about him.

As I have indicated, the problem which education faces is one of the organization of the home, and especially of the school, so that the child is consciously within a life process in which all his activities have their natural and real place, in which there is ample room for the spontaneous play of the newborn powers, Mother Nature's unbounded love and farseeing intelligence, to recognize and take possession of her own.

Part III

Education from the Kindergarten
to the University

11

The Kindergarten and Play[1]

I take it the great new principle that the kindergarten brought into education was the use of the spontaneous activity of the child. Education in the schools above the kindergarten takes its exercises and methods from adult life, simplifies and adapts them to bring them within the range of the child intelligence, and depends upon their routine repetition for development. The kindergarten takes its methods and exercises from the child. It, too, has adapted and directed these spontaneous acts or plays, but that which the child does in the kindergarten is supposed to spring from his own instincts. In the kindergarten he plays,—when he gets into the grades he works. The opposition, then, between the methods of kindergarten and public school has been diametrical. The primary grade has come in to some extent as a connecting link. Its methods have more and more approached the kindergarten in principle, but it has still been obliged to fit its graduates for the task of acquiring abstract processes and principles from the books, which they must face sooner or later. The demand for a connecting link between the kindergarten and the primary school shows how profound the opposition is and how keenly it is felt, now that the kindergarten has forced itself from the position of an outside nursery into the school system. It is so profound that one feels more and more that it can be overcome only when it has reorganized the whole school as it promises to reorganize the primary grade.

The difficulties, however, in the way of such a reorganization do not arise alone from the resistance offered by the traditional methods of the public school. The kindergarten cannot undertake this task, which is being forced upon it, until it has mastered its own method, and this mastery cannot be attained until a sounder psychology unfolds the processes of child nature. The essence of the child-act is play. But its educational value can only be learned when we understand how the play-acts of the child are gradually organized into the fully developed activity of the grown man, who is conscious of their meaning for himself and society. To get an inkling of this development, our psychology has had to pass from the fixed analytical type of the traditional English school to the dynamic type which is characteristically represented in Professor [William] James [e.g., 1890, 1907]. Universal interest in evolution was needed, that attention might be directed to the natural evolution, for example, of the mouse-catching cat out of the spool-chasing kitten, or, in a word, of the adequate activity of the adult form out of the detached and *immediately* valueless plays of the young.

It should certainly be possible for the kindergarten to analyze and test its methods to-day from a new standpoint—for between us and [Friedrich] Froebel[2] lie evolution and a new psychology. I shall try to indicate the lines along which such an analysis must run. Let me state again what have been the assumptions of the school and of the kindergarten. The school assumes that a child gains the technique of the full-grown man by mastering step by step its different elements, language, number, and the results of past experience. It assumes, also, that the meaning of these cannot be given to the child because he cannot live the life of the man. The spontaneous acts of the child, lying entirely within the range of his own intelligence, cannot therefore become parts of an education which is governed by ends lying beyond. He must wait till he has attained maturity for the comprehension of these steps. Out of school he can be left to himself to play. Within school he must work, not as the man works with a full realization of what he is working for, but with a childlike faith in his parents and teachers that it will in the end all work together for his own good.

The kindergarten has been satisfied to take the child before the school could claim him, before he could be inducted piece-meal into the full-grown man's activity. There were left, therefore, for the kindergarten teacher only the child's plays to deal with. But she[3] has felt that these may have an essential bearing upon his later life, and has taken it as her task to bring this out and to utilize it to the full. She has seen that every play does, or at least may, represent in some degree what is to be done when the child is grown. She has striven to take advantage of this reference in three ways: First, by emphasizing the correct emotional attitude of the child in the act which the play represents; second, by symbolizing in the plays what is going on around and within him, and finally, by a direct education of the sense organs and powers of discrimination and perception.

It will be seen that in a general way this corresponds to the two divisions of the school work. The school aims to give to the child the technique of life work—for example, the use of number and language—and then in history, natural and social, the information which makes the basis for their use. So the kindergarten plays at getting food and shelter, the use of hands, feet, eyes, and ears, and on the other hand symbolizes in games the essential facts of life and nature. It aims to give technique and information. The giving of the technique again is by two different means—by educating hand, foot, eye, and ear in weaving, building, singing, dancing, etc., and by making the child feel the meaning of his plays as representative of what he will do when grown. Out of the first has grown an education of the sense organs, and a primitive artistic and manual training in drawing, singing, sewing, cooking, etc. These by themselves are not essentially kindergarten processes. They become such by their direction and arrangement with reference to the desired emotional attitude.

This emotional attitude is either that of the society to which the child belongs—the family and the state as represented by the family—or that coming with the recognition of the beautiful and orderly. The same is true of the symbolic games, the emotional and aesthetic reference of the play to the playmates and the home is the governing principle in their direction and control. I do not mean the mere ethical correction of the child's way of playing so that he shall recognize the rights and places of his playmates, parents, and teacher, but inducing the emotions that should characterize the life activity which the play symbolizes. In a word, the kindergarten has striven to organize and direct the plays of young children, by making them symbolic of their later life and the world in which they are to live, and has striven to educate the children by inducing the emotional attitude in the midst of these plays which should underlie the activities symbolized.

I wish to emphasize here that the problem which the kindergarten has recognized, and from its standpoint has solved, is not only that of finding the possibilities of beginning a school education earlier than the primary grade. The problem is not simply to find exercises with the hands, eyes, etc., which will start the child's education at the cradle—though the recognition of these possibilities are largely due to the kindergarten—but this would have been without value if it had not discovered a way of setting the children at these exercises and keeping them at them at an age when they could not profitably be subjected to school discipline. The problem is so to organize and arrange the exercises that the child will carry them out through his own spontaneous activity. But, on the other hand, to make them educative they must not be simply plays—they must not only appeal to the child's spontaneous nature—they must lead on to the adult life for which education seeks to prepare the child. A merely sympathetic mother or nursery maid can keep children playing healthfully. This is not necessarily education.

The problem is twofold: to find appropriate processes of education for these early years, and second, so to organize them that they shall be both play for the child and preparatory and educative for adult life. The solution comes back, then, to the question in what sense can children's plays stand for adult activity. The answer to this question gives the principle on which the plays must be organized. The answer of the kindergarten is that, on the emotional and aesthetic reaction of the child within his plays, one finds the element which relates them to adult life. Plays have, then, to be so organized as to bring out the fundamental social and aesthetic emotions. Within such a system an education of sense organs and a primitive manual training may be developed, but these presuppose a system of educationally organized plays.

The only way in which the kindergarten is able to organize them from this standpoint is by a symbolism, to which reference has already been made. The hunting games must be symbolic of the search for food for the self and those dependent upon him in later life, and he must, for example, as father-bird, feel the love for the nestlings which is to prompt him to provide for his children when he becomes an actual father. In the fighting games must be symbolized the defense of home and country, and the little soldier must feel the love for home and fellow citizens which it is assumed should prompt him to offer his life in battle. In the work with colors and forms—the mats, the cubes, and spheres—if they are to be educative, they must be symbolic of the aesthetic value of color and form in art. The aim must be to arouse in the child the emotional reactions upon the primitive colors and forms which afterwards be developed in the adult into aesthetic judgement upon all expressions of beauty.

The psychological test of the kindergarten education of the past will be found in the answer to the question: Can children's plays be thus symbolic to them of later adult activities? Or, in other words, do we develop the native play activities of the young form into the full acts of the adult by bringing to the child's consciousness the emotional phase which represents that underlying the adult act? Can this be the principle by which we organize and arrange children's plays so that they become a part of his education? Do children in this way feel social and aesthetic value of such isolated acts as those of games? For this isolation is the characteristic of play. The act in itself is rational enough. The child hunts for the hidden object just as rationally as the adult searches for the necessary food. But the object for which he hunts has no value for the rest of his life. He fights in principle as rationally as if he were defending his life or those of his family, but his victory or defeat has no relation to his own real independence or that of any one else, and so on through the whole gamut of children's games. He draws a line and calls it a man, but the success in reaching a likeness has at first no connection with his further drawing or his other life processes. He picks out a bright color, but this act has for him no connection with his recognition of a sunset. How are we to set up the necessary connections and so help nature in developing a rationally acting man out of the detached processes, by arranging and controlling his plays that he will feel in the midst of them more strongly his love for the members of his family and playmates? Is this emotional element that which develops the isolated play-act into the full act rationally connected with all other acts in a well-ordered life? I do not think so.

I think the whole evidence of psychology, individual and comparative, is that the detached isolated acts of the young forms—the plays of the lower animal or the child—are developed by objective stimuli that connect the play-act more and more closely with the life activity of the adult. The rolling spool calls forth, in the kitten, the spring and clutch which is just so much nearer the capture of the mouse. The larger meaning of this act of play is found in the control which she gets over a rapidly moving object. When this technique is thus developed, she is in a position to maintain herself by seizing her prey. There is no evidence that her feeling of dependence upon mother *in* the play or *out* of it develops in her a sense of the wider significance of the act of catching the spool. Furthermore, the child advances from his interest in using tools for the fun of it, to the sense of a valuable technique where he sees what he can do with them— and out of the appreciation of his power, and the social position which this gives, comes the recognition of the social relationships which this makes possible. His feeling of affection for his family or playfellows cannot lead him to develop his technique till he feels in the technique the new relation which this sets up. It is impossible for us to evaluate emotionally a social relation until our activity has already set up this relationship in consciousness.

The negro is being taught his duties to himself and his family by an industrial education which really makes of him a self-supporting artisan or farmer.[4] No people have advanced to civic virtues except by acquiring of capacities for independent life within the community. The emotion follows upon the recognition of the situation. The child, recognizing his dependence upon his parents, has an affection for them that must be different from that which arises when he feels within him the capacity for maintaining them in their old age, and no amount of emphasis upon the young child's dependent love for the parents can develop the technique by which he advances to an independent place in the community. It is what we do and can do that determines our relationship to others, and there is no emotional prevision that can push us into it unless we feel the capacity within us of doing what brings responsibilities with it.

The impulses out of which these capacities develop must respond to the objective stimuli that call them out, and their connection with other acts which finally altogether make up the technique of the fully developed man must be recognized before we can feel the emotions that are our valuation of these acts. Our psychology is making it constantly more evident that our emotion follows up on the act not *vice versa*, it is demonstrating that our objective world is known to us in terms of our action—the necessary conclusion from this is that we increase our known world by finding stimuli for further, higher action, and only then can we recognize the value of the larger world in our emotional states. Or, in still other terms, we must first feel in some sense the intellectual meaning of that which is to have emotional value.

If this is true, symbolism cannot be a legitimate means for educating the child. The result of it must be sentimentality, so far as it has any effect—an emphasis upon a sentiment beyond its immediate range. We are, in fact, subject to the psychological fallacy when we try to use it as a means of education. In the child's play we recognize the fully developed act of the adult and feel its emotional value. But, when we try to transfer this emotion to the child, we are emphasizing a sentiment out of its natural sphere, and, if we succeed in making it predominant in the child's consciousness, this must result in making him set up the sentiment for the sake of feeling it, and this is but a definition for sentimentality. What can dying for one's fellow playmates mean to a child who knows nothing of fighting nor the legitimate causes of it, except a mere wave of feeling? I do not imagine that the healthful child is very apt to fall into this sentimentality. He will much sooner build up in imagination some grotesque picture of a battle or funeral in which he is doing something, whatever may be the terminology which he uses. He will play the game, but to luxuriate in the feeling of dying for his playmates and teacher is probably not granted to many children. In exact proportion as this leads to such unreal pictures and ideas, must the child be hindered in the normal development of his powers. He will lose the sense of the real relationships between things when he pictures himself dying in a battle without the necessary concomitant of fighting. To emphasize the sentiment in this one-sided way is necessarily to deprive the child of the logical relation between different acts.

This brings us to the broader question of the use of the child's imagination. As the kindergarten teacher organizes the plays through their emotional reference, the use of the imagination is left largely arbitrary. Indeed, with the child himself the use of the imagination seems arbitrary. Likenesses which are almost beyond our recognition are sufficient for him. He identifies things that for our purposes are without a shadow of resemblance. There are two ways in which you may aim to develop this power. Either a simple facility in finding likenesses, which we may try to make as free and independent of all fixed lines of association as possible, or we may assume that the child always has a sufficient reason for the likeness which he finds, a reason which is founded in his own development.

From this standpoint what we want is not an indeterminate freedom of the imagination, but the association of ideas should enable one to find in the objects about him the stimuli that will call out his whole nature. The child must be free to find in his environment what he needs, and to give him this freedom we must make him conscious of his needs.

This brings us back to the original problem. The child's life is made up at first of isolated detached acts—acts which represent the different sides of what he is to do in later life. His growth brings with it a gradual organization of these isolated play-acts into the rational activity of the full-grown man. If this organization cannot be brought about by emphasizing the social emotion—making the child feel in this way the larger meaning of his play—and this we have seen is impossible—we have left the possibility of organizing his environment. If in this way we can make his plays parts of one large activity that corresponds to the whole life act—within which in reality they all lie—we give him the natural lines of association which he is really seeking. The apparently arbitrary movement of the child's imagination is but the inner expression of the isolation of his acts, and his instinctive groping after the connections between them as the brain and body develop. It lies within the power of parent and teacher to give him surroundings which will naturally assist this growth. For example, he may play at housekeeping, building, making dishes, getting and preparing food. In one way or another all his plays have a bearing upon this.

We can give him the means, arrange them so that the life activity will be called out in all its phases, and the inherent connection of things which the imagination is seeking for will be at hand. There need be no forcing at any stage of the child's growth. We have only to order his world about him so that one play leads on to another— so that the inherent unity between the games which is open to us, but as yet not awakened in his consciousness, will be ready for his intelligence as soon as he is able to grasp it. This is, of course, only carrying the organization of the child's world a little farther than it is in [the] home already. Just such an organization is to be found in the surroundings of the young animal that lies below us. His life is, however, infinitely simpler than ours in its details. The infant beast of prey needs only the moving object, the odor and sight of the prey brought home, and eventually the experience of the hunt by the parent forms to arouse during its short period of infancy the co-ordinated acts by which he is to support himself. The necessities of life keep him within his limits of his ultimate process, and as fast as his development proceeds he finds the appropriate stimuli to call out the larger acts that include isolated processes that preceded them.

The longer period of infancy of the child enables him to await a full development before he is thrown upon his own resources and obliged to differentiate himself in some particular calling. But we are in error if we try to take advantage of this long period of infancy by protracting the isolation of his different acts. Certainly one of the greatest advantages of freedom from the necessity of self-support is the possibility of learning the real interrelation of all individual activities in the whole life of society. Then, when he must concentrate his whole energy in a single calling, he can carry into it a consciousness of its solidarity with every other and be able to control his life by a recognition of its relations to those of all others within the community. The earlier, therefore, the child recognizes the interrelations between his acts the better. And out of the consciousness of this interrelation comes the stimulus of advance. As we have seen, it is characteristic of the child in play that he is interested not in the product, but in the activity. The problem of education is, in one sense, to bring him to the point of criticizing his act by the product. The result must be exact and adequate to the further use to which it is to be put.

The public school forces the child by its discipline to produce a result which the teacher passes upon from the standpoint of the use to be made of it later. The child has but little immediate interest in it. And it is evident that he can have little interest in it until he feels its value in the spontaneous act that follows upon the first. He has no interest in exact measurement. But the exact measurement that is essential to the box he is making at once arouses the interest that the making of the box calls forth. In a word, we must so connect the different acts together in a whole, which the child grasps, that the product of one act becomes the stimulus for the next. From the first the control lies in the feeling of the whole, and education must present wholes within the range of the child's interest and intelligence which will control the separated and at first isolated play-acts.

The principle then, it seems to me, upon which the kindergarten must organize the plays of the child if they are to become educative, is that of giving at every stage of his development a whole life process within which his spontaneous acts fall. The plays must be related from without in a whole which the child can recognize, With this principle—one that is at work within our educational system at many points—the kindergarten will be able to force the public school to adapt itself to its methods. Like all great reforms, this one is coming from below. The kindergarten teacher has felt that in education a little child shall lead us—but we must be able to recognize the child first.

12

The Relation of Play to Education[1]

There are three general types of human activity, work, art, and play. We may define work as an endeavor, in which a definite end is set up, and the means are chosen solely with reference to that end. In art the control of the activity is not a sharply defined end which governs the selection of the means, but the harmony of the means in their relation to each other. A true work of art arouses pleasure because of the perfection of the construction and consequent truth of the representation. But it would be a false psychological analysis to assume that this end is in the consciousness of the artist, consequently guiding his selection of the means at his disposal. In the successful activity of the artist the thought of the public as pleased or bored by his production would be only so much hindrance. He has nothing to depend upon but the feeling of appropriateness and consistency in the means which he uses for the expression of his idea. The expression of the idea is the impulse to his activity, but it is not an end in the sense of a consciously defined ideal object which in itself determines all the means used. The expression of the artist's idea can be clearly defined in his own mind only when the product is practically accomplished. In art, then, we may say that the attention is fixed upon means and their relations, in other words upon the *technique.* Play finally distinguishes itself from both work and art in its absolute spontaneity and in its lack of consciousness of an end in view, of the means used to accomplish an end, or finally of the perfection of the movements and postures, that is of the technique. Of course an end is accomplished by play, but the health and grace of movement, the social ease and general development that follow from play under favorable circumstances can never occupy the attention of the children, nor yet can they select their plays nor the instruments which they use in them with a view to such ends. The whole spontaneity and with it the fascination and value of play, would be lost if such elements were brought to the child's consciousness.

This is not saying that these typical activities do not overlap each other. There are points in all endeavor when either work or art becomes play for the time being. It is an unfortunate workman who is in no sense an artist, and a sorry artist who never works. Finally, it is possible to conceive abstractly of conditions in which all endeavor should have the spontaneity of play, should be accompanied by the artist's consciousness of the harmonious interrelation of all the activities that go to bring about the result, and yet all have the rational consequence of a piece of well-considered and adequately planned work. But this overlapping and conceivable coincidence of these different phases does not blur the distinctions between them as we watch them in the lives of others and ourselves.

Now our education, at least beyond the primary grade and before it reaches the laboratory or the experimental method, depends solely upon the work phase of human activity for the development of the child. I refer here to consciously directed education and to the general drift of our methods and schools. There are notable exceptions to be found here and there, but they remain exceptions. There is as indicated a great deal of wholesome common sense which recognizes, without formulating it, the tremendous value that accrues to children from play and is willing ungrudgingly to sacrifice often the supposed advantages of regulated work in the school room for the freedom of development and generosity of interest which comes with an out-of-door life under favorable circumstances. I know personally a professor in Columbia University whose mother kept him out of school till he was twelve years old and left him with his interests in insects and flowers, in tools and playthings, and withal not very much directed. Similar instances are familiar, I presume, to many of us, but they are still but exceptions to the general principles that guide our education. It is the purpose of this paper to criticize the basing, especially of the earlier education of our children, upon this work phase of our activity.

Two classes of labor from time immemorial have been recognized, the free and the slave labor. Slave labor is no longer recognized in the statute-books of any civilized nation, but in the most highly civilized lands the labor-agitators are never weary of asserting that in character labor remains essentially slavish. What is the fundamental distinction between free and slave labor?

We certainly do not mean by free labor that the workman is to be left free to follow any whim which chances to root itself in his mind. The labor is to be directed as really under a system of free labor as under one of slave labor. The distinction does not lie in the presence or absence of determining direction, but in the nature of the means by which that direction is enforced. The motive of wages, with the consequent support of the laborer and his family and the possibility of rising by accumulations and increased skill, are the means used, instead of the whip. It is, however, evident that the motive power is still outside the activity of the laborer. Hunger or even hope of advancement in life represents still a *vis a tergo* [a propelling force from behind], so far as the particular piece of work is concerned. So long as intelligent interest in the product to be attained is not the immediate motive power in holding the laborer to his work, it is slave labor, according to the definition that Aristotle gave of it. The only distinction lies in the fact that Aristotle supposed that those, whose intelligent interest could not be aroused in the work, must be politically subject to those who directed them.

Although this may not be recognized in so many words, the great advantage which branches of labor have, that involve high mechanical or some artistic power, lies in this interest of the laborer in the work itself. Labor troubles are comparatively absent from these callings, and the relation of employers and employed is much more satisfactory and intimate than in the callings in which the employer can depend only upon the bread-and-butter-earning character of the wage to hold the workman to his task. Profit-sharing means a similar invasion of this field of essentially slave labor, and where it can be successfully undertaken the added zest of the workmen speak eloquently for the opening up of new and more natural motive power.

It is then impossible to get beyond this incomplete and unnatural character of work until the whole man responds immediately to the product upon which he is working, and is not required to seek for impetus in his labor from an interest that lies completely outside his shop or factory and its activities. This does not mean, of course, that the workman is to lose all thought of those that are dependent upon him, and all that flows to him and them from his ultimate success, but that there should be no break between the two sources of interest, any more than there should be in the life of the successful business and professional man, though here the chasm is by no means completely bridged. In other words, in an ideal condition the interest which directs any separate activity should be but an expression of the whole interest in life and carry the momentum with it of this whole. Until this is attained[,] labor cannot become entirely free.

We are not, of course, interested at present in the probability or the improbability of the coming of such a millennium. The advantage for us of the recognition of the different sorts of labor lies in the possibility of discussing the legitimacy of the application of the principle of work to education. We are not able to reconstruct our whole industrial system so that the labor shall be always an expression of the whole man, but we are able to banish this slavish, dwarfing method from our school rooms.

The unfortunate character of the method comes out most clearly when we consider it from the standpoint of the physiology of the nervous system. As we know now, the cells in the brain at birth are practically all complete, but the connections between the cells—the so-called coordinations—have yet to be established, at least in large measure. Indeed this process goes on at least till the age of twenty-five, and perhaps much later. It is the formation of these coordinations that represents on the side of the nervous system the process of education. The question at once suggests itself, how can they be set up? Is the brain an empty country into which the educator can go, like the manager of a telegraph company, and put wires where he will? Is it possible for him to break through paths in the brain at any point that suits his fancy, or, if you like, his pedagogical sense? Is it possible to force a path through by pure force of drilling along lines to which the child shows no capacity? Or is it a question of what the Germans call *Anlage*, or a natural capacity? Or, to put the question in still a different form, is there a[n] essential difference in the development of the body after and before birth? The surrounding mother form affords before birth the appropriate conditions and stimuli for the development of the embryo. Does society do more than to receive the child into favorable conditions and afford the appropriate stimuli for the development of the still imperfect child form? So far as we know the mother form provides simply favorable conditions for development, plus the stimulus of a highly organized food medium. Can society legitimately attempt to do more than the mother form in principle? And yet when society employs the method of work as the method of education it is taking a completely different course from that which is pursued by nature before birth.

To comprehend this we must remember that the brain coordinations are as really organs of the body as the lungs or the heart, that they have their essential value in the development of the whole organism as really as the liver or the intestines. Now, so far as we understand the development of the embryo, the stimulus is at first food, and not until the organ is comparatively highly developed does the stimulus of use come in. This comes out very clearly in the evolution of such functions as those of walking after birth. There is a steady development of the coordinations in the brain which call forth this activity, but the process itself is not called into action until the coordination is practically formed. Take a child seven or eight months old and hold its feet on a smooth table and he will move them rhythmically, showing that the coordination is already largely broken through. But nature does not at once place the necessity of walking upon the child in order to insure the skill of the older child in walking. She lets him kick his legs as much as he will. That is, she allows him to play, and out of this play arises all of the exercise that is needed. What needs to be noticed here is that this play does not direct the child's attention to any end to be accomplished by the use of the limbs. In other words, the stimulus of use does not arise under normal circumstances until the organ is so far developed that its use becomes a natural and essential part of the activity of the whole body. Nowhere in the development before birth and immediately afterwards, nor anywhere, where our instruction does not come in, is an organ *used* simply with a view to a function that is to come later. Or, to put it in terms that we used earlier, nature never compels work with reference to an end which has not direct interest, while the young form is developing. She accomplishes her part of the task by spontaneous activity, in other words by play, while we feel it necessary to arouse the stimulus of use before the organ is capable of being used in the only sense in which an organ should be used. When an organ is properly used, when it is fully and normally developed, any exercise of it should be one of the entire organism through it, that is the whole interest that is involved in the entire life process should come to expression in that one function. Play is the application of this principle to development.

Undoubtedly in play, an exercise is given to as yet imperfectly developed organs, but it never involves a directing end or purpose which lies in it's full expression beyond the capacity of the organism in its present state of development. For example, a kitten playing with a spool undoubtedly represents an exercise of the functions of mouse catching, which is of great value to the full developed animal; but the point is that nature neither makes the kitten dependent upon the use of its yet imperfect capacity in order to stimulate it to higher development, nor yet does she in any way test the success of any separate part of the act by the criterion of adult mouse catching. The playing with the spool stands upon the same plane of development as the kitten, and there is no control exercised over it by the completed act of mouse catching, except in the sense that the spool calls out spontaneously all the mouse-catching capacity of the kitten at her present stage of advancement.

As fast as these coordinations begin to ripen, there is abundance of nerve force to keep them exercised. It is the most evident characteristic of childhood that there is a superabundance of energy, required for no immediate purpose, that brings to expression each new capacity of the infant-form as soon as it is consistent with the entire life-process of the organism. In other words, under normal conditions the child's life should be perfectly homogeneous; either it is made up of the pursuit of ends which are perfectly comprehensible to the child and of native interest to him, or else of spontaneous outbursts of activities that represent newly formed coordinations, whose meaning is not yet fully evident and will not perhaps become so till the form has become adult. So far as the immediate life of the child is concerned and its consciousness, they have no value except as escape valves for the surplus energy. They are purely spontaneous. From the standpoint of the final development of the child they mean the taking possession of and making itself at home in new-won coordinations, that are later to be of the highest value to the man.

It is evident that nature, then, never uses the principle of work as that upon which to forward development. I am referring, of course, to as yet undifferentiated functions. What the child comprehends and can do, it will do with a native interest that requires no continuous spurring. But this occupies but a small part of the child's life. Nature depends upon the presence simply of the right stimuli to call out spontaneous use of new coordinations as fast as formed. And this is, in principle, play. As a part of the supporting and developing social form for the yet dependent child, it is our duty to see that the requisite nourishment and protection for the continued growth of the child is present, and then that those stimuli are not lacking which answer to the developing coordinations of the central nervous system, and which will call out spontaneously the exercise of these functions. In a word, the whole education of a child should be upon the principle of teaching him to walk. We do not put him through a carefully controlled series of leg motions from birth on that he may have the necessary facility later. We simply see that there are an abundance of chairs and other objects by which he can pull himself up, a floor adapted to stimulating the soles of the feet and things that he wants at a distance. There is nothing else to be done in teaching the use of number or any other branch, so far as the principle is concerned.

The matter is simple enough so far as the walking is concerned, for these means are right at hand. The problem becomes much more complicated when we reach higher stages of development. A moving object is all that is necessary for the education of a kitten. But the life of the man is indefinitely complicated in comparison with that of the cat, and the series of stimuli that are needed for his education are proportionately more numerous and complex. I think that it is fair to say that in an ideally constructed society these stimuli would be as naturally present, as are those which bring about the education in walking. But it is just the characteristics of our society that it is not perfect and that it is the child *par excellence*, that forces upon us the recognition of this lack of perfection, and makes us, with reference to him, try to provide a miniature society which shall be as near perfection as possible. The environment of the child, as providing the appropriate stimuli to call out the exercise of all the functions of the child in succession as they appear, would represent, in miniature at least, the normal environments, physical and social, of the man. The problem of educating the child is almost as large as that of accomplishing the full development of society, representing an earlier stage in the accomplishment of the latter. It is still true that "a little child shall lead them."

As far as system is concerned it is a great deal easier to simply drill a child a year on all the combinations of numbers up to five, than it is to find out how and when he naturally begins to recognize the numerical distinctions, and to provide the natural stimuli to which these coordinations will respond. Miss Allyn did it, for example, in Mrs. Quincy-Shaw's school, some years ago, by the use of coins. Upon them as stimuli the child responded gradually with a whole series of combinations. It was not for the purpose of actually buying and selling. It was simply playing at buying and selling. It was a purely spontaneous activity, but one that was essential for the child, if he was to take possession, so to speak, of these new brain coordinations, just as a smooth floor and objects by which to pull himself up are essential to the child if he is to walk. No one can tell him how to use his limbs, but one can put chairs in his way and hold out to him an apple at a little distance. If he have no stimuli he will never walk, but the stimuli do nothing more than enable him to do what he is all ready to do.

The problem is to find the appropriate stimulus which naturally calls out the activity as far as it is then developed, not to get hold of motives which will force the child to work where he has and can have no interest. The final solution of the problem is surrounding the child with the life process in such a form that it will appeal to him. In Sloyd work or the simple use of carpenters' tools,[2] in molding objects from the history of the race, in the presentation of industrial processes, in the watching and care for insects and animals, there lies an abundance of stimuli for all the developing child's powers, not presented in a helter-skelter fashion but arranged and united in such a way that the child responds to their values for life as he gradually awakes to them. For, to continue our terminology, a child is forming, in the central nervous system, not only simple coordinations, but coordinations of coordinations, and there must be the stimuli for these latter as much as for the former. The problem is by no means a simple one, but this is no excuse for continuing the old method of giving him his whole technique of life in advance, before he can have any objects on which to use them.

For this is our method at present. We aim to give a child *methods* while his interest is all in objects. He wants the natural stimuli, and we insist on forcing through coordinations of our own making. This method is, of course, subject to a fundamental psychological fallacy. We try to fix the child's attention upon the problem we set him, and really we are fixing it upon the external motives which are to keep him at work. The result is that he loses, frequently, the power of real concentration. How many of us can add a long column without making a number of errors? We are unable practically to keep the attention upon so simple a process continually, while in something that has our whole interest from the start, which we have learned under the influence of this interest, there may be no break in the process from beginning to end. I am sure that this very common disability comes from the constant break that must take place in the child's study of arithmetic as it is usually taught. He must be continually jumping back from the study that has no interest for him to the discipline of the school that keeps him at work. We are setting up coordinations here, but, instead of their being between the different steps of the problem, they lie from one step to the teacher's eye or the fear of staying after school and back again. Those we set up are making constant breaks in the coordinations we wish to form.

In referring to play, then, as the principle upon which education should be conducted[,] we do not mean that the child should be left to the chance influence of what may be about him, but that we should so arrange these stimuli that they will answer to the natural growth of the child's organism, both as respects the objects he becomes successively interested in and the relations which they have to each other in the life process that he will have to carry out.

13

On the Social Situation in the School[1]

I have been asked to present the social situation in the school as the subject of a possible scientific study and control. The same situation among primitive people is scientifically studied by the sociologist and folkpsychologist.[2] They note two methods in the process of primitive education. The first is generally described as that of play and imitation. The impulses of the children find their expression in play, and play describes the attitude of the child's consciousness. Imitation defines the form of unconscious social control exercised by the community over the expression of childish impulse.

In the long ceremonies of initiation, education assumed a more conscious and almost deliberate form. The boy was induced into the clan mysteries, into the mythology and social procedure of the community, under an emotional tension which was skillfully aroused and maintained. He was subjected to tests of endurance which were calculated not only to fulfil this purpose, but to identify the ends and interests of the individual with those of the social group. These more general purposes of the initiatory ceremonies were also at times cunningly adapted to enhance the authority of the medicine man, or the control over food and women by the older men in the community. Whatever opinion one may hold of the interpretation which folkpsychology and anthropology have given of this early phase of education, no one would deny, I imagine, the possibility of studying the education of the savage child scientifically, nor that this would be a psychological study. Imitation, play, emotional tensions favoring the acquirement of clan myths and cults, the formation of clan judgments of evaluation, these must be all interpreted and formulated by some form of psychology. The particular form which has dealt with these phenomena and processes, is social psychology. The important features of the situation would be found not in the structure of the ideas to be assimilated, considered as material of instruction for any child, nor in the lines of association which would guarantee their abiding in consciousness. They would be found in the impulse of the children expressed in play, in the tendency of the children to put themselves in the place of the men and women of the group, i.e., to imitate them in the emotions which consciousness of themselves in their relationship to others evoke, and the import for the boy which ideas and cults would have when surcharged with such emotions.[3]

If we turn to our own systems of education, we find that the materials of the curriculum have been presented as percepts capable of being assimilated by the nature of their contents to other contents in consciousness, and the manner has been indicated in which this material can be most favorably prepared for such assimilation. This type of psychological treatment of material and the lesson is recognized at once as Herbartian.[4] His associational type of psychology, its critics add[,....] is intellectualistic. In any case it is not a social psychology, for the child is not primarily considered as a self among other selves, but as an *apperceptionsmasse*.[5] The child's relations to the other members of the social group to which he belongs have no immediate bearing on the material nor on the learning of it. The banishment from the traditional school work of play, and any adult activities in which the child could have a part as a child, i.e., the banishment of processes in which the child can be conscious of himself in relation to others, means that the process of learning has as little social content as possible.

An explanation of the different attitude in the training of the child in the primitive and in modern civilized communities is found, in part, in the division of labor between the school on the one side and the home and the shop or the farm on the other. The business of storing the mind with ideas, both materials and methods, has been assigned to the school. The task of organizing and socializing the self to which these materials and methods belong is left to the home and the industry or profession, the playground, the street, and society in general. A great deal of modern educational literature turns upon tile fallacy of this division of labor. The earlier vogue of manual training and the domestic arts, even before the frank recognition of their relation to, industrial training took place, was due in no small part to the attempt to introduce those interests of the child's into the field of his instruction which gather about a socially constitute self, to admit the child's personality as a whole into the school.

I think we should be prepared to admit the implication of this educational movement:— that however abstract the material is which is presented, and however abstracted its ultimate use is from the immediate activities of the child, the situation implied in instruction and the psychology of that instruction, that it is impossible fully to interpret or control the process of instruction without recognizing the child as a self and viewing his conscious processes from the point of view of their relation in his consciousness to his self among other selves.

In the first place, back of all instruction lies the relation of the child to the teacher and about it lie the relations of the child to the other children, in the schoolroom and on the playground. It is, however, of interest to note that, so far as the material of instruction is concerned, an ideal situation has been conceived to be one in which the personality of the teacher should disappear as completely as possible behind the process of learning, in the actual process of instruction. The emphasis upon the relation of pupil and teacher in the consciousness of the child has been felt to be unfortunate. In like manner, the instinctive social relations between the children in school hours is repressed. In the process of memorizing and reciting a lesson, or working out a problem in arithmetic, a vivid consciousness of the personality of the teacher in his relationship to that of the child would imply either that the teacher was obliged to exercise discipline to carry on the process of instruction, and this must in the nature of the case constitute friction and division of attention, or else that the child's interest is distracted from the subject-matter of the lesson to something in which the personality of tile teacher and pupil find some other content; for even a teacher's approval and a child's delight therein have no essential relation to the mere subject-matter of arithmetic or English. It certainly has no such relationship as that implied in apprenticeship, in the boy's helping on the farm or the girl's helping in the housekeeping, [it] has no such relationship as that of members of an athletic team to each other. In these latter instances the vivid consciousness of the self of the child and of his master, of the parents whom he helps, and of the associates with whom he plays is part of the child's consciousness of what he is doing, and his consciousness of these personal relationships involves no division of attention. Now it has been a part of the fallacy of an intellectualistic pedagogy that it divided attention was necessary to insure application of attention-that rewards and especially punishments of the school hung before the child's mind to catch the attention that was wandering from the task, and through their associations with the school work brought the attention back to the task. This involves a continual vibration of attention on the part of the average child between the task and the sanctions of school discipline.

It is only the psychology of school discipline that is social. The pains and penalties, the pleasures of success in competition of favorable mention of all sorts, implies vivid self-consciousness. It is evident that advantage would follow from making the consciousness of self or of selves, which is the life of the child's play—in its competition or cooperation,—have as essential a place in instruction [as discipline has]. To use Professor Dewey's phrase, instruction should be an interchange of experiences in which the child brings his experience to be interpreted by the experience of the parent or the teacher. This recognizes that education is *interchange* of ideas, is conversation—belongs to a universe of discourse. If the lesson is simply set for the child,–is not his own problem,–the recognition of himself as facing a task and a task-master is no part of the solution of the problem. But a difficulty which the child feels and brings to his parent or teacher for solution is helped on toward interpretation by the consciousness of the child's relation to his masters. Just in so far as the subject-matter of instruction can be brought into the form of problems arising in the experience of the child, just so far will the relation of the child to the instructor become a part of the natural solution of the problem. Actual success of a teacher depends in large measure upon this capacity to state the subject matter of instruction in terms of the experience of the children. The recognition of the value of industrial and vocational training comes back at once to this, that what the child has to learn is what he wants to acquire to become the man. Under these conditions instruction takes on frankly the form of conversation, as much sought by the pupil as by the instructor.

I take it, therefore, to be a scientific task to which education should set itself, that of making the subject-matter of its instruction the material of personal intercourse between pupils and instructors, and between children themselves. The substitution of the converse of concrete individuals for the pale abstractions of thought.

To a large extent, our school organization reserves the use of the personal relation between teacher and taught for the negative side, for the prohibitions. The lack of interest in the personal content of the *lesson* is, in fact, startling when one considers that it is the personal form in which the instruction should be given. The best illustration of this lack of interest we find in the problems which disgrace our arithmetics. They are supposed matter of converse, but their content is so bare, their abstractions so raggedly covered with the form of questions about such marketing and shopping and building as never were on sea or land, that one sees that the social form of instruction is a *form* only for the writer of the arithmetic. When, further, we consider how utterly inadequate the teaching force of our public schools is to transform this matter into concrete experience of the children, or even into their own experience, the hopelessness of the situation is overwhelming. [Wilhelm] Ostwald[6] [1909] has written a textbook of chemistry for the secondary school which has done what every text-book should do. It is not only that the material shows real respect for the intelligence of the student, but it is so organized that the development of the subject-matter is in reality the action and reaction of one mind upon another mind. The old dictum of the Platonic Socrates that one must follow the argument where it leads in the dialogue, should be the motto of the writer of text-books.

It has been indicated already that language being essentially social in its nature, thinking, with the child, is rendered concrete by taking on the form of conversation. It has been also indicated that this can take place only when the thought has reference to a real problem in the experience of the child. The further demand for control over attention carries us back to the conditions of attention. Here again we find that traditional school practice depends upon social consciousness for bringing the wandering attention back to the task, when it finds that the subjective conditions of attention to the material of instruction are lacking, and even attempts to carry over a formal self-consciousness into attention, when, through the sense of duty, the pupil is called upon to identify the solution of the problem with himself. On the other hand, we have in vocational instruction the situation in which the student has identified his impulses with the subject-matter of the task. In the former case, as in the case of instruction, our traditional practice makes use of the self-consciousness of the child in its least effective form. The material of the lesson is not identified with the impulses of the child. The attention is not due to the organization of impulses to outgoing activity. The organization of typical school attention is that of a school self, expressing subordination to school authority and identity of conduct with that of all the other children in the room. It is largely inhibitive—a consciousness of what one must not do, but the inhibitions do not arise out of the consciousness of what one is doing. It is the nature of school attention to abstract from the content of any specific task. The child must give attention *first*, and *then* undertake any task which is assigned him, while normal attention is essentially selective and depends for its inhibitions upon the specific act.

Now consciousness of self follows upon that of attention, and consists in a reference of the act, which attention has mediated, to the social self. It brings about a conscious organization of this particular act with the individual as a whole–makes it his act,—and can only be effectively accomplished when the attention is an actual organization of impulses seeking expression. The separation between the self implied in typical school attention and the content of the school tasks makes such an organization difficult, if not impossible. In a word, attention is a process of organization of consciousness. It results in the reinforcement and inhibition of perceptions and ideas. It is always the part of an act and involves the relation of that act to the whole field of consciousness. This relation to the whole field of consciousness finds its expression in consciousness of self. But the consciousness of self depends primarily upon social relations. The self arises in consciousness *pari passu* [equally everywhere, universally] with the recognition and definition of other selves. It is, therefore, unfruitful, if not impossible, to attempt to control scientifically the attention of children in their formal education unless they are regarded as social beings in dealing with the very material of instruction. It is this essentially social character of attention which gives its peculiar grip to vocational training. From the physiological point of view, not only the method and material, but also the means of holding the pupils' attention must be socialized.

Finally, a word may be added with reference to the evaluations— the emotional reaction—which our education should call forth. There is no phase of our public-school training that is so defective as this. The school undertakes to acquaint the child with the ideas and methods which he is to use as a man. Shut up in the history, the geography, the language and the number are the values that gather about the country and its human institutions, about beauty, in nature and art, and the control over nature and social conditions. The child, in entering into his heritage of ideas and methods, should have the emotional response which the boy has in a primitive community when he has been initiated into the mysteries and the social code of the group of which he has become a citizen.[7] We have a few remainders of this emotional response in the confirmation or conversion and entrance into the church, in the initiation into the fraternity, in the passage from apprenticeship into the union. But the complexities of our social life, and the abstract intellectual character of the ideas which society uses, has made it increasingly difficult to identify the attainment of the equipment of a man with the meaning of manhood and citizenship. Conventional ceremonies at the end of the period of education will never accomplish this,[8] and we have further to recognize that our education extends for many far beyond the adolescent period to which this emotional response naturally belongs. What our schools can give must be given through the social consciousness of the child as that consciousness develops. It is only as the child recognizes a social import in what he is learning and doing that moral education can be given.

I have sought to indicate that the very process of schooling in its barest form cannot be successfully studied by a scientific psychology unless that psychology is social, i.e., unless it recognizes that the processes of acquiring knowledge, of giving attention, of evaluating in emotional terms must be studied in their relation to selves in a social consciousness. So far as education is concerned, the child does not become social by learning. He must be social in order to learn.

14

The University and the School of Education[1]

In the two general types of Schools of Education in the country there is evident the same tendency to make closer the work of the School and of the University. These two types are that represented by the Teachers' College in Columbia University and that to be found in a number of State Universities in the West. The Teachers' College has had a quite separate existence from that of the University of which it has become a technical school. But the policy of the institution at present is to identify its work with that of the University us far as possible. There is a steady pressure brought to bear by the School of Education upon the University to introduce members of its faculty into the faculty of the University, in so far as they are not specifically teachers of pedagogy, theoretical and applied. In the other type, which is by no means so developed as that of the Teachers College in New York, the schools have been organized by the addition to the Department of Education of members from the other departments, who are a asked to give courses in the teaching of their respective subjects. It is clear that the trend in both Schools is to merge as largely as possible the work of the technical school and the University in so far as it has to do with the subject-matters that are taught in both. One can discover the same tendency in the development of technical schools of other sorts, especially in medicine and engineering. But in these cases the identification of work done in the technical school and in the University does not cover nearly as large a field, and does not seem to have as great importance for the definition of the work of the School as in the case of the Teachers College.

The difference lies in the fact that there is no clear and generally accepted theory of the teaching of teaching. The teaching of medicine and of engineering and law stand to-day upon very clearly defined and eminently successful methods. One cannot say as much for pedagogy. Pedagogy is to no small extent an application of psychology, and yet we find that dominant type of psychology among pedagogues is Herbartian. Herbart's (e.g., 1891, 1902) psychology could possibly be presented as the basis for work in psychology itself in any scientific institutions, and yet it is resurrected from the history of psychology to become the controlling theory is no insignificant part of our educational theory. The explanation for this may be found, I presume, in the present condition of psychology. So-called structural psychology, which has offered a convenient statement of the phenomena of consciousness for the purposes of experimentation, does not offer any workable doctrine of the *development* of consciousness which takes place in the child. It is easier to make use of the confessedly outworn doctrines of Herbart or that of [Alexander] Bain [1897], than it is to adapt the doctrines of [Wilhelm] Wundt [e.g., 1894, 1902, 1912], of [Oswald] Külpe [1895, 1904], of [Edward Bradford] Titchener [1898, 1909], or [Hugo] Münsterberg [e.g., 1912, 1920] to educational theory. To tell the truth, their psychological doctrines are at bottom the statement of the as yet unsolved problems of psychology. On the other hand, the functional psychology which is represented by [William] James [1890, 1907], [John] Dewey [1900/c. 1899], and Professor [James Rowland] Angell [e.g., 1907, 1918] here has from the start offered new life to educational theory, but it has not itself so formulated its educational doctrine for publication that it can speak with final authority to what should be this applied science of psychology.

Apart from the work which has been done in the philosophy of education by Professor Dewey, and the scientific work which is being carried on in the history of education, and the study of specific problems in child-psychology by experimental methods, e.g., some of the work that is being done at Clarke [University] under the direction of G. Stanley Hall [e.g., 1890, 1904], and at Columbia [University] by [Edward Lee] Thorndike [1898, 1901], there can hardly be said to be any work going on in the country in theoretical pedagogy which we can feel has any very vital importance for the control over the training of our teachers; and the pedagogy to which I have referred above is as yet too fragmentary in its published form, and in the type of problem that it attacks, to guide those who want to give the right direction to a School of Education.

It is because the prophets of education themselves, with a few exceptions, give such uncertain messages, that I want to call especial attention to the tendency mentioned at the opening of this letter. It seems to indicate that the training of teachers calls for control over subject-matter. If I am not mistaken, this is and is likely, for a long time to come, to remain the key to the pedagogical situation. For, while our pedagogical theory is by no means self-consistent and adequate, the abandonment of earlier pedagogical tradition, the advance to a new point of view, have made a rearrangement and enrichment of the subject-matter of the curriculum necessary not only in the Teachers College, but also in the elementary and secondary schools.

The new attitudes, to which reference is made, is, in general, that of taking the student's point of view. It means in the schoolroom stating the subject-matter in terms of the experience of the child, and making problems, which are his own problems, the medium of his education. A survey of our schools at present would show them pretty generally the battlefield between this point of view and the old formal education, which cared nothing for the meaning of the training to the immediate experience of the child, but was satisfied with his acquiring facilities in number and language, and certain facts, all of which he was expected to comprehend only when he had reached man's estate.

It is hardly necessary to point out that the advance in the pedagogical point of view is due fully as much to the dominance of scientific method in all of our intellectual processes as to the application of a more modern psychology to process of [the] process of teaching. It is an invasion of the lower schools not simply by University standards of results, but the invasion by University methods. We can hardly shirk the responsibility which our own successful research, and the inspiration of its example and methods, has put upon us. A second very evident result of this change of point of view is that an indefinitely greater control over the subject-matter is required of the teacher than was necessary under the older system. Just because the child gets at the world in a different manner from that of the adult, and because different children will approach it from different points of view, the teacher must have such a comprehension of the subject that he can select and present what is adapted to the specific problem with which he is concerned. It is furthermore,

I think, a mistake that we all recognize at present, to suppose that the child's problem is a superficial one which can be dealt with by a teacher who is superficially trained. Many of the problems which arise on all subjects in children's minds and which are very real to them, and which can therefore be made the media of the most successful education, can be dealt with only by the very competently trained teachers in their own fields.

Again, it is evident that the use of what is at bottom scientific method in the education of children is bound to involve as great a change in methods of teaching, in the apparatus used, in the opportunities offered out of the schoolroom as well as within it, as has taken place within our colleges during the past generation.

While there is a contest going on between the old and new point of view in teaching children, it would be a mistake to assume that the modern attitude is regarded with a considerable hostility. The opposition is that which arises from the difficulties in the way of the change, and the uncertainty as to what can be done if a change is made. It is a problem of subject-matter and the control over it, not a problem of methods.

Every step that is made in the adequate training of our teachers is a step in advance in the solution of this educational problem. The specific problems that arise as to methods of instruction are, to a great extent, those involved in the handling of material, and the solution of these problems will come through wide acquaintance with the material itself.

It would be possible to multiply examples. I will simply refer to a few. Professor W.G. Hale [1907] has constructed an ideal beginning book in Latin because he has taken the most advanced standpoint in the theory of Latin syntax, and worked it out with beginning classes himself and through his own students. [Wilhelm] Ostwald [1908] has made use of his revolutionary conceptions in chemistry to present the most comprehensive statement of chemical phenomena for children that I have seen. Professor E[liakim]. H[astings]. Moore [1910][2] has pointed out the possibility of introducing children at the earliest periods of instruction to the parallel expression of discrete and continuous quality, and the employment of the concept of the function.

In these instances, and many more that might be adduced, it has been the comprehensive grasp of the subject, that belongs to a mind that has mastered the subject and its treatment, that has made possible the presentation of new and immensely valuable material for the child, and the discovery of the channels through which it could be got to him.

It seems, then, highly important that a School of Education should take advantage of this position of affairs and make the adequate training of teachers in subject-matter its specialty, and that the departments whose subject-matter is taught in elementary and secondary schools should face the responsibility for them which the presence of a School of Education here carries with it. This responsibility cannot be questioned when we recognize that methods in teaching depend, and are going to depend principally, upon the matter presented and the control over it which the student gains.

Finally, it appears most important that the dominant influences in the School of Education, in shaping its policy, in inspiring its work, in informing its students, should be university influences rather than those of the technical Normal School.

I would not, of course, belittle the importance of educational theory and practice considered by themselves. They have to state first of all what has already been accomplished, and to generalize and bring to consciousness methods which are already in existence.

But I would suggest that it follows logically from the educational situation sketched above that educational progress in the School of Education is more likely to come from a faculty of teachers who would have the thorough training in their own subject-matter, which a member of a University faculty must have, as well as a profound interest in the problems of teaching, than from the direction of a professional pedagogue taken among those we could find and secure at the present time.

Present advance in education must come from the side of the content, not from the formal side, and it is safer to trust the development of the School to men interested in teaching and scientifically trained in their departments than to the so-called educational expert, who would be apt to be formal in his attitude, and to subordinate the real problems in education to problems of administration.

There appears to be here a unique opportunity before the University of Chicago, which made use of with comprehension would make her the most important educational center in the country.

15

The University and the
Elementary Schools[1]

The parents' Association of the University, Elementary, and High Schools may legitimately ask what advantages it gets from the connection between these Schools and the University. We are certainly attracted by the fact of this connection. It serves to justify the tuition we pay for our children's instruction. We feel that in some way the methods used and the studies pursued are guaranteed by the larger institution of learning which takes the responsibility for these lower schools. It is assumed that we have a favorable conjunction of supply and demand. On the one side we ask for the best education which can be given our children, while on the other side stands the University with not only its body of learning but its educational ideals, its methods, and its departments of education seeking to prove by theory and practice, and by actual experiment, that the training it gives shall square with what we want and with the canons of pedagogy.

While this is the face value of our connection with the University, I presume that we all of us recognize that it stands not so much for an accomplished fact as the statement of the problem with which the University has to deal.

We all know that both elementary and secondary education grew up apart from the University. That they stand upon traditions that are centuries old. That there has been in the past little or no community of life between the schools and the University. And those of us who are at all familiar with the sentiment of the members of our Universities recognize that very few there feel the necessity, or even naturalness, of any close connection between the higher and lower branches of our educational structure. At most, many of them would say the University can pass upon the results which the schools attain.

They can set standards for admission to college which the lower schools must respect. The pedagogical staff of the University will also discuss the methods which are used in these schools, but beyond this they feel that the connection of the schools with the University can only be an administrative one.

In the largest School of Education in the country, that of Columbia University in New York, the secondary and elementary schools are not in as close connection with the University as that which subsists here in Chicago.

So far as I know, the only other large schools of a similar character are those connected with Normal Schools, and serve primarily the purpose of practice teaching (and these do not generally include High Schools).

The University, Elementary, and High Schools are not primarily practice schools. Certainly the intention with which these schools have been brought into the University has been that they should be vital parts of [the] whole institution. The question arises, then, in what sense this can be accomplished. It has never been assumed that these schools were to be simply supervised by the members of the College of Education and the Department of Education. Both the University, through its officers and members of its faculties, and those who have been part of the Schools themselves have maintained that there was to be a continual organic relation between the Schools and the other parts of the University. We do not, therefore, have to ask the question whether there is willingness to co-operate upon both sides. The history of the Schools and the University emphatically affirms the purpose of maintaining this cooperation. We may assume that the University is willing to give anything that it can give, and the Schools to receive anything that they can profit by.

I do not think, however, that it is quite clear in our minds just what this cooperation can be, and it is this lack of clearness which constitutes the problem with which both the Schools and the University are face to face.

The easiest answer to the question would be that the University has no other organic relation to these schools except through its departments of theoretical and practical pedagogy. If that were the case, the responsibility could be loaded onto certain shoulders, and the rest of the University would have its skirts quite free.

It is, however, not difficult to see that such an answer is really dodging the whole issue. If the Elementary and High Schools had no other connection with the University than the Departments of Education, they would never have come into it. They are not necessary for teaching theoretical pedagogy, and the University is not undertaking to simply train School Teachers. It has not simply added a Normal School to its departments. The reason that the Schools have arisen within the University is, that we are beginning to recognize that the problems of Elementary and Secondary education cannot be solved apart from the subjects that are taught and investigated within the University; that there is the same justification for a laboratory of Education within the University that there is for those of Chemistry, Physics, or Biology. These exist within the University because no one can pursue any of these subjects apart from the others. The scientist in one branch must have connection with the scientist in other branches. They are naturally necessary to each other.

There have been two problems in elementary and secondary education. One was the problem of the way that which is to be learned should be presented. The other is the problem of the subject-matter of the curriculum itself, what shall be taught.

We are all of us pretty conscious of the revolution that has been taking place in the methods of teaching. We know, in the words of G. Stanley Hall,[2] that the Renaissance of Childhood has come. We have heard from early morn till dewy eve that the child can only assimilate what comes to him in terms of his own experience. That it is only in so far as the problems of the schoolroom are his problems that he can gain any real education through them. Child-study has brought our teachers close to the child, and psychology has demonstrated that only in so far as what the child learns interprets his own experience can it be educative. Here we have a comparatively sure platform to stand upon. But when we go beyond this platform, that of the attitude which the school and the teacher should occupy toward the child, when we advance beyond what has become the commonplace of Teachers' Institutes and Parents' Associations, Life with the Child in the School— we find no sort of uniformity of theory or practice. What shall we teach? Is it to be the same content which is contained in the old-fashioned text-books, enlivened, illustrated, revivified by our newer pedagogy? Or is it to be something new? And, if it is to be something new, what will it be and where will it come from?

The problem is a somewhat more serious one than it seems to be at first blush. Take a group of text-books that were in use in our schools a generation ago, [Dana Pond?] Colburn's[3] or [Sir Benjamin] Thompson's[4] or [Joseph] Ray's[5] Arithmetics, or [William Holmes] McGuffey[']s[6] or [Edward Austin] Sheldon's,[7] or [Lucy Langdon Williams?] Wilson's Readers [e.g., 1898], or [Arnold] Guyot's [1849] or [Samuel Augustus] Mitchell's [8] [?] Geographies, and you will find no material differences. The doses were differently divided, but the contents of the prescriptions were the same. Any one with a good general education and that sort of common sense which was called the endowment of the born-teacher, could write a text-book on any subject, and publish it, too. But this subject-matter has no sort of natural relation to the child's experience or life, and was made up of a body of facts which were so commonplace and generally accepted that no one felt called upon to investigate their truth or pertinency. In fact, the question of the reliability of the statements made in these text-books was not raised, for they were after all written for children, and if the children learned to read and write and figure out of them, what they read and wrote and figured night as well be one thing as another. Which is another way of saying that, when the education is largely of a formal character, the content of what is taught is generally neglected. If the child questioned it, of course he was brought up with a sharp turn for an unwarranted questioning of his elders and betters. This was supposed to be particularly good for his moral development. It formed character.

I think that any one will agree that this was an ideal situation for the text-book writer, and that this highway, where he that runs may read, becomes at once precarious and uncertain when one has entered the field of the Newer Pedagogy, The only demands that were made upon the former text-books were that they should train the children in the formal processes and should not be at variance with generally accepted views and ideas of the community.

Now we demand, in the first place, that the subject-matter should be true for the child; that is shall be fair essential part of his experience; and, in the second place, that it shall be as rich and varied in its contents as the kaleidoscopic consciousness of the child, for it must appeal to his interest, and for that purpose to the varied activities, especially constructive activities, of the child. A great mass of material has been brought in this way which is quite foreign to the text-book world, which does not always square, by any means, with the commonly accepted views and opinions of the community, and which has very varying success in interesting the children. (The teacher and text-book writer are still possessed with that somewhat easy conscience in regard to that which they present to the children. From their point of view, it does not make so much difference what is presented, provided it holds the children's attention.)

The situation has completely changed: while formerly what was thought was of minor importance provided the formal part of the work was satisfactory, now we are depending upon the content of what is given to insure success in the schoolroom work. We have got to justify what we give the children, first by its success in appealing to them, and controlling their attention, in the second place because of its value for its own sake. This new material does not belong to it traditional mass of text-book material. It is so novel that after all nothing but the imprimatur of scientific testimony can assure its place in the schoolroom.

I think it has been this unwieldy character of the material with which he is dealing that has driven the driven the pedagogue to seek the assistance and support of the University, that has made situation out of which Elementary and Secondary Schools in University pedagogical departments have arisen. The newer educator has felt that he or she was quite competent to deal with the child if they could live together in the schoolroom, there was no call for intermediation by an institution of higher learning. It has only been gradually that these school teachers have come to recognize that the new material which they wish to use in the schoolroom has got to come from the researches and investigations of the institutions of higher learning and that these investigators have got to give the stamp of scientific accuracy to this new subject-matter before it can have currency.

In a word, a content teaching in the place of the formal teaching has been bringing Elementary and Secondary Schools constantly closer to the University, because the University has in the end to pass upon the contents used.

I have dwelt upon this phase of the movement, because it has not been so evident as the other current which flows in the channel of educational theory. As I indicated above, the old-fashioned teacher was born and not made. It was the text-book that was made, sometimes out of whole cloth. Now the material of the text-book is born or supposed to be out [of] scientific researches, while the teacher is made in a training school. Teaching, instead of being a natural-born talent, is found to be the product of applied psychology, and the teacher has had to come to the University for the psychology. But, while the teacher has had to come to the University for his scientific pedagogy, it is not so evident that he must bring his school with him. Indeed, such all active educational University center as Clark University has gathered the teachers without the Schools. The problems that have given rise to University Elementary and High Schools are not those of the training of teachers through scientific psychology, it has been rather the problems of what can be taught. I do not think that Colonel Parker felt that the School of which he was the head had so much to gain from the educational theory to be found in the university as from the materials which the scientific departments should put at their disposal. I know that Professor Dewey felt that the important problems with which the Laboratory School could deal were those of the subject-matter of the curriculum rather than those of the theory of teaching.[9] To get a subject-matter which would be worthy of the intelligence of the child he felt to be the pedagogical demand that could not be silenced. These and all other educational thinkers who have thought their way out have recognized that such subject matter could only be secured at the fountainhead of scientific research.

I can see no other adequate justification for the presence of our Elementary and High Schools as parts of the University of Chicago, than this demand which the Schools are making upon the university, to work out a curriculum which shall square not only with educational theory, but which shall in every grade bring in that which stands the test of scientific criticism, and those ideas and newly discovered truths which are bound to be most interesting and valuable even to children, if expressed in the language of their experience. We are only just beginning to appreciate how much material the competent expert can put at the disposal of the schoolroom, that we can make better use of one-sided competency in graduate work in the University than we can in the elementary and secondary schools.

We have yet to appreciate that the highly trained expert in higher mathematics is the man who can free the child with his Square-paper from the divorce between his number and his geometry; that it is only the trained Biologist who can safely make use of the conception of Adaptation to present the facts of life to children, that it is only an Ostwald [1909] that can present the essential concepts of Chemistry to the child of the secondary-school period, in conversations that neither impoverish the subject nor lose contact with the child's intelligence; that it is only the first Latinist in the country who could make use of his point of view in his theory of structure of the Latin language, to construct an ideal beginning book in Latin; that it has required a historian in the country, who is in the first rank of research men, to produce the text-book of medieval history which guides the secondary school pupil through the intricacies of that period. You are perhaps unaware that in three cases University men have worked out text-books in the High School here that are as legitimate tests of their competency in their own fields as any work they could publish, and the converse of this is true, that men who were less competent could not have accomplished what they did for the child.

We are only just beginning to comprehend that truth is an organic whole, that, therefore, it has to be taken into account as a whole when we make use of it in the instruction of children.

We have attained the standpoint which recognizes the experience of the child as the field within which education of the child must take place. And the simple use of this pedagogical point of view has reached the limit of its reforming power. Unless I am very much mistaken, the great and important steps in development of our school-system in the immediate future are going to be taken by the scientifically trained men in our Universities reorganizing the curricula from the point of view of the truth which makes children as well as men free.

This is, then, what we have a right to demand of the University, because it harbors the Schools to which we send our children. We may ask for the cooperation of every department in the University that deals with that which our children are taught. And when we ask for the mint, anise, and cumin[10] of administrative reform, let us not forget these weightier matters of the law.

16

Science in the High School[1]

The science in the high school that flourished a generation or two ago is best known to us as "natural history." It is as far away from the science that flourishes in our universities and colleges, or even our high schools, as the *Gentleman's Magazine* is from a *wissenschaftliches Centralblatt* [German scientific newsletter or journal].

It is not difficult to regret this passage, to recognize the human interest, the power of inspiring healthful curiosity, the fact that it was on all-fours with even adolescent intelligence; to recognize, in a word, that it possessed reality for the student, and quickened rather than deadened his interest in the sciences to which it served as a humble portico. Our regret may even pass over into a program, an extension of the culture-epoch program. We can point out that it was out of beginnings such as these that the most scientific of modern sciences arose; that, further, the concrete interest, the shrewd guesses, the search for tangible causes, which a [Benjamin] Franklin incarnates, is just the attitude which high-school boys and girls can take toward the physical world around them. And the conclusion to be drawn seems to be that secondary-school science should return to natural history as the proper introduction of the secondary-school child to science properly so called.

It does not seem necessary that the natural history of a modern-school curriculum should embody the mistakes and crudities of an earlier phase of the science. What is necessary rather is that the immediacy, the tangibility, the comprehensibility of the older natural history should replace the technical introduction to university sciences which have ousted it from its former place. That is, there is seemingly no necessity for the loss of immediate touch with the experience of the child.

Certainly the same problems face him which faced his father and grandfather, and there is unquestionably in him as in them the same native interest in the solution of these problems. Perhaps we should add: There is the same interest, provided they remain as concrete and comprehensible as those which his predecessors found or accepted when presented.

It is equally necessary to recognize, however, that while the same problems arise from one generation to another, the solutions differ with each scientific generation; and the fallacy of a culture-epoch theory lies in the assumption that, because the problems seem to be identical, it is possible to give the modern child the antiquated solution. We state only half of the educational problem when we emphasize this identity of attitude of the boy in his teens with that of the old-fashioned natural history. In spite of ourselves, we are compelled to answer his questions in the language—the scientific language—of to-day. And it is upon this difficulty that as yet our high-school science has been wrecked.

We cannot speak of fluids and forces and substances in what to us is the nonchalant manner of earlier days. The phenomena of the world about us have been translated into facts of motion, and the very things themselves—their substances and attributes—are defined in terms of motions. The teacher who has been adequately trained in his subject-matter cannot project himself into outworn theories, simply because they are more comprehensible to his students.

It is then only natural that he should assume that his task is to train the student to understand the language which he must eventually use in the solution of the problems he meets. He must understand and speak this language, if he is to solve the problems, so that it becomes of the first importance to master the vernacular. The problems—the familiar experiences of light, of heat, of electricity, of chemical change, of growth and reproduction in plant and animal—can be safely postponed till he understands how so to state them that he may then satisfactorily answer them.

There have been, of course, many compromises offered, lying between the two positions suggested above: that science in the high school should be adapted primarily to the immediate interest of the child, being taught only in so far as it is stated in terms which he understands, and only those problems being presented which arise naturally in his own consciousness; and that science can be profitably presented only in so far as it is expressed and received in the language which sciences uses; that it is a body of truth that cannot be diluted nor flavored to suit the taste of the child; that, on the contrary, it is the child's first duty to acquire that language, and put himself by this and similar training in a position to comprehend the actual problems of science, when presented to his more matured intelligence.

It cannot be said, however, that these compromises have succeeded. And it is natural that, on the whole, the scientific expert should carry the day. He stands for the university requirement in the first place; and, though but relatively few of the high-school students enter colleges or universities, the college requirement is, after all, a standard that is explicit and definite; while the world into which the majority of the students pass from the high school sets no explicit standards, and takes in general very little interest in the high-school curriculum.

The result is that at the present time science means from one to three possible units. University prescription lays the emphasis upon physics. Chemistry is but slightly encouraged, for college instructors in chemistry prefer commencing *de novo* [from the beginning] to building upon foundations that can be laid in the high school. Biology may be represented by a general course which is an introduction to botany and zöology, or by a half or entire unit given to either. Here the modern physiological method is superseding the older systematic method, and there is present the somewhat unsatisfactory leaven of evolutionary ideas, which are either too dogmatic or too vague to serve the purpose for which they are used. The absence of mathematics favors biological science in the mind of the high-school student, but its position is too isolated, and the demand for it in entrance requirements not general nor peremptory enough, to give it the importance which physics has obtained. Physiography, the lineal descendant of the older physical geography, is acquiring a growing importance, for reasons which will be discussed later; but it uses ideas which require training in physics and chemistry for comprehension, and, as generally taught, lacks the concreteness of experimental sciences.

The university influence upon the study of science has not been fortunate. Even its power to introduce definite standards has been attended with grave misfortunes. Entrance requirements present alternatives. The high school is encouraged to expend the money and hours at its disposal for science upon some one branch, and the result is that, even if a number of branches are represented, they are treated as units with little or no relationship to each other. And, as above noted, the university is the only power that comes forward with definite demands that have penalties attached to them. Thus the sciences in the high school are hopelessly isolated. They exist in water-tight compartments, with none of the interrelationships which are implied in their own subject-matter, and which are essential to their comprehension, especially for the student of this period. The textbook writer or the teacher trained in his subject unwittingly uses ideas belonging to a world of science, which his own specialty implies, and forgets that his students have yet to build up that world in their own experience.

That isolation is most felt in the separation between mathematics and those sciences of which it is the language. The students pursue algebra, geometry, and, reaching physics, where they meet the abstract quantity to the measurement of which these branches of mathematics are fitting them or should fit them, they do not and perhaps cannot feel the connection. The subject has been presented to them as a study quite by itself, much as grammar in the study of a language with which one is not familiar. As we have discovered that it is impossible for a child to learn the rules for the use of a language first, and then apply them in speech afterward, so we have to learn that the rules for mathematical processes cannot be acquired in advance of the application of these processes.

It is at least a fact which no one familiar with the teaching of physics will deny that the training, which children receive in algebra and geometry, as it is now taught, does not assist them in stating in mathematical terms the problems which physics presents. If there is any preparation which the teacher of physics would ask for, if he could get it, it would be that his students should come to him with the power of stating a physical problem in exact quantitative terms. But the formal training in adding, subtracting, multiplying, dividing, of whole numbers and fractions in algebra, does not advance a whit toward this end. The problems of physics call for the statement of continuous processes in discontinuous terms, of movements in number. The mathematical discipline that accomplishes this is algebra applied to geometry. But in high-school mathematics there is no suggestion that these two branches have any relationship with each other. And no training that the child receives in them there assists him in bringing the two together. They are completely isolated from each other and from physics.

This is so apparent that the demand on the part of the educational authority is for physics which shall not be predominantly mathematical, that there shall be a return to the standpoint of the old natural history.

This is, however, but a single illustration of a situation which embraces the whole field of science in the high school. That the child may really comprehend any of the phenomena which he studies in any field of science, it must be stated in terms of a world in which he lives and moves and has his being. That world is the *näive* world of the child, and he cannot live in it and learn something that belongs to another world, the world of science. His whole world must be in some sense transformed before he can approach the problems of the separate sciences in a scientific fashion. The result of the type of teaching which is now predominant in our secondary schools is that, what the child learns does not interpret his own world at all. A teacher of psychology has recently complained that his classes have not the faintest knowledge of the physical phenomena of sound and light, though in the high school a very large proportion of them have studied these very topics. What they learned there did not enter into their own experience and become an interpretation of the sounds that they heard, of the light that they saw.

The conclusion of this seems to be, not that we should turn to an antiquated method of presenting science, but that the child should be carried into the world of science before he is dispatched into the separate divisions of that world. And the high-school student should be brought into this world, not simply that he may overcome the isolation of the separate sciences in his curriculum, but because he has reached a period at which he naturally analyzes and refers the results of his analysis to some whole to which they belong.

The child below the high-school period has, as a rule, no such interest. Each experience is to him a matter of interest in itself, and though it is unconsciously interpreted by what he sees and hears and reads, still his interest does not lead him to make it consciously a part of some larger whole. All that he has learned or experienced converges upon the immediate thing before him. It does not radiate out into a new world which his thought constructs.

The predominant intellectual characteristic of the adolescent age is that the child wakes up to the existence of a world about him that he belongs to, but of which he is as yet ignorant.

Adequate materials for the reconstruction of his social world are placed at his disposal. Literature, history, stories of adventure and travel, especially novels of all descriptions, are in these days within easy reach, and are made so tempting in style, illustration, and content that the process of building up the new social world is pushed too fast, and the child becomes socially over-stimulated.

Something of the same opportunity is offered in popular works on scientific subjects. Boys' books of inventions and discovery, Jules Verne's [Costello 1978] stories, and the articles in our countless magazines popularizing scientific discoveries and methods, awaken an interest which the applications of steam and electricity keep alive. With these interests come the instincts for constructions and collections of various sorts, out of which a scientific spirit and a wide acquaintance with the world of science should result.

The result, however, is not what it should be. The study of science in the school is neither extensive enough, nor does it grow out of the instincts and interests of the children. While the language of his new social world is that of everyday life, that of the science he studies is a mathematical vernacular, which is not even comprehended without serious effort, and, as we have indicated above, he is not even allowed to use the language till he has mastered its grammar and syntax. There is nothing into which he cannot enter by the door of his vivid imagination, if it is presented to him in terms of human experience. He acquires almost unconsciously the political and social structure of this world. It is essentially comprehensible to him from the start; while most scientific concepts and laws are acquired with painful effort. And this effort is requisite, not because the concepts and laws are incomprehensible in themselves, but because they belong to a different world from that of the child's immediate experience, and one that does not grow up naturally and unconsciously out of that experience.

It is this background of a scientific world which the high school must supply if it is to give the child the same natural attitude toward the scientific studies in the curriculum, as that which he occupies toward the studies in language, literature, and history. It cannot be given him as the *fait accompli* [established accomplishment] of the trained mind. It must grow out of the immediate experience of the child, and yet it must stand out as a whole within which lie the fields of the different sciences. It is impossible that the child should comprehend the meaning of a physical, as distinct from a chemical or a biological problem, unless he has felt them arise out of a common matrix of experience.

Such a common matrix is suggested in physiography, not as it is presented in the textbooks of the subject, but as it might be presented in a course which would be an introduction to science. Physiography at least takes its world as a whole, and the world is in the main that which appeals to the direct sense-perceptions of the children. It presents that as a subject for investigation, and for the time being all the scientific problems are there lying side by side, and mutually conditioning each other. Problems of pressure and precipitation, of electricity, of solution, of plant and animal growth, and distribution, of commerce and land formation, all arise from the study of the habitat within which the human race is found. That habitat has a meaning as a whole for the child, and the problems that grow out of it are not isolated. On the contrary, they can be kept in intimate interrelation with each other and with the world within which they appear.

Physiography as presented in our textbooks assumes rather than develops the scientific conceptions. The students receive without any concrete experience terms such as "solutions," "precipitations," "warmth," "electricity," [and] "disintegration of rocks through weathering." The opportunity of making the important conceptions of science fundamentally real at the very outset is lost. They become terms with little meaning, that are oppressive rather than enlightening thereafter. The beginnings of scientific work with children must be field and laboratory work. Such a course in the introduction to science would be given best of all without a text-book. Taking as its starting-point the problems of erosion and weathering that are to be found on the large and small scale everywhere, coupling with this some of the problems of plant distribution and dependence upon surrounding conditions, field-work would be the beginning, while the questions of the effects of cold and heat, of solution and precipitation, the physical processes involved in wind and the change of the seasons, would present opportunities for laboratory experiment; in other words, for the development in the children's concrete experience of the conceptions necessary for the study of the physical environment as a whole. At the same time, it would be the differentiation of physical, chemical, and biological problems as distinguished from each other.

The problem of the proper relation of mathematics to the sciences is a much more serious one, and one that will involve a very considerable reorganization of the study of mathematics from the beginning. For the purposes of application to science, mathematics must be considered as the theory of the measurement of motion. Geometry and algebra—the continuous and the discrete—can never be separated from each other if this point of view is to be maintained. It is a point of view which should be maintained from the start—not one that has to be achieved with pain and effort later. The equation presented in the form of the graph is the natural tool, more easily grasped when properly presented than the complicated manipulations of algebraic symbols in the processes of addition, subtraction, multiplication, [and] division, with their applications in fractions and factoring. If mathematics were approached from this standpoint from the beginning, its value as the language in which scientific meaning is to be expressed would be won; instead of being a subject-matter largely incomprehensible because hopelessly abstract, it would become a transparent medium within which the concrete contents of science would appear.

There are, then, two great separations that have to be overcome in bringing science in the high school to its legitimate position, to its rights: (1) the separation between the science and the world to which it belongs—the isolation of the science—an isolation from the experience of the child, the isolation from the other sciences which leaves them each abstract and helpless within its own compartment; (2) the separation of the sciences from the language in which to so large a degree they must be expressed—a separation which is rendered necessary by the manner in which the mathematics is taught. It is this separation which constitutes especially the middle wall of division between the child and his expert instructor; it is this separation which calls for a physical science which shall be non-mathematical. The instructor has learned that his physical problem can be stated only in terms of mathematics, and is helpless when he is deprived of the medium in which alone he is able to express himself.

There is no question that the highly abstract form in which the mathematical statements of university physics are given is unnatural to the boy and girl of the high school; but this is quite a different thing from the statement that their physical science should be presented without mathematics. It is not necessary that mathematical statement should be eschewed because the child is not interested in the niceties of exact mathematical statement. The graph remains a mode of presenting continuous change which is graphic and concrete, and which welds together what must be presented together if physics is to have the value of scientific training-motion measured in discrete terms.

There is another respect in which the influence of the university upon the high-school science has been unfortunate. In its sense of competency and the incompetency of the high school and the high-school child to deal with science, the influence of the university has inevitably been to restrict the extent of the field of science in the high school. Let science be confined to that which the child in these years can accomplish in accordance with exact methods. It does not matter so much how much the child learns. The important thing is that he should make use of the proper method. The amount that he can adequately conceive is very small; let him, therefore, confine himself to that and do it correctly, leaving the rest to a period which is equal to the more difficult task. Thus he will at least bring to later study an unspoiled mind, and what method has been acquired will not have to be unlearned. From this standpoint it makes very little difference what a child learns, if he only does it in a really scientific manner. Let him keep the tentacles of observation sensitive. Whether his few observations are made in one subject or another is unimportant. The important thing is that he has learned to observe, to distinguish between what is uncritical assumption and what is fact. Science in the high school can almost be left to the chance of the equipment of the teaching force. If the science teacher is especially well equipped in biology, let the subject-matter be botany or zoology, if he is a physicist or a chemist, let one of these be the scientific pablum of the child. What must be insisted upon is that the instructor be competent to direct the child's work in the scientific spirit and method, giving him the doctrine pure and undefiled.

I have already indicated that this is theoretically almost impossible, because the fundamental conceptions of all the sciences are so interwoven that it is impossible to pursue one branch by itself, without making use of conceptions which are to the child abstract and meaningless. If the position taken above is correct, it is necessary that these fundamental scientific conceptions be developed out of the experience of the child in a course which shall be introductory to all the sciences. But this isolated manner of giving a child his science does him a wrong that is more serious than that of forcing him to use conceptions that he does not comprehend. It deprives him of the world of science, to which he has as incontestable a right in his years as the adult in the university or elsewhere.

It has been already indicated that the child finds a literature so adapted to his intelligence that he is capable of fashioning in the adolescent period a social world into which all his experiences and acquirements fit naturally. It is not the world which he will have in his maturer years, when he has learned to apply historical criticism and literary judgment to the subject-matter of his study, but it is a world which is a whole, and which as a whole serves to interpret the individual things that he learns and experiences. Ancient history dovetails with the ancient languages and literature. Whether he is studying one or the other, it remains all a part of one organized piece of human experience. Each element serves to interpret the other. In the same way there arises very soon a medieval period, even if it is gained only through the sources of Walter Scott.[2] The Reformation, and the wars and struggles that gathered around it in England and the Netherlands and America, constitute another whole into which the different facts of history, modern institutions, and movements of population and commerce fit naturally enough, and from which they get their interpretation. There is no necessity of any fact or change standing shivering by itself. They can all have their relations brought out through the whole movement or situation to which they belong.

We should at once cry out that the child was being cheated if our high schools should deprive him of this whole, and the interpretation which it carries with it; if we should attempt to isolate history from language and literature, to isolate the study of institutions from that of biography, discovery, and warfare; if we should say the child cannot take the attitude of the historical critic as yet, but what he must learn at present is to use properly the method on a small scale, with a few facts. Let him then take some isolated problem in history and gather the data from sources; when he is older he will be able to comprehend what he has done. Let him simply keep his capacity for observation keen, and later he will come with a matured mind to grasp the import of what he observes. We should reply that, no matter if he does revise his judgments of men and affairs, their history and achievements, when he is older, he has an unquestioned right to comprehend and think them earlier according to his powers. He has a right to the world as he can present it to himself, and especially to the interest and meaning which this carries with it. He has an equal right to the world of science as a whole for the meaning and interpretation which it carries with it; and a high-school curriculum which gives him some of the fragments of this world only, and does not allow him to form such an idea of it as an entirety, is cheating him out of what belongs to him at that time.

It is a commonplace of the times that we are living under the sign of science, that greater changes have been brought about by the applications of science to human affairs and apparatus than have ever been wrought before in human history. We recognize also that the discoveries of science have made the reconstruction of institutions, governmental and religious, necessary; that the bringing together of the ends of the earth, by steam and electricity, has presented us with entirely different moral problems, has reconstructed the theory of who is my neighbor. We know that change in scientific hypothesis has brought with it a new era even in philosophy. And yet, while the high-school student gets the sweep of the development of democracy as a whole, of the long struggle for liberty, of growth of empires and the spread of commerce; and while these vast organic wholes rest in the back of his mind to correlate the events of yesterday and today, he is not helped to a view of the scientific world as a whole. What he gets in this way is confined largely to the popular articles in the magazines, and the science he has in the school is so isolated that it does not even dovetail into this. It follows that, at a period when he is peculiarly sensitive to moral forces and ideas, he does not come into touch with the high morality of science, with its decalogue of disinterested exactness, its idealistic hypotheses, its gospel of human intelligence. Furthermore, the set he gets against science in the high school follows him into the university or out into the world. The scientists in the university complain that scientific courses are not placed upon the same level with the language and literature courses. They fail, however, to recognize that back of these latter courses lies a whole organized world of human experience that takes up into itself history, philology, [and] literature; while back of their scientific studies lies at first almost nothing. The beginning is a difficult reconstruction of current conceptions, or an equally difficult discovery of meaning in terms and phrases which have been loosely and uncomprehendingly used before.

The preliminary work should be done in the secondary school, not simply for the sake of the university, but for the sake of the student himself. For it is science that carries with it the most modern and the most profound culture, for the simple reason that it is science which is the source of our ideas and ideals, at least of the formative ideas and ideals.

17

The Teaching of Science in College[1]

I wish to call attention to a situation which seems to me unnatural and unfortunate. It is unnecessary to present it in statistical form. No one will question that science in the colleges of this and other universities has not the importance and popularity that it should have, that this element of our modern education is by no means represented in the results of education in accordance with its importance.

It is not, however, to the failure to elect scientific courses as they are to-day or to enroll themselves for science devotees on the part of our students that I think especial attention should be directed. Nor do I think that we can explain this and other evidences of the deficiencies in this regard by the traditional prestige of the so-called humanity, or the prejudicing of the students' minds by preparatory courses inimical to scientific interest.

Scientific courses have not become popular as the old requirements in the languages have been decreased. It is rather the other courses such as the Ph.D. that have profited by the greater freedom of election. With considerable freedom of election in the preparatory schools, the scientific courses are not sought out there by the children at a period when the concrete subject-matter of science properly presented should be immensely more attractive than the languages and many more abstract objects of study. The science courses in the high school are not at the present time popular, nor is the money spent upon them, either in equipment or in teaching force, comparable with their educational importance.

The result of this is that the majority of our students leave our colleges and universities, without being able to grasp the most important achievements in modern thought, without being able to take the point of view of those thinkers who are reconstructing our views of the physical universe and its constituent parts, and without being able to interpret what they see and hear and feel by means of the profoundest and most magnificent generalizations which the world has ever known.

I wish to present two reasons for this condition which seem to me more fundamental than those usually presented, and to discuss in connection with them the possibility of removing them or at least to invite discussion on the subject.

It is natural to compare the sciences so-called with the humanities. And yet in one respect the distinction between them has much decreased of late years and promises to continue to decrease. The method of study of the languages, history, literature and the so-called social sciences has become to a large degree that of the natural sciences. There is certainly no fundamental distinction between the researches of the historian, the philologist, the social statistician and those of the biologist, the geologist or even the physicist and chemist, in point of method. Each is approaching problems which must be solved, and to be solved must be presented in the form of carefully gathered data. For their solution hypotheses must be constructed and tested by means of experiment or observation. With the complexity of the phenomena, of course, the application of the scientific methods will vary. The processes of observation, for example, will vary enormously in the study of a historical problem in the ancient world, and in the study of the problem of variation where the material is immediately at hand. The methods of historical criticism—lower and higher—are nothing but methods of observations under conditions which are peculiarly difficult of access.

While it is true that in literature and other arts we do not go back of the aesthetic reaction in the judgment of beauty, or the study of this reaction in others as presented in literary criticism; outside this field of appreciation and criticism, the methods of study in the field of the humanities is just as scientific as the subject matter with which it deals.

This means for one thing that we no longer regard the acquirement of information as the legitimate object or method of education. The ideal of modern education is the solution of problems, the research method. And this research method is no less dominant in the humanities than it is in the natural sciences, so far as the subject matter permits.

The ground for the difference in attractive power of the natural sciences and the humanities can not be laid up, therefore, to a difference in method. And if it could the prospect would be discouraging indeed and the judgment upon the students most unflattering, for the research method is, after all, nothing but the elaboration of the simple processes of perceiving and conceiving the world, elaborated in such a way that it can be applied to the complex and subtle problems of the physicist, the geologist, the biologist, *etc.* If the scientific method were the cause of unpopularity we should have to assume that the process of knowledge itself, the very function of cognition, was disagreeable to the average student.

If, however, we examine these two types of studies, we do meet a distinction which holds for many if not for all. In the physical sciences the process of investigation involves the analysis of the objects, which are studied, into elements which are not present to immediate experience and which are with difficulty conceived and presented to the mind. The resolution of nature into atoms and molecules or corpuscles is an undertaking presenting itself at the beginning of scientific investigation, that is not forced upon the social sciences. Here the elements into which analysis reduces its objects are at bottom, but more or less reproducible states of our own consciousness, or still more direct objects of possible sense-perception. This was a difficulty that did not inhere in the old-time natural history. There the problem that aroused investigation was stated in terms of everyday experience, and for this very reason natural history was a more successful subject in the curriculum than our physics and chemistry. Its problems were real problems in the minds of the students. They were not located in a field as yet foreign to their acquaintance and, therefore, artificial and unmeaning.

The problems of biology and geology do not suffer as much from this remoteness, for to a large degree they can be stated in terms of a possible immediate experience of the student, and it is true that they make a more immediate appeal to the student than do the physical sciences. But it must not be forgotten that these biological and geological sciences are to no small degree applied physics and chemistry, and that this tendency is steadily increasing. That is, it is increasingly difficult to state the problems of these sciences in terms of immediate experience; their problems do not arise of themselves in the consciousness of the student; in other words, he is not immediately interested in the study.

We can generalize this in the following form: the result of the development of our sciences has been that their problems are no longer within the immediate experience of the student, nor are they always statable in terms of that experience. He has to be introduced to the science before he can reach the source of interest, i.e., problems which are his own and which he wants to solve by the process of his own thinking.

On the whole, the problems of the social sciences have a meaning to the student when lie meets them, i.e., they can be his own problems from the start, and they do not have to be translated into terms which must be somewhat painfully acquired before they can be used.

In a certain sense mathematics has become the language of the physical sciences, and the student must have a command of this vernacular before he can read with interest that which is writ in the sciences, before he can attack their problems. But even where the vernacular of the science is not that of mathematics, it is still true, to a large extent, that the field of the real problems in the science lies outside of the direct experience of the student.

It hangs together with this, in the second place, that the natural sciences are not interconnected in the minds of the students, that they exist in water-tight compartments. There is no common field out of which they all spring. It seems to me that in this lies the great advantage which the humanities so-called have over the natural sciences in the curriculum. They all of them belong to one piece of human experience, and it remains true *nil humanum nihi alienum est* [nothing human is foreign to me], not simply because of the immediate human sympathy which unites men and women who are distant not only in space, but also in time, not only in speech, but also in state of civilization; there is a still more important hold which the social sciences and humanities have upon the interest of the student. It is that human history, human development, human institutions, its arts, its literature, its achievements, are so bound up together with each other, with the languages in which thought has been expressed, with the literature in which achievements have been recorded, with the movements of trade, commerce, colonization and discovery which have motiv[at]ed historic changes, that wherever one begins, problems of all sorts arise at once, interlacing with each other, so that the pursuit of one subject reinforces the interest in another, and *vice versa*. The whole group represents one social world which can not be picked up piecemeal nor divided up into separate compartments, but is bound to exist in the mind as a whole.

This is not simply an advantage of an external sort. The logician tells us that, if we would expand it, the subject of every judgment would be found to be the universe itself, individualized in some immediate experience, but implying the whole world in its implicit relations. If we express this somewhat more modestly it would run, in educational terms, that it is only the implicit relation to other things that makes any subject teachable or learnable, and that the more evident and more pregnant these relations are the more readily is it assimilated. In a certain sense the more complex a thing is the more readily it is acquired, while its simplicity leaves it bare, without lines of connection, without retaining points. Of course this would not be the case if education were merely a process of storing away, a process of piling learning into the mind. But as the theory of science instruction, as well as scientific advance, is that of research, it is evident that the richer an object is in relation to other things the more suggestive it will be of solutions for problems, the more fertile it will be in arousing associations of kindred data. To bring out a problem, then, in a field which is already rich in interest is to insure not only its immediate attractiveness, but to provide the ideas and connections through which the problem may be studied and a solution reached.

It is this wealth of associations, this complex interrelation with a mass of other things, which the student fails to secure when he is introduced to modern science, through one door at a time, and that door leading into a specialized subject-matter whose relations with immediate experience are of the slightest character. A new subject should not be presented by itself, but in its relation to other things. It must grow in some fashion out of the student's present world.

The problem of college science is, therefore, very intimately connected with science in the secondary school. If the child were introduced to it in the proper way there the situation, which has just been described, would not exist in the college. He would come up into the college with the world of science already in existence, and that world as a field of his own experience. He would find problems arising there for whose solution he must look to the more specialized sciences. But the opposite of this is the case. Science in the high school, at the present time, is in a more parlous condition than it is in the college, because the child is farther away from the field of exact science than in the later college years. He finds fewer points of connection. His sciences remain for him located between impassable barriers. The college, therefore, at least until a reform can be wrought in the secondary school, is forced to face the problem within its own walls.

Its solution calls for introductory courses which will lead the student into the field of science, which will show the problems of his own experience in terms of this new field, and show them there capable of solution. There are two points of view from which such courses could be naturally presented; that of history, and that of a survey of the world analogous to what is given in introductory courses in sociology or social institutions.

The peculiar appropriateness of a course in the history of science for the junior college students, lies in the fact that the special character of modern science would grow out of the conditions that made it natural and necessary. There would be in it the inspiration of the personalities of the great scientific men, and the romance of their struggle with difficulties which beset their sciences from within and without. The conceptions of to-day would be found motived in the struggles of yesterday. But still more important[,] the relations which have subsisted between scientific investigation and the whole field of human endeavor would appear—its relation to commerce, industry, the geographical distribution of men, their interconnection with each other, and the other sides of their intellectual life. Science would be interwoven with the whole human world of which it is actually a part. It is true that something of this is found in general history. It is there, however, presented not to lead up to further study of science, but to merely fill out the entire picture—a picture which is so crowded that many features are bound to be slighted, and among those which are slighted, science, just because it is a subject somewhat apart, is sure to be found.

We have, of course, the evidence of the import which such a course would have in the biographies of our scientific men—such as [Charles] Darwin [e.g., 1872], [Thomas Henry] Huxley [1894], [Louis] Pasteur, and [Hermann] von Helmholtz [e.g., 1895, 1896]. But few of our students in that period read them, and taken by themselves they do not have the educative power which the story of their efforts would have when presented in a course on the history of science. It is not, however, principally the personal note, which comes from the account of the men who have been the heroes of science, that would be found in such study. It is rather the form in which the scientific problem arose and the methods used for its solution which will carry the most valuable instruction. One scientific theory swallows up into itself what has preceded it, and the traces of the situation out of which the later doctrine arose are washed away. While our historical atlases present us in flaring colors the political situations out of which sprang present political conformations, the younger student of science must pick up, as best he may, without assistance or interpretation, the explanation and historical interpretation of the conceptions he is forced to use. If an adequate comprehension of the powers of the American executive can not be gained without a knowledge of the situation which preceded the formation of the constitution, no more can the uninstructed student comprehend the value of such terms as forces, energies, variations, atoms, or molecules without understanding what the problems were which brought forth these hypotheses and scientific conceptions.

And there is no study like that of history to bring out the solidarity of human thought. The interdependence of scientific effort and achievement, and the interrelationship which exists between all science in presenting its world as a whole, can be brought out vividly only when its history is being presented, while in the midst of the arduous struggle with a single science these profound connections are quite overlooked. It is a fact that science is, from an important point of view, a single body of knowledge, whose different parts determine each other mutually, though this mutual influence is often overlooked. When the historian comes forward with the picture of a past age, such as [Theodor] Gomperz has given us in his *Grieschische Denker* [1903-1909], we recognize these interconnections and see that what has been done in one line has been now advanced because of the achievement of another, and now has been thwarted by the backwardness in still another. The *Weltanschauung* of any age is at once the result of all its scientific achievements and a cause of each, by itself. We can not finally understand any one without the comprehension of the whole, and it is the whole which is more comprehensible than any single science. It is a great deal easier to present the problem of evolution in the world as a whole than it is in the specific instance. It is easier to recognize the problem of matter, as it is presented in the book entitled *The New Knowledge*[2] than it is to present the specific problem with which the physicist or chemist must wrestle. It may be a Hegelism, but it is good educational doctrine that the whole is more concrete than the part. A student who has first followed out the results of scientific evolution through the preceding centuries, in their interconnection with each other, and meets then the problems of modern science as the growing points of the past, who understands somewhat what the controlling meanings are behind scientific concepts and terminology, who feels that he is entering into a battle that is going on, whose field he has surveyed before he has lost himself in the particular brigade, such a student is bound to enter into his study with both a comprehension and an interest which his brother will lack—his brother who must get the parts before he can have an inkling of the whole.

I am aware that, in the minds of a great many of you, there has arisen a spirit of contradiction to what has been presented, a spirit of contradiction which arises out of the very competency and exactness of the scientist. Such a type of instruction as that suggested above is felt to be superficial, inexact, and bound to be misleading to the person who is not scientifically trained. It would be information in a word, and the scientist does not hold it to be his position to impart information, nor can he promise any valuable educational result from a course whose content is one of information.

I wish to bring out the point because it seems to me fundamental to the question which has been broached. We need, in the first place, a definition of what information is and what knowledge is, as distinguished from it. I would suggest toward such a definition that nothing is information which helps any one to understand better a question he is trying to answer, a problem he is trying to solve. Whatever bridges over a gap in a student's mind, enabling him to present concretely what otherwise would have been an abstract symbol, is knowledge and not mere information. Whatever is stored up, without immediate need, for some later occasion, for display or to pass examinations is mere information, and has no enduring place in the mind. From this standpoint nothing is superficial or inexact which gives concreteness and meaning to the problem before the student. Truth is a relative thing. We none of us have exact knowledge in the sense that our knowledge is exhaustive, and we none of us know the full import of what we do grasp. There can be no objection to the young student having a broad if seemingly superficial view of the scientific world, if it helps him to approach with more understanding the particular science he has before him. It is also certainly the pedagogic duty of the instructor in science to get far enough into the consciousness of the student to present the part to him by means of the whole.

The second point of view suggested for approach to the specialized study of science was that of the survey of the present field. If we can find the counterparts of the historical course in the biographies of great scientists, we can find that of the survey course in such treatises as the popular lectures of eminent scientists, such as those of [John] Tyndall on *Sound* [1877], or many of the popular lectures of men like [Hermann] von Helmholtz [1895], [Emil] du Bois-Reymond [1843-1894] and a score of others. We highly approve of such lectures when they appear on the lyceum or the university extension platform. We encourage the reading of such books, considering them distinctly educative, but we deny that they have a place in the university curriculum. The prevailing assumption is that when one can not follow out the scientific process by which the results are reached, it is indeed better that he should have the result presented in a form which he can understand than not to have them at all, though it is not the place of the university to perform this function, except through its extension department. This statement, however, overlooks the fact that such acquaintance with the results of scientific research is also the source of interest in the research itself. What is merely keeping up with the progress of the world on the part of the business man is preparation for the student who has to approach a new field. I presume that no one would question that those who had listened with intense interest and enthusiasm to an extension lecture upon the solar system would be better prepared for the study of astronomy. Indeed, we assume that university extension will serve in this fashion as a feeder of the university, but for some reason we feel that this same sort of preparatory work has no place inside of the university itself. From the point of view of education we are mistaken, for nothing is out of place which makes the approach of the students to the subject-matter a normal one. And until the student feels the problem of the science he undertakes to be a problem of his own, springing out of his own thought and experience, his approach is not a normal one.

One or two courses, then, from the standpoint of the history of science, and from that of the survey of the scientific field of to-day in the junior college, would organize the vague information of the student, would correlate it with the political and literary history with which he is familiar, would give him the sense of growth and vitality, would state the problems of science in his own terms, and awaken in him the passion to carry on the investigation himself which might otherwise remain dormant. They would be feeders to the specialized scientific courses that follow. They would break down the prejudice which most students bring against science from the high school. But not least, they would be as educative as any course in history could possibly be. They would serve as valuable a function as those courses which aim to acquaint the student with the social and political forces which dominate the world into which he is to enter.

What has been said so far has borne directly upon introductory courses in the junior college. It is only in the last remark that I have touched upon the demands which the university may make upon its scientists for the interpretation of the world for those who do not follow its special courses. If in the present day, under the sign of science in nature and society, any one leaves an institution of higher learning without a comprehension of the results of science, which he can grasp in their relationship to the rest of human history and endeavor, he is certainly cheated out of one of the most valuable of the endowments which he has a right to demand from that institution. As I have already indicated, scientific method is dominant not only in the study of nature, but in the study of all the social subject matters, in religion, politics, [and] all social institutions. Scientific discoveries have made over the answer even to the fundamental question of who is my neighbor. Science is responsible for the view of the universe as a whole which must be the background of our theology as well as our philosophy and much that is finest in our literature. Science has changed sentiment to intelligence in divine charity, and has substituted the virtue of reformation of evil for that of resignation thereto in religion. And yet a large percentage of our students leave the university without having any better opportunity of coming to close quarters with this science than those who are outside the university. They are compelled to get their science from the extension platform, or from the popular magazine. There should be unspecialized science for those who do not specialize in science, because they have the right to demand it of an educational institution.

There is still another demand that should be made upon the science faculties of the university, and that is that they should so organize the courses which their students take, that they will get the unity which every college course ought to give.

That unity of the social sciences which is given in subject-matter and human nature itself is, as has been pointed out, absent from modern sciences which have become largely what Professor [Wilhelm] Wundt calls conceptual sciences. The interconnections are not apparent to the students who are in the special groups. Their attention is fixed within too narrow boundaries, the demands of their own subject is so great that they have no time to go beyond. They have a wealth which they can not realize because they can not put it into circulation.

Through the history of science, especially of the other sciences which they do not specialize in, through lecture courses which give them the results of these other sciences, they should be able to get the unity of *Weltanschauung*, which is requisite for any college course.

It is requisite at the end as at the beginning that the student should see his world as a whole, should take up into it what he has acquired, and should get the mutual interpretation which the relation of his subject-matter has to what lies beyond it.

There is certainly no agent that can carry more profound culture than the sciences, but our science curriculum is poor in what may be called culture courses in the sciences, and the import of science for culture has been but slightly recognized and but parsimoniously fostered.

18

Industrial Education, the Working-Man and the School[1]

The education of a workman has always been very close to his trade. The dependence of his training upon his trade is expressed in the word apprenticeship. The apprentice has been trained by helping under the direction of a master in the trade. If we go back far enough we find apprenticeship as a necessary introduction to every trade, and indeed the only introduction. The elementary school appeared in the first place to train the clerk and accountant. It was part of the apprenticeship of the commercial trades. In the seventeenth and eighteenth centuries the artisans and laborers were not taught to read, write, and figure. The extensive commercial activity, the constantly increasing use of money, and the growing importance of reading for political and social life, gradually carried the demand for control over the three R's throughout the whole laboring class; though it remained for America in the early decades of our republic to inaugurate the common school with universal education. Under these conditions, the master artisan was expected to allow his apprentices to attend the common schools, but there was little or no connection between the schooling and training in the trade.

The school taught the use of language and number. Apprenticeship taught the vocation. It was true that the exercise of the trade demanded reading, writing, and figuring, but the apprenticeship system simply left training in these to the school. The two vehicles of education remained separate and influenced each other either indirectly or not at all.

This was partly due to the function of the common school in America. It opened the door to all avenues. Our democracy elected men to office who had no more than a common school education. It is not very long ago that boys left the common school to read law and medicine. In a country in which everything was open to everyone, and the common school was the door to all opportunities, the relation of schooling to the work of the apprentice was lost in its relation to more ambitious callings. The common school has retained its stamp of the first step toward the learned professions and political preferment.

Thus the education of the workman has been and has remained divided into two parts, the formal training in the three R's and the apprenticeship to a trade. These two parts have not been parts of a whole. The schooling has remained formal, bookish, and literary in its interest. The apprenticeship has suffered severely in the change of modern industry, but even in its better days, it did not awaken any interest in its own history, nor in its social conditions, nor in the technique of better methods. The schooling taken by itself was narrow and unpractical, the apprenticeship had no outlook and wakened no interest, outside itself. The two did not reinforce and interpret each other. In a certain sense they ought to have been in the relation of theory and practice. The apprenticeship should have presented the problems which the school solved, and the interest in the solution of these problems should have made the work of school vivid and educative. But while it is easy to pick flaws in this training, its results were admirable, especially in comparison with the training which children of today get who work with their hands.

Apprenticeship remains in many trades, especially in those under the control of organized labor. The interest of organized labor has been, however, very largely that of keeping down the number of skilled artisans to that which the trade can profitably absorb. Organized labor has not accepted the control over apprenticeship to make out of it a better education. Nor is there uniformity in the trades. In many the apprenticeship system has quite gone by the boards, in others it is not at all adequate. As a system of training skilled laborers the old system of apprenticeship has disappeared and no consistent new system has arisen to take its place. The cause of the changes is evident enough. It is the machine that has taken possession of the trades, has displaced the artisan, and has substituted for the artisan, who makes an entire article, a group of laborers who tend the machines.[2]

The effect of this upon the training of the laborer has been most deplorable. The more the machine accomplishes the less the workman is called upon to use his brain, the less skill he is called upon to acquire. The economics of the factory, therefore, calls for a continual search for cheaper and therefore less skilled labor. The success of the modern type of wholesale manufacture of inexpensive goods has depended upon the vast numbers of unskilled laborers. Women and children have been swept into the factories to displace the more expensive labor of men. We are accustomed to recognize that the sudden use of this type of factory production was made economically possible by the huge markets which steam transportation brought to the doors of the factory. The other determining factor, the surplus of unskilled labor that could be absorbed by the factory and the mine, we are not so conscious of. We are also very well aware of the nicety with which the inventor can adjust the machine to a product which the market demands. We are not so aware of the equal nicety with which the inventor adjusts his machine to the cheapness of labor. The most serious handicap under which labor suffered with the opening of the modern period of factory industry was the lack of any connection between the training of its apprentices and the technique of the machine. The intelligence of the artisan who made the whole article made of him an admirable citizen of the older community. It was this intelligence very largely which made the success of our early democratic institutions. The apprenticeship system made practical, intelligent, self-reliant men, as well as good workmen, who did not have to blush for the work of their hands. The training was not, however, adaptable. The very skill of the artisan stood in the way of his adapting himself to the new regime. The skilled artisan was no more but rather less valuable than the untrained man. And machines invented to exploit unskilled and unintelligent labor in so far fixed the condition of the workman that were thereafter to tend these machines.

It is perhaps idle to speculate as to what the form of the machine, and the method of industry would have been if the laborer had had the training, the science, and the sort of skill which enabled the merchant, the manufacturer, and the engineer to make use of the advent of steam in manufacture and transportation; but we can recognize that invention has shown a suppleness in adapting itself to any kind of product or market, in using every sort of science and technique, and that there is every reason to believe that adaptable intelligence, skill that could be generalized and applied in various ways, if found at that period in the artisans would have been a more profitable field for invention than the lack of intelligence and adaptability which our present machines are built to use and exploit.

A skill that can be adapted must be based upon some theory. The shop must be reinforced by the school. Such skill can turn from one form of manufacture to another, as the manufacturer himself can turn from sewing machines or steam locomotives to automobiles. Such dependence of the shop upon the school, of practice upon theory, we find in our most up-to-date apprenticeship schools. In those of the General Electric Company, of the New York Central Company, of the Houston, Stamwood, and Gamble Company at Cincinnati, the schooling represents by and large a half of the preparation. The apprentice must understand the technique that he acquires so that he can apply it with intelligence, and this means power to do many things, not one thing alone. It means the creation of intelligence rather than speed in the apprentice. These apprenticeship schools will not allow the foreman to hold the apprentice to a machine because he operates it with greater speed, i.e.: these schools recognize that the man must not be subordinated to the machine if he is to acquire the sort of skill they wish in these upper-class workmen. The school and the shop must go hand in hand in modern artisanship. Their lack of connection in the old system spells the disappearance of the old-time system as the old-time artisan has disappeared. There can be no question that the modern artisan demands schooling if he is not to be a mere creature of the machine. He needs the mathematics and drawing out of which the machine has arisen. He must know the formulas which are expressed in the tools that they may be his tools and adapt them to his uses. He must be able to read the blue-prints that are the language into which the engineer translates the formula to carry it over into bodily form. This sort of training is the only kind that will free the artisan. It is not until he can comprehend the machine as a tool that he will not be a part of it. Not that the employer desires in his high laborers ignorance. He is building up expensive schools because skill here is money in his pocket. The history of the technical schools at Fall River, Massachusetts, demonstrates that the employee, the employer, and the community all recognized the need of this training in the artisans who were to employ the high grade machines.

It is in the economic struggle that organized labor fears the apprenticeship school. It has fought to keep down the number of apprentices in order that their wages might be kept up, and their working hours more occupied. Industry being organized on the basis of surplus labor supply, it is natural that labor should suspect the employer of aiming to bring about a surplus of skilled labor not only to make sudden increase in production possible, but to enable the employer to fight the labor union. That many employers have this in view is, of course true.

However, as long as advance in wages means skill[,] there will be an inevitable demand among laborers for industrial training. Correspondence schools are profiting by this demand at present, at the expense of the laborer. In the end it would be hopeless for labor to maintain its economic position by entrenching itself behind lack of skill. If the apprenticeship school is the best method of learning the trade, it will be adopted. The restriction of the number of apprentices must arise in some other fashion, for with these schools, whether in the hands of employers or in our public school systems, the numbers cannot be fixed by the labor unions, and skilled labor outside the union will be more dangerous than inside the organization.

Inevitably, the manner in which the commodity of skilled labor is to be controlled will be changed. It will be controlled because it is an economic waste to the country to have a surplus of labor. Our present industries adapt themselves to this surplus and, of course, exploit it, but this does not in any sense justify it nor make it permanent. Industry has adjusted itself to and exploited child labor.[3] The remedy for this exploitation is not to be found in reducing the birth rate, and thus the number of children. The community itself, becoming intelligent, refuses to permit such economic and human waste as that involved in child labor. It must reject as decisively a system by which industry drops its adult labor into misery when for the time being it is not needed, to pick it up again at a reduced rate when there is a demand for increased production. The social control we demand will come through increase in intelligence, and the laboring class is the last class that can afford to restrict its own intelligence. In our present industrial evolution the race is to the technically equipped or to those who can command such equipment, and in a competitive society those who lack such equipment must be subject to exploitation. The tremendous revolution brought about by the factory system, the machine, has found every group in society equipped with sufficient free intelligence to enable them to adapt themselves to the changes incident to the revolution. The investor, the producer, the middle man, the technical expert, the engineer, the banker fitted in with no friction with the new order and have profited financially. The capital of the artisan alone has been lost. His capital is his acquired skill. If this is simply in the form of a fixed group of habits, every change in the method of manufacturing will consign workmen to the human scrap-heap.

The financial disability of the laborer is that which is generally contrasted with the greater freedom of the capitalist or those who can accumulate a financial reserve. A revolution in industrial methods may annihilate the investment of the capitalist, and even wipe out of existence the occupations of officers and employees. Still those whose incomes have permitted the accumulation of a reserve, have an indefinitely better chance of getting upon their feet again. There is room for them in which to move. They can seek opportunity at a distance. They can wait for it. They can prepare themselves for new and unaccustomed occupations. While the laborer whose income is swallowed up day by day in the necessary outgoes for his and his family's daily bread must do anything or nothing as, it presents itself, at the moment, at his own door. There is no reason to depreciate this disability of the day laborer. It only emphasizes the other disability which has been above presented; the disability of skill without adaptive intelligence. The man who knows why he does what he does, is better able to do something else. Intelligence, the ability to see the relation of means and end in conduct, is the fundamental form of freedom—"and the truth shall make you free." A laborer with acquired skill for which he has no theory approaches the condition of the purely instinctive animal. He becomes helpless the moment he is out of the environment to which his habits are adapted.

To these general propositions, which may be summed up in the old adage that knowledge is power, the reply comes in the form of our technical schools and our universities. Only a select few can afford to know. Our life has become so complicated that it must be governed by the highly trained expert. It is the age of the expert, who dominates our industry as really as he does our medical practice. And there are social philosophers willing to accept this judgment and build their conceptions of the future of society upon it.

We are, according to them, to pass from the control of the political and financial aristocracy to that of the technical expert. Only they will be able really to understand why anything is done in the growing complexities of our society, and they will rule. And the answer to this philosophy is that the expert does not[,] and in human history has not[,] ruled. He has served. His greatest effectiveness is found among those who are intelligent. The expert even in industry demands not blind obedience but intelligent cooperation, and the more intelligent the cooperation can be the higher the efficiency of the expert. What is wanted in an ideal machine shop, where the tools are made to do certain work, is that the man who uses the tools should be able to criticize the tools. He should be able to go to the man who planned and made them and tell him how they work, and where the test of use shows that they fail and need to be improved. If human intelligence consisted in the knowledge of fixed laws and methods[,] the man who knew them would be king. It consists in the constant interaction of theory and practice. Theory is called in to tell us how to act, and what we do shows us where the theory was defective. As long as we have got to check up and reconstruct our theories, our plans, our models by their working, there is going to be as great [a] need of intelligence in those who use the tools, who install the machinery and fit the pipes, as in those who think them out and make the blue-prints.

No one can estimate the loss which our industry suffers from the lack of trained intelligence among the workmen. The loss arising not simply from injuries and wear and tear due to ignorance, but from the suggestions of inventions that have not been made, from the opportunities for saving, and for increased efficiency of equipment that have not been used, can never be estimated. The exploitation of ignorance and misery which is involved in machines tended by the unintelligent, the children, the physically and mentally unfit represents losses none the less real because they are not recognized. Any process that adjusts itself to the lack of intelligence is in just so far wasteful—if it might be served by intelligence. If human invention has been able to make use of the ignorant and stupid, it certainly could have adjusted itself the more to those who were informed and skilful.

There is nothing more democratic than intelligence, because the higher the intelligence the more it demands of others for its best exercise. It is true that intelligence may be used to manipulate brute matter, and brutalize men, and it may so adjust itself to this task that it conceives its function is to use the unintelligent. Those who possess it may conceive themselves an aristocratic class apart, but this only indicates their false and inadequate conceptions. When intelligence goes into action of any sort it demands all the intelligence it can find. It seeks comprehension in its agents; because it never can keep tab upon itself, it can never adjust itself and its constructions to their purposes without working with people who are in so far on a par with itself that they can judge the workings of the machinery and the execution of its plans.

This needs to be emphasized not only to make evident the importance to society of the widest possible spread of intelligence and the fact that industry can afford to pay for it, but especially to indicate the nature of the intelligence and the manner in which it should be acquired. It is the sort of intelligence that is close to its application. Its results are the criticism of methods and means as well as their use, and the suggestions of improvements and economics. This calls for an interest in theory just as far as that is involved in understanding what is being done. Many of our best mechanics get it without going to a technological school. They find out what they need to know and get the textbooks, the formulas, the tables that are necessary for this purpose. It is a result to which many a more ambitious education reduces itself in practice.

It is just the type of education which higher apprentice schools in this country and in Europe give to those whom they expect to be the *élite* of their workmen. It involves a knowledge of a whole process, if one is to comprehend any part of it. Thus, in the approved apprentice school a boy may not be held to a single machine because he shows speed in running it. He must be familiar with all the machines. Mathematics and drawings are necessary for such a training, at least so far as the control over them helps on [sic] with his task. A large part of mathematics is a language in which one can best state his problem. If his work brings problems with it, the workman must have the appropriate language in which to state them. It is also a language in which the results of the work of others can be conveyed in the form in which they will help toward the solution of the problems. The same thing can be said of the blue-print. The competent workman must be able to read his tables, his formulas, his blue-prints. It is fair to assume that any workman who has had the right training can reach this goal. It is important to notice that so much theory as this does more than make an expert workman in a definite calling. It also gives the skill he possesses adaptability and pliability. When he has met problems and has solved them in his own occupation he gains a confidence in his ability to solve the problem brought by a change of occupation. Theory, after all is, nothing but the consciousness of the way in which one adjusts his habits of working to meet new situations. The man who has never made such readjustments is discouraged at the mere presence of the new situation. The man who has done it, who has some acquaintance with the processes and technical expressions by which it is accomplished has his interest aroused by the new situation. The acquaintance with, and use of, so much of the theory of an occupation as the exercise of the man's own function in it calls for, means that his habits are not fixed, that the man has an adjustable nature. His chances of fitting into a new economic situation are a hundred times better than those of the man who has simply the facility of a single process. In the exigencies of the shop such a man can pass from one machine to another. His speed is not at first what it will be when his reactions become almost automatic, but the knowledge which he has of the whole process and the ability he has of stating the new and the old jobs in the same terms render him a vastly more valuable man than the workman who is nothing but a part of a single machine. The amount of training which an operative, a workman in any trade, should have, is that which will acquaint him with all the processes of his trade, and so much theory of his trade which will enable him to understand the tools he uses and the manner in which they operate, that he may both use the tool to the best advantage and be able to check up its efficiency and suggest the sort of changes and improvement that should in his judgment be made.

So much training a mechanic, a farmer, a mill operative, a plumber, every artisan should have. In the bill of rights which a modern man may draw up and present to the society which has produced and controls him, should appear the right to work both with intelligent comprehension of what he does, and with interest. For the latter one must see his product as a whole, he must know something of the relation of the different parts to the whole, and he must know enough of the language in which the problems of his trade are stated and solved to be able himself to criticize his own work and his own tools. This indicates also the manner in which this training should be acquired. The apprenticeship school in which school work and shop work balance each other, in which the school provides the method of stating and meeting the problems which arise in the shop, has become the modern system of apprenticeship. As we have seen, it is distinguished from the older apprenticeship system by its school, and from the later system by the organic relation between the school and the shop. The school work demands attention because shop problems appear there. And the shop becomes educative because its processes are comprehended and thought out. This educational method is ideal from the psychological point of view, for the acquirements of the school are demanded by the practical activities of the boy. This result has never been attained in other public or private schools. The training in the latter schools has been planned largely with reference to occupations which are not to be undertaken until the pupil has left school. Hence, language and number have been dry, formal studies, meaning little or nothing to the child.

Some schools have attempted to meet this difficulty by introducing what have been called constructive activities in the school, so that the problems of the children might be real problems. The measurements of the box they were making should give them their arithmetical problems. In solving the problem they would also be learning what amount of lumber they would need and what lengths they would have to cut off, etc.

With this in view, very varied activities have been introduced in certain private schools. The results have not been what was anticipated. The children's work has not the compulsion which the apprenticeship offers. The actual products of the factory set not only problems, but they carry with them a discipline that the apprentice accepts. They set the standard which becomes the boy's standard because he wishes to succeed in his calling. No task which the child sets to himself, and no task which the school sets as a school, has this meaning to the child. His own task makes no demand upon him that is bigger than himself, and sets no standard that comes upon him with compelling power from the great world of which he wishes to be a part. No tasks of a school can be made [to] take hold upon the child as the training does [,] which is to admit him to the rank of men. Even in the college the students will not work as they will in the law and medical schools where they get their professional training.

In an industrial democracy the citizen must sufficiently understand the tools and the processes to comprehend and criticize the tool and its use. This is not only necessary for the technical efficiency of the industry. It is equally essential for the social control of the conditions of labor. At present the workmen undertake this by controlling labor as a commodity in the market. The artisan has lost the vantage-point of the medieval guild. Their control was over the product and the process. It is neither possible nor desirable to reproduce the medieval guild. It *is* possible and logical to make the workman's skill the basis of his social position and financial competence. Where labor appears only as a commodity, the unit being any man, the group of laborers can protect their wage only by protecting the weakest man. His wage must be theirs, and it follows that their individual outputs must be his. On the other hand, the more highly skilled workmen tend to get out of the unions, because on the one hand they do not need its protection and on the other their own earning power is restricted. Or the unions of the more highly skilled trades are able to pursue so different a policy in protecting their wage and hours of labor that they lose touch with the unions of less skilled labor. This break emphasizes the attitude of the unions of the relatively unskilled trades. It is of the first importance that the workingmen recognize that skill—developed intelligence—brings an entirely different factor into the economic situation, from that of the so-called supply and demand of a commodity. That other factor is described somewhat vaguely as the standard of life. It is recognized in the higher salaries of skilled employees—of professional men. When you demand skill you must make possible the conditions under which that skill can be obtained and exercised. Those conditions involve not simply technical training. Intelligence depends upon conditions of physical and social well-being. Every new demand for skill will inevitably carry with it the conditions under which that skill can be obtained. The manner in which a community responds to this obligation will be varied, and will appeal to many motives beside the economic interests.

There is no community in which a more conscious demand is being made for larger skill on the part of its workmen than Germany. There is no community in which society has faced more definitely the necessity of raising the standard of life of its working classes. State insurance seeks to meet the unavoidable accidents and disabilities. Supervision of hygienic conditions undertakes to eliminate the evils to which economic inferiority exposes great masses of men. Universities and schools of every character aim to put the intelligence of the laborer upon the higher level demanded by the self-conscious industry of Germany. And Germany has but begun to recognize the consequences which will follow with unavoidable logic upon her demand that her laborers be adequately instructed. Society cannot demand intelligent workmen without accepting the policy of rendering the acquirement of such intelligence socially possible. What the laboring classes have to fear, at least for the immediate future, is that the demand for skill will be too restricted; that our community will conceive that it can fulfil its industrial functions with an *élite* of trained workmen and a proletariat of the ignorant and unskilled. If organized labor can raise its eyes for the moment beyond its immediate quarrels with its employers, it will recognize that its most strenuous efforts must be directed toward the widest possible industrial education, and that this demand must be made on behalf of all labor.

There remains the school itself. The apprenticeship system, as it has been worked out by the General Electric Company,[4] is pedagogically and technically admirable. It is possible and probable that such schools will be multiplied among large concerns throughout the country. But even with such extension of the system, the demand for this apprenticeship will not and cannot be met. Every laborer who is going into mechanical industry or into allied trades should have this training. It will be a training, if we may judge from the experience already gathered, which will accomplish its task of instruction as the public schools have never been able to fulfil theirs, for it will, under proper conditions, draw upon the interest of all professional training, and it will always have the discipline which contact with the actual process and product brings with it.

Such training cannot be confined to those whom our great industrial companies educate for their shops and designing-rooms. It must be the demand of labor that this system of apprenticeship training be taken into the public schools. Manual training high schools[5] should become apprentice schools. But in this case, the curriculum should be one so far liberalized that the history and geography of the trades connect the apprentice's skill with the social and physical conditions out of which it has sprung, and in which it at present exists. The curriculum should also contain the study of the social community into which the graduated apprentice will go. He should comprehend the central and state government not only, but the legal and administrative features of the city within which he is to labor. He should understand the laws that protect him as well as those which threaten him with pains and penalties. He must know to what officials he can appeal, and he should have some comprehension of [the] operation of the courts and the city council. He should know something of the conditions which control wages, and their relation to the calling he expects to exercise. If his years and interests admit, such a course should be one in elementary sociology, such as are already to be found in French industrial secondary schools, in which the ideas of social obligations, the meaning of social standards, and the relations of man to the community can be discussed. What the child expects to do and what he expects to be provides adequate motive power for study and application. They provide also the natural center from which his relation to the past, in history, and to the present, in the study of society, can be brought within his field of interest and comprehension, and through which he can form those fundamental conceptions of social rights and obligations which constitute our morality.

There remains, however, the still more difficult question of the elementary schools, where at the present time the vast majority of Americans get all their formal education [Mead, Weidt, Broggan 1912].

As has been indicated earlier, the rest of the community have suffered because the curriculum of the elementary schools has been fashioned to meet the demands of a commercial class, and for those who expect to pursue literary and professional studies. The arithmetics do not present the type of problem that the average child meets when he leaves school. The history, instead of bearing on the occupation and phenomena with which the child is familiar, and toward which he is attracted, are hopelessly political. One would assume, from the study of our school histories, that politics is the only phase of human society that has a history. Geography is abstracted from the actual relation of industry and commerce, which would give it meaning to the child living in a world that is given over to the production of wealth.

How the elementary schools will finally adjust themselves to an education that faces toward the occupations which its pupils will enter remains to be seen. It is, however, beyond question that the training on the farm and in the shop, even of the child who is not yet old enough to enter upon definite apprenticeship, indicates the direction toward which educational theory and practice must turn.

Two great facts stand out. One is that we are forced to reconstruct our whole apprenticeship training, and that when this is satisfactorily accomplished it will carry with it not only satisfactory technical training, but a much broader and more liberal education than our schools at present can give to those who enter industrial occupations. The other is that apprenticeship provides an adequate, and indeed almost the only adequate method of instructing children. When we recognize that this instruction need not be narrow nor unenlightened, the objection to the application of the principle in our public schools finally disappears.

Notes

Notes to Introduction

1. The galleys are printed with either "2 November" or "5 November" at the top of each page. There is a stamp for November 1909 and another for November 1910 on the back of one set of galleys. This stamp is for the faculty exchange at the University of Chicago, the internal sign of a mailing received. See Mead Addenda, Series III box 1, folders 10, 12, and 14. Folders 9, 11, and 13 contain copies of the chapters, sometimes as reprints and sometimes as handwritten or typed originals.

2. I asked librarians at Love Library, the University of Nebraska-Lincoln and at Regenstein Library at the University of Chicago to check their references and resources for any indication that this book was published. I also visited the Library of Congress and asked their staff to search for any record of this book as published. Everyone concluded that there is no evidence of such a publication.

3. Postmodernists believe that any modern perspective that supports the Enlightenment's values, such as Mead's, is in error. I do not share the postmodernists' critique. Like Mead, I do not reject the assumption of human rationality, but I do argue that his examination of emotions and motivations in these chapters provides a needed balance to his overemphasis on rational behavior in the previously available literature.

4. I believe Wilhelm Dilthey, Mead's doctoral chair, and his analysis of psychology and experience is fundamental to Mead's essays and ideas in the 1890s and early twentieth century. Mead does not footnote these influences, however, while he does frequently mention Wundt and even more frequently discusses topics that are identifiably in Wundt's area of expertise, such as *rite de passage* and early, nonmodern social institutions. Establishing the Mead/Dilthey connection would bring in the "interpretive" tradition of Max Weber to Meadian scholarship, a task beyond the scope of this introduction.

5. There are other posthumous publications. David Miller's *Self, Language and the World* (Chicago: University of Chicago Press, 1982); and *The Individual and the Social Self* (Chicago: University of Chicago Press, 1982). Anthologies of Mead's work include collections introduced and edited by Andrew Reck (Mead 1964), John Petras (Mead 1968a), and myself (Mead 1999).

6. Mead's depression followed a "typical" pattern found in many of his later colleagues and friends who shared his questions about personal placement in a rapidly changing world. For example, his later friend, Jane Addams, and her friend, Charlotte Perkins Gilman, suffered deep depression in the 1880s as well. These depressions were gendered, however, and Mead's conflicts may have been more similar to those suffered by William James, the psychologist and pragmatist. On "typical" generational patterns, I draw on the insights of Alfred Schutz (e.g., 1967, 1971) and Erik Erikson (1958, 1969).

7.   Gary Cook (1993, 200 n. 35) documents a funny story of Mead trying to "harden" a brain through heat, but he inadvertently had a fire in his laboratory and lost a valuable microscope among other things.

8.   Helen paid a considerably higher price for her career interruption than George, for she never translated foreign books as she had intended while he became an eminent philosopher. Helen's intellectual influence on Mead has never been examined, and there is little evidence now for such an analysis. She did share his interests and training for years, nonetheless.

9.   This kindergarten and other related family efforts dramatically shaped early childhood education in Hawaii from the 1890s until the present (Castle 1992; Deegan 1999).

10.   Elizabeth Storrs lived here, with her daughter Alice and son-in-law, Albert Swing. She died in 1917 and was buried in Andover, Massachusetts (Benson 1971).

11.   Alice Chipman was a central figure at the Laboratory Schools and her role in progressive education is discussed in greater detail in Deegan (1999, lxvii-lxxiii).

12.   Most importantly for sociology, Albion Small was another student of Wundt and the first chair of sociology at the University of Chicago.

13.   I am not aware that Wundt argued for kindergartens in this way. Perhaps Mead first encountered kindergartens during his studies in Germany, but he clearly encountered kindergartens as a social movement in Chicago in the 1890s and this became a foundational element in the Laboratory schools at the University of Chicago (Deegan 1999).

14.   The pedagogist and later president of the University of Chicago, Charles Judd, also studied with Wundt.

15.   Mead had this division within his galleys but did not name them. I added the topic titles.

16.   [Hans Joas (1985, 64-89) argues this article is of fundamental importance in Mead's thought, but it has been systematically overlooked].

17.   I analyze a Meadian letter where he discusses his enjoyment of good food, and criticism of a poor cook, in Deegan (1999, xxv-xxxi).

18.   This argument complemented Mead's more general analysis in "Suggestions toward a Theory of the Philosophical Disciplines." *The Philosophical Review* 9 (January 1900): 1-17.

19.   British sociologists like Herbert Spencer, Patrick Geddes, and J. Arthur Thompson influenced Chicago sociologists during the 1890s and were concerned about the human/animal connection. W.I. Thomas, one of Mead's students and a later Chicago sociologist, was profoundly influenced by Geddes and Thompson in the early 1890s. See Deegan 1988, 202-205, for a fuller discussion.

20.   The Philosophy Department also published the *International Journal of Ethics* in which Mead was also engaged. Mead sometimes edited issues of *The Psychological Bulletin*, too [e.g., Mead was the editor for the *Psychological Bulletin* 8 (15 December 1912)].

21.   The members of the Parents' Association at the University of Chicago, with Mead as its first president (Mead 1904, 1999, 97-106) also wanted to know the relationship between the academy and the elementary schools. This academic versus pedagogist debate was waged at this School of Education for a century. The institution was internationally pre-eminent from the time of Mead's and Dewey's work in 1894 until the latter institution closed it in 1996, to the dismay of many people, including me.

22.   Many scholars from this era took up this cause of writing high school textbooks, but this literature is usually not critiqued in contemporary scholarship on intellectuals. See E.A. Ross' *Civic Sociology* (1935) for this type of textbook.

23. Peter Costello (1978) considers Jules Verne the inventor of science fiction in the former's review of his novels.
24. The history of the school is documented more fully in Deegan and Burger (1978, 363-65).

Chapter 1: The Social Character of Instinct

1. [Never published essay. Mead published an abstract of a different, now lost, paper on emotions in 1895.]
2. [I identify works that may be the ones that Mead was reading or that are similar to Mead's topics and era whenever possible. I bracket these references.]
3. [James Rowland Angell wrote a book on psychology in 1918, after Mead's essay was written.]
4. Lange and James (1967/c. 1922) published their work separately before 1922, but they were published together in the latter year.

Chapter 2: Social Psychology as Counterpart to Physiological Psychology

1. *The Psychological Bulletin*, 6 (15 December 1909a), 401-408.
2. Mead's review of E.A Ross' *Sin and Society* (1907) was published for the first time in 1998, *Sociological Origins* 1 (Summer), 22-26.
3. [Mead reviewed this book in the *Psychological Bulletin*, 6 (15 December 1908), where he makes many of the same points found in this chapter, but expands upon them. Thus the review is a helpful compliment to this chapter.]
4. [Apperception was used by Dewey to refer to an active mind that integrated the self in a dynamic process of interaction. Andrew Feffer (1993, 58-64) has an instructive analysis of the term. Mead used Dewey's meaning here.]
5. [Mead wrote a highly critical article of Cooley in 1930(a), showing his continuing dissatisfaction with Cooley's ideas after this chapter was written.]
6. [When I introduce a new paragraph into Mead's often lengthy paragraphs, I indicate this change with brackets.]
7. [Mead positively reviewed an English translation of this book in 1919.]

Chapter 3: What Social Objects Must Psychology Presuppose?

1. Read before the American Philosophical Association, Boston, 31 December, 1909. [Later published in *The Journal of Philosophy*, 7 (31 March 1910a), 174-180.]
2. "The Definition of the Psychical," *University of Chicago Decennial Volumes*. [see ftn. 16 above.].
3. [Wundt defines "apperception" as the relation of a perception to other, related perceptions arising from experience. Mead (1906) discusses Wundt's concept in "The Imagination in Wundt's Treatment of Myth and Religion."]
4. [See Mead's discussion of similar points in Chapter 2 above.]
5. [See Wundt (1973) for a compilation and translation of his different writings on the relation of language and gesture.]
6. [All these ideas on the phases of the act are developed further in Mead (1938)].
7. [See also Mead, "Image or Sensation." *Journal of Philosophy* 1 (1904), 604-7.]
8. [Mead later compared "The Philosophies of Royce, James, and Dewey in Their American Setting." *International Journal of Ethics* 40 (January 1930b): 211-31.]

9.   [Mead appended the following two paragraphs in his version of this paper published in 1910, the approximate date of his unpublished first book:
        If we may assume, then, that meaning is consciousness of attitude, I would challenge any one to show an adequate motive for directing attention toward one's attitudes, in a consciousness of things that were merely physical; neither control over sense-perception nor over response would be directly forwarded by attention directed toward a consciousness of readiness to act in a given situation. It is only in the social situation of converse that these gestures, and the attitudes they express could become the object of attention and interest.
        Whatever our theory may be as to the history of things, social consciousness must antedate physical consciousness. A more correct statement would be that experience in its original form became reflective in the recognition of selves, and only gradually was there differentiated a reflective experience of things which were purely physical.]

Chapter 4: Emotion and Instinct

1.   [Never published essay.]
2.   Spinoza (1632-1677) was a Portuguese Jewish philosopher who assumed humans were antisocial and social organization arose from the search for individual profit and prestige (Bogardus 1960, 200-201).

Chapter 5: A Psychological Study of the Use of Stimulants

1.   [Never published essay.]
2.   [Mead is probably referring here to the ancient Greek epic of the *Iliad*(e.g., 1886-1888) by Homer.]

Chapter 6: The Problem of Comparative Psychology

1.   [Never published essay.]
2.   "Suggestions toward a Theory of the Philosophical Disciplines." *The Philosophical Review* 9 (January 1900), pp. 1-17.
3.   [*Principles of Psychology*, 1890].
4.   *Mental Evolution in Man* [1884].
5.   *Introduction to Comparative Psychology*, [1894], p. 47.
6.   I have in this bare statement of the act omitted those processes in which the order seems to be reversed, in which we move and manipulate that we may see or hear or smell—the processes out of which aesthetic experiences, both appreciative and constructive, arise. These aesthetic experiences are most intricate and subtle. Their organic value to the system is very difficult to discover and define. We recognize in general that they are but functions of the distance senses, the eye or ear, for example; that the selective process, by which the eye and ear recognizes and in some sense constructs its object, is that which is developed more fully in artistic construction and appreciation; that the value the object of aesthetic appreciation has for us must come back to our possible movements with reference to it, our organic response to those movements, and the contact experiences it may give rise to. In a word, the distance value which the object of art has for us must be interpreted ultimately in terms of the act as we have defined it. Thus music has in it the sound values which give the spoken word its power of calling out action, together with the rhythms of that action. Listening to music is a further evolution of a capacity to recognize this

distant object and move toward it. And the value which the music has for us lies in responses, however they may be inhibited, which these sounds call out in the bodily system—responses which must follow the lines which the reactions to sounds have already drawn.

Finally, a word should be said with reference to social processes by which one form communicates with another, whether through sounds or gestures or movement. The value of these signs and signals is found in providing an object for a distance sense of the other form, but it has its value for the animal that makes it in term of possible movements toward and contacts with still more distant objects. In a word, the processes to which we have referred are but complications of the act as we have defined it, i.e., movement with reference to an object recognized by a distance sense, leading to contact experience. It is evident that a statement made as simple as this applies not only to our own experiences, but also to all animal life. There is no form which we may wish to bring into comparison with man to which such a definition of the act would not suffice. There would be more hesitation in applying it to human experience than to the life of the lower animals.

7. *Mental Evolution in Animals*, [1883], p. 48.
8. *Habit and Instinct*, [1894], p. 264.
9. I am for the present leaving out of account the abstractions of scientific thought which present relations and uniformities as objects, and am dealing with that more primitive analysis which gives what we term physical reality to what later may be presented as law. This Is allowable, as we are as yet discussing the most primitive stage of human intelligence, that we may bring it into connection with that of lower forms.

Chapter 7: Concerning Animal Perception

1. [*The Psychological Review* N.S. 14 (November 1907), pp. 383-390. A note follows this chapter: "The MS. of this article was received September 18, 1907."]
2. *Mind in Evolution*, p. 117. [The footnotes in this chapter are found in the published article but not in the galleys.]
3. *Manual of Psychology*, [London, W.B. Clive, 1899], pp. 84 ff.
4. "Animal Intelligence," *Psychological Review, Monthly Supplement, II.* No. 4, pp. 65:ff.
5. *Loc. cit.*
6. *Loc. cit.*, pp. 326 ff.
7. ["The Reflex Arc Concept in Psychology."] *Psychological Review*, 3, [July 1896], p. 359.
8. *Loc. cit.*

Chapter 8: On Perception and Imitation

1. [Never published essay.]
2. *Mind in Evolution*, [1901], p. 150.
3. *Ibid.*, p. 207.

Chapter 9: The Relation of the Embryological Development to Education

1. [Never published essay.]

Chapter 10: The Child and His Environment

1. [Published in *Transactions of the Illinois Society for Child Study* 3 (April 1898): 1-11.]
2. [See Mead, 1899.]

Chapter 11: The Kindergarten and Play

1. [Published for the first time in *Play, School, and Society*, by George Herbert Mead, introduced and edited by Mary Jo Deegan (New York: Peter Lang, 1999), pp. 23-32.]
2. [See discussion of Froebel, Mead, and the Laboratory Schools in Deegan (1999).]
3. [Mead assumes the female pronoun here.]
4. [Mead is probably referring to the work of Booker T. Washington and industrial education for African Americans at Tuskegee Institute. Washington did not capitalize the word "negro" but his opponent W.E.B. Du Bois (1899) did.]

Chapter 12: The Relation of Play to Education

1. [*The University Record* (Chicago) 1 (22 May 1896): 141-45. Address delivered at Chicao Commons at a conference co-sponsored with Hull-House on 1 May 1898.]
2. [By 1900 manual education in the U.S. had adopted a series of woodworking exercises called *Sloyd* that were developed in Sweden and were keyed to stages of neurological development in the child (Feffer 1993, 139).]

Chapter 13: On the Social Situation in School

1. [Never published essay.]
2. [Wilhelm Wundt was a leading folkpsychologist. Mead reviewed a translation of Wundt's *Folk-Psychology* in 1919, long after Mead wrote this essay. Mead found the book useful but it lacked a sound sociological perspective.]
3. [See a complimentary discussion in Mead, "The Imagination in Wundt's Treatment of Myth and Religion," (1906).
4. [Johann Friedrich Herbart (1776-1841) was a German philosopher and educator who influenced educational theories during the later nineteenth and early trentieth centures. Mead frequently drew on Herbart in the 1890s.]
5. [*Apperceptionsmasse* was a Herbartian term referring to the individual's mental predisposition which was created through human perception. Dewey transformed this concept so that it referred to an active mind that integrated the self in a dynamic process of interaction. See Andrew Feffer (1993, 58-64).]
6. [Ostwald was a Nobelist chemist who taught as the University of Leipzig. He believed in the unity of man and nature and their governance by common laws. He popularized these views in a number of writings. Wundt was a colleague of Ostwald and Mead probably learned of Ostwald through his studies at Leipzig (Whimster 1987, 274-75).]
7. [Mead is referring to some type of *rite de passage* in his contemporary society and to Wundt's interest in nonmodern rituals. Mead does not footnote Wundt's interests here, however.]
8. [This supports my analysis of contemporary rituals, see Deegan (1989, 1998).]

Chapter 14: The University and the School of Education

1. [Never published essay.]
2. Moore offered a course on general analysis at the University of Chicago, autumn, 1908, and typewritten notes on it remain at the Department of Special Collections, Regenstein Library, at that university. Mead probably knew Moore at this time.

Chapter 15: The University and the Elementary Schools

1. [Never published essay.]
2. [I have not located this concept of "the Renaissance of Childhood," but Hall is famous for his study of youth (see Hall 1904).
3. [There were two famous, American authors of arthimetic and algebraic textbooks named Colburn: Warren Colburn (1793-1833) and Dana Pond Colburn (1823-1859).]
4. [Sir Benjamin Thompson (1753-1814) was an English educator who wrote many important, early, scientific textbooks.]
5. [Joseph Ray (1807-1857) was an Ohio educator who wrote several textbooks in elementary school arithmetic.]
6. [William Holmes McGuffey (1800-1873) wrote many famous textbooks, and his reader spread throughout the United States school system.]
7. [Edward Austin Sheldon (1832-1897) was the founder of the Oswego movement in education based on Pestalozzian methods of education. It stressed nature study and introduced this subject to many public schools. Oswego Normal School, where Shelton was the first principal, trained and influenced many school teachers.]
8. Samuel Augustus Mitchell (1752-1868) was a geographer who wrote many classic textbooks including important maps and atlases.
9. [A discussion of Dewey, Parker, and Mead at the Laboratory School is found in Deegan (1999).]
10. [These are spices.]

Chapter 16: The University and the Elementary Schools

1. [*The School Review* Vol. 14, No. 4 (April 1906a), pp. 237-249. A lengthy section, "Discussion," pp. 249-253, followed the article and is not reproduced here.]
2. [Sir Walter Scott (1771-1832) was a famed poet and novelist. One of his famous adventures is the tale of *Ivanhoe* (1998/c.1883).]

Chapter 17: The Teaching of Science in College

1. [An earlier version of this chapter was published in *Science* N.S. Vol. 24, No. 613 (September 28, 1906b), pp. 390-397. This was also an address delivered before the Chicago Chapter of Sigma Chi, March, 1906.]
2. [I was unable to locate the author for this book.]

Chapter 18: Industrial Education, the Working Man, and the School

1. [Published in *The Elementary School Teacher*, Vol. 9, No. 7 (March 1909); pp. 369-383.]

2. [The Chicago Arts and Crafts Society employed this argument and was founded at Hull-House in 1897. See "Chicago Arts and Crafts Society." *Hull-House Bulletin* 4 (Autumn 1900): 8.]

3. [Hull-House residents fought hard and successfully against child labor (see Addams 1910).]

4. [The owner of this company, Gerald Swope, was a Hull-House resident from 1897-1899 and a friend of Addams for decades. Given the friendship between Mead and Addams, it is logical that Mead knew Swope as well.]

5. [The Manual high school in Chicago merged with the Chicago Laboratory Schools in 1894, so Mead was already familiar with this model and its operation. For an excellent discussion of manual education in the thought of Mead and Dewey, See Feffer, 131-41.]

Bibliography

Archival Collections

Chicago, Illinois
University of Chicago, Regenstein Library, The Department of Special Collections
- George Herbert Mead Papers
- George Herbert Mead Papers Addenda

Mead's Bibliography

Mead, George Herbert. "A Theory of Emotions from the Physiological Standpoint." *Psychological Review* 2 (March 1895): 162-64.

_____. Review of C.L. Morgan, *An Introduction to Comparative Psychology*. *Psychological Review* 2 (July 1895): 399-402.

_____. "The Relation of Play to Education." *University Record* (Chicago) 1 (22 May 1896): 141-45.

_____. "The Child and His Environment." *Transactions of the Illinois Society for Child Study* 3 (April 1898): 1-11.

_____. "The Working Hypothesis in Social Reform." *American Journal of Sociology* 5 (November 1899): 367-71.

_____. "Suggestions toward a Theory of the Philosophical Disciplines." *Philosophical Review* 9 (January 1900): 1-17.

_____. "The Definition of the Psychical," *University of Chicago Decennial Volumes*, 1st Ser., 3 (1903): 77-112.

_____. "The Relations of Psychology and Philology." *Psychological Bulletin* 1 (15 October 1904b): 375-91.

_____. "Image or Sensation." *Journal of Philosophy* 1 (27 October 1904): 604-7.

_____. "Science in the High School." *School Review* 14 (April 1906a): 237-53.

_____. "The Teaching of Science in College." *Science* 24 (28 September 1906b): 390-97.

_____. "The Imagination in Wundt's Treatment of Myth and Religion." *Psychological Bulletin* 3 (15 December 1906c): 393-99.

_____. "Concerning Animal Perception." *Psychological Review* N.S. 14

(November 1907): 383-90.

_____. Review of William McDougall, *An Introduction to Social Psychology. Psychological Bulletin* 5 (15 December 1908): 385-91.

_____. "Social Psychology as Counterpart to Physiological Psychology." *Psychological Bulletin* 6 (15 December 1909a): 401-8.

_____. "Industrial Education, the Working Man, and the School." *Elementary School Teacher* 9 (March 1909b): 369-83.

_____. "What Social Objects Must Psychology Presuppose?" *Journal of Philosophy, Psychology, and Scientific Methods* 7 (31 March 1910): 174-80.

_____. "Josiah Royce—A Personal Impression." *International Journal of Ethics* 27 (January 1917): 168-70.

_____. "A Translation of Wundt's *Folk Psychology.*" *American Journal of Theology* 23 (October 1919): 533-36.

_____. "Mary E. McDowell." *Neighborhood* 2 (April 1929): 77-8.

_____. "Cooley's Contribution to American Social Thought." *American Journal of Sociology* 35 (March 1930a): 693-706.

_____. "The Philosophies of Royce, James, and Dewey in Their American Setting." *International Journal of Ethics* 40 (January 1930b): 211-31.

_____. *The Philosophy of the Present*, ed. and intro. by Arthur E. Murphy, pref. remarks by John Dewey. Chicago: University of Chicago, 1932.

_____. *Mind, Self and Society*, ed. and intro. by Charles Morris. Chicago: University of Chicago Press, 1934.

_____. *Movements of Thought in the Nineteenth Century*, ed. and intro. by Merritt H. Moore. Chicago: University of Chicago Press, 1936.

_____. *The Philosophy of the Act*, ed. and intro. by Charles W. Morris, in collaboration with John M. Brewster, Albert M. Dunham, and David L. Miller. Chicago: University of Chicago Press, 1938.

_____. *The Individual and the Social Self*, ed. and intro. by David L. Miller. Chicago: University of Chicago Press, 1982.

_____. "E.A. Ross on *Sin and Society.*" *Sociological Origins* 1 (Summer 1998): 22-26.

_____. *Play, School, and Society*, ed. and intro. by Mary Jo Deegan. New York: Peter Lang, 1999.

Ickes, Harold, George H. Mead, and Irwin St. J. Tucker. *Brief History of the Clothing Strike in Chicago*. Pamphlet. 15 October 1915.

Mead, George Herbert, and Helen Castle Mead, eds. *Henry Northrup Castle: Letters*. London: privately printed, 1902.

Mead, George Herbert, Ernest A. Weidt, and William J. Broggan. *A Report on Vocational Training in Chicago and in Other Cities*. Chicago: City Club of Chicago, 1912.

General Bibliography

This section includes editions that were most likely used by Mead by reason of availability during the period. I often used the catalog at Regenstein Library, at the University of Chicago to help increase the likelihood that these were the editions available to Mead. Mead often only refers to the name of an author, however, so this reference list is suggestive rather than precise. I indicate years of birth and death for Mead's cited authors and contemporaries.

Addams, Jane (1860-1935). *Twenty Years at Hull-House.* New York: Macmillan, 1910.
_____. *The Spirit of Youth and the City Streets.* New York: Macmillan, 1909.
_____. *The Second Twenty Years at Hull-House.* New York: Macmillan, 1930.
Angell, James Rowland (1869-1949). "The Province of Functional Psychology." *Psychological Review* 14 (1907): 61-91.
_____. *An Introduction to Psychology.* New York: H.H. Holt, 1918.
Annual Register, July 1893-July 1894. Chicago: University of Chicago Press, 1893.
Bain, Alexander (1818-1903). *Education as a Science.* New York: D. Appleton, 1897.
Baldwin, James Mark (1861-1934). *Mental Development in the Child and Race.* New York: Macmillan, 1895.
_____. *Social and Ethical Interpretation in Mental Development.* New York: Macmillan, 1897.
Barnes, Charles R. (1898-1910) "Discussion." *School Review* 14 (April 1906): 252-53. Robert Andrews Millikan (1906),
Barnes, Elmer, ed. *An Introduction to the History of Sociology.* Chicago: University of Chicago Press, 1948.
Bernard, Luther Lee. (1881-1951) *Instinct: An Introduction to Social Psychology.* New York: Henry Holt, 1907.
Benson, Mary Sumner. "Mead, Elizabeth Storrs Billings." Pp. 519-20 in *Notable American Women,* ed. by Edward T. James, et al. Cambridge, MA: Belknap Press of Harvard University Press, 1971.
Blumenthal, Arthur L. "Introduction." Pp. 11-19 in *The Language of Gestures* by Wilhelm Wundt, Intro. by Arthur L. Blumenthal and add. essays by George Herbert Mead and Karl Buhler. The Hague: Mouton, 1973.
Blumer, Herbert. *Symbolic Interactionism.* Englewood Cliffs, NJ: Prentice-Hall, 1969.
Breckinridge, Sophonisba, and Edith Abbott. *The Delinquent Child and the Home,* intro. by Julia Lathrop. New York: Charities Publication Committee, 1912.
Buhle, Mary Jo. *Women and American Socialism, 1870-1920.* Urbana: University of Illinois Press, 1981.
Campbell, James. *The Community Reconstructs: The Meaning of Pragmatic Social Thought.* Urbana: University of Illinois Press, 1992.
Campbell, Mary Rachel. *Report on an Investigation Concerning the Present Technical Status of Educational Work with the Deaf, Blind, Subnormal*

and Feeble Minded in the United States. Baltimore: Department of Special Education of the National Educational Association, 1905.

Charon, Joel. *Symbolic Interactionism,* 5th ed. Englewood Cliffs, NJ: Prentice Hall, 1995.

Castle, Albert L. *A Century of Philanthropy: A History of the Samuel N. and Mary Castle Foundation.* Honolulu: Hawaiian Historical Society, 1992.

Comte, Auguste (1798-1857). *The Positive Philosophy of Auguste Comte,* 2 vols. Freely translated and edited by Harriet Martineau. London: John Chapman, 1853.

Cooley, Charles H (1864-1929). *Human Nature and the Social Order.* New York: Charles Scribner's Sons, 1902.

_____. *Social Organization; A Study of the Larger Mind.* New York: Charles Scribner's Sons, 1909.

_____. *Human Nature and the Social Order.* Intro. by Philip Rieff. Foreword by George Herbert Mead. Chicago: Schocken Books, 1964/c. 1922 rev. ed.

Cook, Gary A. *George Herbert Mead: The Making of a Social Pragmatist.* Urbana: University of Illinois Press, 1993.

Costello, Peter. *Jules Verne.* New York: Charles Scribner's Sons, 1978.

Cremlin, Lawrence A. *The Transformation of the School: Progressivism in American Education.* New York: Vintage Books, 1964/c. 1961.

Darwin, Charles (1809-1882). *The Origin of Species by Means of Natural Selection and the Preservation of Favoured Races in the Struggle for Life,* 6th ed, with add. and corrections. London: John Murray, 1872.

_____. *Expressions of the Emotions in Man and Animals,* 2nd ed. London: J. Murray, 1890/c. 1872.

Deegan, Mary Jo. "Symbolic Interaction and the Study of Women." Pp. 3-15 in *Women and Symbolic Interaction,* ed. by Mary Jo Deegan and Michael R. Hill. Winchester, MA: Allen and Unwin.

_____. *Jane Addams and the Men of the Chicago School, 1892-1920.* New Brunswick, NJ: Transaction Publishers, 1988.

_____. *American Ritual Dramas: Social Rules and Cultural Meanings.* New York: Greenwood Press, 1989.

_____, ed. *Women in Sociology: A Bio-Bibliographical Sourcebook,* intro. by Mary Jo Deegan. New York: Greenwood Press, 1991.

_____. "Play from the Perspective of George Herbert Mead." Pp. xix-cxii in *Play, School, and Society,* ed. and intro. by Mary Jo Deegan. New York: Peter Lang, 1999.

_____, ed. *The American Ritual Tapestry: Social Rules and Cultural Meanings.* New York: Greenwood Press, 1998.

Deegan, Mary Jo and John S. Burger. "George Herbert Mead and Social Reform: His Work and Writings." *Journal of the History of the Behavioral Sciences* 14 (October): 362-72.

Deegan, Mary Jo and Michael R. Hill, eds. *Women and Symbolic Interaction.* Boston: Allen and Unwin, 1987.

De Pencier, Ida B. *The History of the Laboratory Schools.* Chicago: University of Chicago Press, 1967.

Dewey, John (1859-1952). "The Theory of Emotion, I." *Psychological Review* 1 (November 1894): 553-69.

_____. "The Theory of Emotion, II." *Psychological Review* 2 (January 1895a): 13-32.

_____. "The Synthesis of Emotions." *Psychological Review* 2 (January 1895b): 13-32.

_____. "The Reflex Arc Concept in Psychology." *Psychological Review* 3 (July 1896): 357-70.

_____. *School and Society*. Chicago: University of Chicago Press, 1900/ c. 1899.

_____. *Studies in Logical Theory*. Chicago: University of Chicago Press, 1903.

_____. "Play." Pp. 725-27 in *A Cyclopedia of Education*, Vol. 4, ed. by Paul Monroe. New York: Macmillan, 1913.

Dewey, John and Evelyn Dewey. *Schools of To-morrow*. New York: E.P. Dutton, 1915.

Dillon, Mary Earhart. "Willard, Frances Elizabeth Caroline." Pp. 613-19 in *Notable American Women*, Vol. 3, edited by Edward T. James. Cambridge, MA: Belknap Press of Harvard University Press, 1971.

Diner, Stephen. "George Herbert Mead's Ideas on Women and Careers: A Letter to His Daughter-in-Law, 1920." *Signs* 4 (Winter 1978): 407-409.

_____. *A City and Its Universities: Public Policy in Chicago, 1892-1919*. Chapel Hill: University of North Carolina Press, 1980.

Du Bois-Reymond, Emil (1818-1896). *Collected Papers on Physiology*, 5 vols. 88 pamphlets, 1843-1894.

Faris, Robert E. L. *Chicago Sociology: 1920-1932*. Chicago: University of Chicago Press, 1967.

Feffer, Andrew. *The Chicago Pragmatists and American Progressivism*. Chicago: University of Chicago Press, 1993.

Ferguson, Kathy E. *Self, Society, and Womankind*. Westport, CT: Greenwood Press, 1980.

Fine, Gary A., ed. *A Second Chicago School?: The Development of Postwar American Sociology*, ed. by Chicago: University of Chicago Press, 1995.

Fiske, John (1842-1901). *Darwinism and Other Essays*. New edition, revised. Boston: Houghton Mifflin, 1893.

Gomperz, Theodor (1832-1912). *Grieschische Denker*, 3 bds. Leipzig: Velt, 1903-1909.

Guyot, Arnold (1807-1884). *The Earth and Man. Lectures on Comparative Physical Geography, and Its Relation to the History of Mankind*. Translated by C.C. Felton. Boston: Gould, Kendall, and Lincoln, 1849.

Hale, William Gardner (1843-1928). *A First Latin Book*. Chicago: Atkinson, Mentzer, and Grover.

Hall, G[ranville]. Stanley (1844-1924). *How to Teach Reading, and What to Read in School*. Boston: D.C. Heath and Co., 1890.

_____, *Adolescence*. New York: D. Appleton, 1904.

Helmholtz, Hermann von (1821-1894). *Popular Lectures on Scientific Subjects*, New Ed. Edmund Atkinson. With an introduction by Professor Tyndall. New York: Longmans, Green, 1895.

_____. *Handbuch der Physiologischen Optik*. Leipzig: L. Voss, 1896.

Herbart, Johann Friedrich (1776-1841). *A Text-book in Psychology*. New York: D. Appleton, 1891.

_____. *The Science of Education*. Boston: D.C. Heath, 1902.

Hobhouse, L(eon) T(welawney) (1864-1929). *Mind in Evolution*. London: Macmillan, 1901.

Hochschild, Arlie Russell. "The Sociology of Feeling and Emotion." Pp. 280-307 in *Another Voice*, ed. by Marcia Millman and Rosabeth Moss Kanter. New York: Doubleday, 1975.

_____. *The Managed Heart*. Berkeley: University of California Press, 1983,

Homer. *Iliad*, ed. with English notes and intro. by Walter Lead. London: Macmillan.

Huxley, Thomas Henry (1825-1895). *Science and Education*. New York: D. Appleton, 1894.

James, William (1842-1910). *The Principles of Psychology*. New York: Henry Holt and Co., 1890.

_____. "The Chicago School." *Psychological Bulletin* 1 (15 January 1904): 1-5.

_____. *Pragmatism*. New York: Longmans, Green, & Co. 1907.

Joas, Hans. *G.H. Mead: A Contemporary Re-examination of His Thought*, tr. by Raymond Meyer. Cambridge, MA: MIT Press, 1985.

_____. *Pragmatism and Social Theory*. Chicago: University of Chicago Press, 1993.

Judd, Charles Hubbard (1873-1946). *Genetic Psychology for Teachers*. New York: D. Appleton, 1903.

Karpf, Fay. *American Social Psychology*. New York: McGraw-Hill, 1932.

Kelley, Robert L. "Psycho-Physical Tests of Normal and Abnormal Children— A Comparative Study." [Studies from the Physiological Laboratory of the University of Chicago: IV, communicated by James Roland Angell]. *Psychological Review* 10 (July 1903): 345-72.

Külpe, Oswald (1862-1915). *Outlines of Psychology*. Tr. by Edward Bradford Titchener. New York: Macmillan, 1895.

_____. *Introduction to Philosophy*, 2nd Ed. Tr. by Walter Bowers Pilsbury and Edward Bradford Titchener. New York: Macmillan, 1904.

Kurtz, Lester R. *Evaluating Chicago Sociology: A Guide to the Literature, with An Annotated Bibliography*. Chicago: University of Chicago Press, 1984.

Lange, Georg Carl (1834-1900) and William James (1842-1910). *The Emotions*. New York: Hafner, 1967/c. 1922.

Lewis, J. David, and Richard L. Smith. *American Sociology and Pragmatism*. Chicago: University of Chicago Press, 1980.

McDougall, William (1871-1938). *An Introduction to Social Psychology*. London: Methuen, 1908.

_____. *Introduction to Social Psychology*, 4th Ed. rev. Boston: J.W. Luce, 1911.

Manis, Jerome and Bernard Meltzer, eds. *Symbolic Interactionism,* 2nd Ed. Boston: Allyn and Bacon, 1972.

_____. *Symbolic Interactionism,* 3rd Ed. Boston: Beacon Press, 1980.

Matthews, Fred. *Quest for an American Sociology: Robert E. Park and the Chicago School.* Montreal: McGill-Queens University Press, 1977.

"Mead, George Herbert." P. 825 in *Who Was Who, Vol.1, 1897-1942.* Chicago: Marquis, 1943.

Mead, Henry C.A. "Biographical Notes." Pp. lxxv-lxxix in *The Philosophy of the Act,* ed. and intro. by Charles Morris. Chicago: University of Chicago Press, 1938.

Mead, Elizabeth Storrs (Billings). "President's Annual Report, 1899-1900." South Hadley, MA: Mt. Holyoke College, 1900.

"Mead, Elizabeth Storrs (Billings)." Pp. 463-64 in *The National Cyclopedia of American Biography.* New York: James T. White, 1893.

_____. P. 825 in *Who Was Who, Vol.1, 1897-1942.* Chicago: Marquis, 1943.

Miller, David L. *George Herbert Mead: Self, Language and the World.* Chicago: University of Chicago Press, 1973.

_____. "Introduction." Pp. 1-26 in *The Individual and the Social Self,* by George Herbert Mead. Chicago: University of Chicago Press, 1982.

Millikan, Robert Andrews (18//-19//) "Discussion." *School Review* 14 (April 1906): 250-52.

Moore, Eliakin Hastings (1862-1932). *Introduction to a Form of General Analysis.* New York: Yale University Press, 1910.

Morgan, C[onway]. Lloyd. (1852-1936). *An Introduction to Comparative Psychology.* London: W. Scott, 1894.

_____. *Habit and Instinct.* London: E. Arnold, 1896.

Moulton, Forest Ray. "Discussion." *School Review* Vol. 14 (April 1906a): 249-50.

Münsterberg, Hugo (1863-1016). *Psychologie und Wirtschaftsleben.* Leipzig: J.A. Barth, 1912.

_____. *Psychology and the Teacher.* New York: D. Appleton, 1920.

Oswald, Wilhelm (1853-1932). *The Fundamental Principles of Chemistry,* tr. by Harry W. Morse. New York: Longmans, Green and Co., 1909.

Petras, John W. "George Herbert Mead: An Introduction." Pp. 1-23 in *George Herbert Mead: Essays on His Social Philosophy.* New York: Columbia University, Teachers College Press, 1968.

Romanes, George John. (1848-1898). *Mental Evolution in Animals, With a Posthumous Essay on Instinct by Charles Darwin.* New York: D. Appleton, 1884.

_____. *Mental Evolution in Man: Origin of Human Faculty.* New York: D. Appleton, 1889.

Ross, Edward A(lsworth) (1866-1951). *Social Psychology.* New York: Macmillan, 1908.

_____. *Sin and Society: An Analysis of Latter-Day Iniquity.* With a letter from President Theodore Roosevelt. Boston: Houghton, Mifflin, 1907.

_____. *Civic Sociology*. Yonkers-on Hudson: World Book Co., 1935.
Royce, Josiah. *Studies of Good and Evil: A Series of Essays upon the Problems of Philosophy and Life*. New York: D. Appleton and Co., 1898.
_____. *Outlines of Psychology: An Elementary Treatise on One Practical Application* (12th ch). New York: Macmillan, 1903.
Rucker, Darnell. *The Chicago Pragmatists*. Minneapolis: Minnesota Press, 1969.
Schutz, Alfred. *The Phenomenology of the Social World*, tr. by G. Walsh and F. Lehnert and intro. by George Walsh. Evanston, IL: Northwestern University Press, 1967.
_____. *Collected Papers, I: The Problem of Society*. Edited and Introduced by Maurice Natanson and preface by H.L. van Breda. The Hague, Holland: Martinus Nijhoff, 1971.
Scott, Walter (1771-1832). *Ivanhoe*, ed. by Graham Tulloch. Edinburgh, UK: Edinburgh University Press, 1998/c. 1893.
Shils, Edward. "The Sociology of Robert E. Park." Pp. 15-34 in *Robert E. Park and the "Melting Pot" Theory*, edited by Runzo Gubert and Luigi Tomasi. Trento, Italy: Departimento di teoria, storia e ricerca sociale dell Universita degli studi di Trento.
Smith, Dennis. *The Chicago School: A Liberal Critique of Capitalism*. New York: Macmillan, 1988.
Stone Gregory P. and Harvey Farberman, eds. *Social Psychology Through Symbolic Interaction*. Waltham, MA.: Xerox College Publishing, 1970.
Stout, George Frederick (1860-1944). *A Manual of Psychology*. London: W.B. Clive, 1899.
Thomas, W.I. (1863-1948). "The Relation of the Medicine-Man to the Origin of the Professional Occupations." *University of Chicago Decennial Volumes*, 1st Ser., 4 (1903): 241-56.
_____. *Sourcebook for Social Origins*. Chicago: University of Chicago Press, 1909.
Thorndike, Edward Lee (1874-1949). "Animal Intelligence," *Psychological Review, Monthly Supplement,* 2 (No. 4): 65:ff.
_____. *Animal Intelligence*. New York: Macmillan, 1898.
_____. *Notes on Child Study*. New York: Macmillan, 1901.
Titchener, Edward Bradford (1867-1927). *The Primer of Psychology*. New York: Macmillan, 1898.
_____. *A Textbook of Psychology*. New York: Macmillan, 1909.
Tyndall, John (1820-1893). *Sound*, 3rd ed., rev. and enl. New York: D. Appleton, 1877.
Whimster, Sam. "Kurt Lamprecht and Max Weber." Pp. 268-83 in *Max Weber and His Contemporaries*, ed. by Wolfgang J. Mommsen and Jürgen Osterhammel. London: Unwin Hyman, 1987.
Willard, Frances. *Glimpses of Fifty Years: The Autobiography of an American Woman*. Introduced by Hannah Whitall Smith. Chicago: Woman's Temperance Publications Association, 1889.
Wilson, Lucy Langdon Williams (1864-1937). *History Reader for Elementary Schools*. New York: Macmillan, 1898.

Wundt, Wilhelm (1832-1920). *Ethics: An Investigation of the Facts and Laws of the Moral Life: The Facts of the Moral Life* , vol. I. Tr. by Julia Gulliver and Edward Bradford Titchener. London: Swan Sonnenschein, 1897a.

_____. *Ethics: An Investigation of the Facts and Laws of the Moral Life: Ethical Systems*, vol. II. Tr. by Margaret Floy Washburn. London: Swan Sonnenschein, 1897b.

_____. *Ethics: An Investigation of the Facts and Laws of the Moral Life: The Principles of Morality and the Departments of the Moral Life*, vol. III. Tr. by Margaret Floy Washburn. London: Swan Sonnenschein, 1901.

_____. *Völkerpsychologie: Eine Untersuchung der Entwicklungsgesetze von Sprache, Mythus und Sitte*, 2 vols. Leipzig, Germany: W. Engelmann, 1900-1909.

_____. *Lectures on Human and Animal Psychology*. Tr. by J.E. Creighton and E.B. Titchener. New York: Macmillan, 1894.

_____. *Outlines of Psychology*. Tr. by Charles Hubbard Judd. 2nd rev. English ed. of the 4th rev., German ed. New York: G.E. Stechert, 1902.

_____. *Elements of Folk Psychology: Outlines of a Psychological History of the Development of Mankind*. Authorized tr. by Edward Leroy Schaub. New York: Macmillan, 1916.

_____. *The Language of Gestures*. Intro. by Arthur L. Blumenthal and add. essays by George Herbert Mead and Karl Buhler. The Hague: Mouton, 1973.

Subject Index

Adaptation, xxiv, 61, 134-35; and intelligence, 163-64, 166, 160. *See also* Evolution.

African American, xvii, 100

Alcohol, xxxiv-xxxv, 31-41; temperance, xxii, xxxiv, 32-33

Alteri, 7, 16

Apperception, 21

Art, xxix, xxx, 105; psychology of, 8. *See also* Play; Work.

Association, 68-69

Attention, 64, 117-18, 133

Beginning of Social Acts, xxxv-xxxvii, 43-92

Biologic individual, xiii, xix, xxv, xxxii-xxxv, 3-41

Chicago pragmatism, xxiii-xxiv, xxv; World of, xxv, xxxix

Chicago sociology, lxiii

Child, xiv, xviii; and environment, 83-92; experience of, 132, 135, 137, 138-39, 141, 143-46; labor, 165; and modern pedagogy, 125-27; -Study, 141. *See also* Kindergartens; Mothers; Progressive Education; Dewey, John

Christianity, 39; Methodism, 40; Puritan 37; revivals, 32; Roman Catholic, 39

Comparative psychology, xxxi, xxiv, xxxv-xxxvi, xlii, 23-24, 45-57; and animal perception, 59-65. *See also* Functional Psychology, Wundt, Wilhelm

Consciousness, xxiii, xxiv, xxv, xxxiii, xxxiv; appearance of, 46-47; objective and subjective, 25; of meaning, 15-16, 18, 24, 169; self-, 118, 119-120; social, 14, 124, 151-52; types

of, xxxviii. *See also* Alcohol; Emotions; Functional Psychology; Instincts

Co-operation, xxix, 15

Cult, 35

Democracy, 147, 161-62; and artisan, 163; industrial, 171

Economic man, 21-22

Education, and play, 105-113; as apprenticeship, 161-62, 164, 168-69, 172-74; and work attitudes, 31; from kindergarten to the university, xxxvii-xli, 93-174; manual, 97, 98, 116; science and the high school, 137-48; sex, 78-79, 87; social situation of, 115-21; the university and the elementary school, 129-35; the university and the school of education, 123-27; vocational/industrial, xxv, xl-xli, 119-20, 161-74. *See also* Embryo; Kindergarten; Parent; Progressive Education; Dewey, John

Embryo, 86, development and education, 73-82

Emotions, xii-xiii, xviii, xxx, xxxviii, 97, 98-99, 120-21; expressions of, 4-6, 22; follow the act, 100; function of, 36, 175, n. 3. *See also* Alcohol; Instincts; Darwin, Charles

Expert, 166-67

Folk-psychology, xxvii, xxxi, 115. *See also* Education, primitive; Wundt, Wilhelm

Functional psychology, xxiii-xxiv, xxxii, xxxiii, xxv, lxi, 19-25, 124; definition of, 5-6. *See also* Instinct; Angell, James Rowland; Dewey, John; Mead, George Herbert

193

Name Index

Addams, Jane, xxii-xxiii; 175, n. 6; and *Twenty Years at Hull-House (1910), xxii. See also Hull-House*
Angell, James Rowland, xxi, xxiv, xxv, xxxiii, xli, 24, 124; and Robert Kelley, xli;
    on emotions, 4. *See also* Chicago Pragmatism
Aristotle, 107

Bain, Alexander, 124
Baldwin, James Mark, xv, xxiv, 3, 10, 11, 13, 15. *See also* Wundt, Wilhelm
Barnes, Charles R., xl
Blumer, Herbert, xiii, xiv, xl
Breckinridge, Sophonisba, and Edith Abbott, xlii

Calhoun, Dana Pond, 132, 180, n. 3
Calhoun, Warren Colburn, 180, n. 3
Castle, Helen (see Mead, Helen Castle)
Castle, Henry, xvii, xviii, xix, xxi
Cattell, J.M., xxvii
Campbell, Mary R., xli
Comte, August, 10
Cooley, Charles H., xxiv, xxxiii, 10; *Human Nature and the Social Order*, 21

Darwin, Charles, xiii, xxiv, 4, 22, 27, 31-41, 154. *See also* Emotions; Evolution; Instincts; Fiske, John
Dewey, Alice Chipman, xxiv, 176, 176, n. 11
Dewey, John, and Chicago Physiology School, xl, 179, n. 7; and functional psychology, xxiii, xxxii, 24, 124; and the Laboratory Schools, xxiv, xxxviii; and progressive education, xiv; and Wundt, Wilhelm, xxvii, xxxi.

See Dewey, Alice Chipman; Laboratory Schools; Wundt, Wilhelm
Dilthey, Wilhelm, xix, 175, n. 4
Donaldson, Henry H., xli
Du Bois-Reymond, Emil, 157

Ebbinghouse, Herman, xix
Einstein, Albert, xl
Erikson, Erik, 175, n.6

Fiske, John, xxiv, xxxvi, 73. *See also* Darwin, Charles; Evolution
Froebel, Friedrich, xxxviii, 96, 179, n.2. *See also* Kindergarten; Laboratory schools; Mother-play
Franklin, Benjamin, 137

Geddes, Patrick, 176, n. 9
Gilman, Charlotte Perkins, 175, n. 6
Gomperz, Theodor, 155
Guyot, Arnold, 8, 132

Hale, William Gardner, 126
Hall, G. Stanley, xv, xxvii, 124. *See also* Wundt, Wilhelm
Harper, William R., xli-xlii
Helmholtz, Hermann von, xxi, 154, 157
Herbart, Johann Friedrich,
Hobhouse, L(eon) T(welawney), xxxvi, 59, 67-68, 70
Homer, 34, 178, n. 2.
    See also Greeks
Huxley, Thomas Henry, 154

James, William, xv, xviii, xxiv-xxv, xxxiii, 45-46, 96, 124, 175, n. 6; and the James-Lange theory of emotions, 4, 179, n. 4. *See also* Wundt, Wilhelm
Judd, Charles, 14. *See also* Wundt, Wilhelm
Külpe, Oswald, 124

197

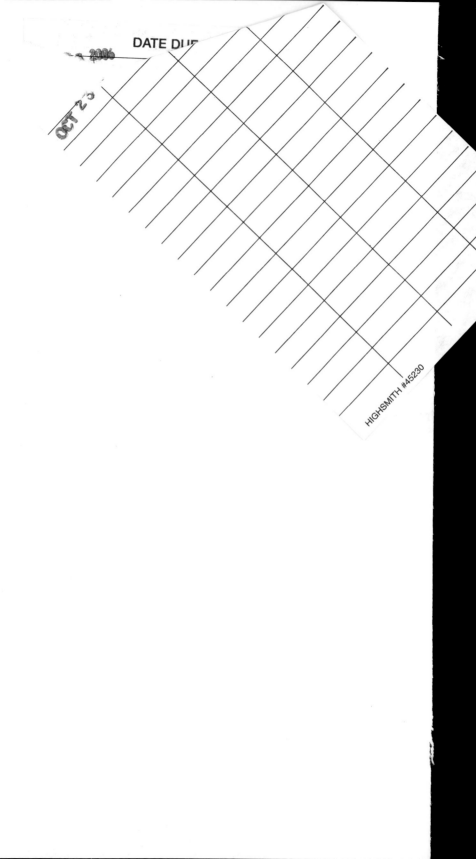

DATE DUE

OCT 2 3 2006

HIGHSMITH #45230